Speaking of Earth

Speaking of Earth

ENVIRONMENTAL SPEECHES THAT MOVED THE WORLD

Edited with Commentary
and Biographies by

Alon Tal

Rutgers University Press

NEW BRUNSWICK, NEW JERSEY, AND LONDON

A British Cataloging-in-Publication record for this book is available from
the British Library

Manufactured in the United States of America

Library of Congress Cataloging-in-Publication Data

Speaking of Earth : environmental speeches that moved the world / edited with
commentary and biographies by Alon Tal.
    p.   cm.
Includes bibliographical references and index.
    ISBN-13: 978-0-8135-3726-9 (hardcover : alk. paper)
    ISBN-13: 978-0-8135-3727-6 (pbk. : alk. paper)
1. Environmental literature.   2. Environmentalism—Social aspects.
3. Nature—Effect of human beings on.   I. Tal, Alon, 1960–

   GE35 .S64   2006
   333.72—dc22

                                     2005016866

For my parents David Tal and Yonina Rosenthal,
who taught me how to speak,
and what was worth speaking out about

"For I shall always speak,
And cry out about the destruction and shout against the plunder . . .
There is in my heart as it were a burning fire,
Locked up in my bones,
And I am weary with holding it in,
And I cannot"

Jeremiah 20:8−9

Contents

Acknowledgments

Writers are often warned about a dangerous tendency to get "too close" to their subject matter. In the spirit of transparency and equitable disclosure, readers should be forewarned that a healthy distance was never a possibility in a book of this type. To be truthful, I never even tried. And so, during the past year, while writing and compiling, I often found my thoughts drifting, perhaps during a run or a shower or merely a slow moment at the keyboard. Quite involuntarily, my imagination would sweep me away to a retreat in a remote lodge high up in some alpine park. I would look around the rustic lounge, fire blazing, and smile at these great environmental heroes of whom I was writing, who had so graciously agreed to join the gathering I convened.

Zulu King Buthelezi would be sharing anecdotes with Prince Charles about the lighter side of modern royalty. At the bar, conservation icon David Brower with his irrepressible ecological curiosity would be plying former Prime Minister David Lange with questions about the evolution of New Zealand's flightless birds. A fascinating tactical debate has ensued among Petra Kelly, Chico Mendes, and Wangari Maathai, all environmentalists who found very different roads to politics, about Ralph Nader's obsessive presidential campaigns and the potential and price of green political parties. Thor Heyerdahl and Ian Kiernan, the resident sailors, are regaling Rachel Carson (whose initial fame came from turning oceanography into poetry) with bawdy tales of human life on the high seas. Vandana Shiva and Margaret Thatcher are arguing about the merits and pitfalls of a scientific education, and about whether chemistry or physics was a better way to start a career. Ken Saro Wiwa and Yizhar Smilansky, who both began as politically engaged novelists, are talking about their remedies for writer's block and about obtuse publishers. Lois Gibbs and Karl-Henrik Robert are locked in a spirited discussion on the nature of industry and whether it will ever change. Old pals Maurice Strong and Mostafa Tolba seem lost in nostalgic stories about the days when the United Nations Environmental Program was trying to open its offices in

Kenya. Despite their formal religious regalia, the Dalai Lama and the Ecumenical Patriarch Bartholomew seem the most relaxed participants, chuckling in a corner, in no hurry to begin their shared convocation that will start the meeting. And I too am there, delighted simply to be a "fly on the wall" and have had the opportunity to make their acquaintance.

It would seem, therefore, that acknowledgments should begin with this book's protagonists, the sundry environmental champions who have so enriched my days in preparing this anthology. They or their descendents have graciously agreed to let me reprint their speeches. For this, I am grateful, as without their concurrence there could be no book. Obviously, it is much more than these heroes' words that I appreciate; it is what they chose to do with their lives and what they stood up for. I hope that this gratitude is reflected in the twenty profiles.

There were many, many individuals who helped me to identify, track down, translate, prioritize, and select the speeches for this book—or at least to locate other persons who would know where to find these. Several other individuals critiqued and corrected early drafts of the chapters. Most of these coconspirators remain "virtual penpals," and I fear that I shall never have the chance to thank them in person. I am also certain that any attempt to name them all will result in a few awkward omissions, and for this I am truly sorry. Yet it seems well to invoke the adage that has become something of a personal axiom, "Perfection is the enemy of the good." I should like, therefore, to take my best shot and express my gratitude to as many of these fine folks as I can. My thanks go to: Kirsten Abrahamsson, Dr. Mary Allegretti, Richard Aylard, David Baldock, Prof. John Bonine, Dr. Klaus Bosselmann, the Brazilian Embassy in New Zealand, Kenneth Brower, Robert Brower, David Burchett, Tom Burke, Carole Camille, Robert Camp, Shmuel Chayin, Dr. Mark Chernaik, the Chico Mendes Foundation, Fran Colin, Chris Collins, Mikhail Davis, Brock Evans, Sharon Franklin, Paul Gikas, Dr. Michael Graber, Julia Hagl, Dan Haig, Jan Flood, Terrie-Ann Johnson, the Kon-Tiki Museum, Dr. Adeline Levine, Wanjira Mathai, Ferdinando Milanez, Stephen Mills, Fernando Milnaz, Asher Minns, The Nobel Foundation, Priya, the Venerable Thupten Rinpoche, Ruth Rominger, Julia Scherf, Rob Schneider, Stephen Seidel, Dr. Henrik Selin, Giora Shapira, Julia Sharp, the South African Embassy in Israel, Sondra Sullivan, Dr. Bron Taylor, Tendar (the First Secretary of the New York Office of Tibet), Sir Crispin Tickell, Dr. Manal El Batran-Tolba, Adam Werbach, Ken Wiwa, Olivia Wiwa, Dr. Owens Wiwa, and Frieder Wolf.

Many people beyond the speakers granted rights to reprint photographs, and for this I am grateful. Andy Blau and *Life Magazine* top the list. The Brazilian Embassy in Tel Aviv, the British Embassy in Washington D.C., Dennis Cunningham, Dr. Yossi Leshem, Rivka Marcus, Werner Schuering, Halfdan Tangan Jr., and Sonam Zoksang were also generous in this regard. Anna Palamarchuk was extremely efficacious and ever cheerful as a research assistant, in the book's final stages, chasing down the last of these photographs and reprint permissions. Florencia Bellesi did a superb job of expeditiously compiling the index.

At Rutgers University Press, Dr. Audra Wolfe, science editor, was invaluable in many ways. Above all, her enthusiasm and faith in the project from the inception were extremely encouraging and important to me. Her professional skills at trimming and correcting the manuscript were only exceeded by her general wisdom, as a historian of science, in considering the larger picture. Beth Kressel at Rutgers was a most patient and helpful force in tying together the attributions and credentials. The technical assistance in copyediting provided by Paula Friedman was both meticulous and inspired. Without the patience and professionalism of Nicole Manganaro and the production team, this would be a far poorer final product.

My wife Robyn Tal was my favorite, as well as most accessible, advisor about the relative oratorical virtues of candidates for inclusion. She let me know which speeches and profiles resonated, and which droned on. More important, she believed in the book from the second she heard of the idea. The superb and detailed comments of my mother, Dr. Yonina Rosenthal, sometimes merciless but always on the mark, are reflected throughout, as she put her professorial red pen to every chapter.

This book was written at the University of Otago Faculty of Law during an academic leave, in between a half-dozen other publishing projects and a course in international environmental law. Since this was my second stay in Dunedin, I should not have been surprised at the warmth and congeniality that so contributed to a perfect writing environment. But the remarkable hospitality extended by the dean, Professor Mark Henaghan, and support from Marie-Louise Neilsen, Tracy Thompson, Lucy Gray, and the many other able staff members remains a source of wonder. Without Matt Hall's wizardry at solving every computer glitch and recovering every lost file, the project would most certainly have been abandoned. The invariably helpful, cheery, and clever personnel at the University's Central, Law, and Science Libraries always managed to find the appropriate book somewhere in New Zealand. I am grateful to Professor John Smiley's insights into the vagaries of copyright law, almost as much as for his wit and erudition at morning tea. And, of course, without Jim Allan's friendship and encouragement, I would never have made it back to Dunedin in the first place. So I salute the Otago University Law School for tolerating me and my guitar once again. Not only the southernmost law school in the world, but the best.

Preface

No single factor is responsible for the environmental achievements of the past forty years. Many of the secrets to green successes are somewhat prosaic: a growing information base, a responsive media, expanded legal standing, the growth of foundation support for activism, and very often the severity of an ecological insult itself. But at the end of the day, it was, I believe, the hard work of extraordinary individuals and the resonance of their message that were ultimately responsible for heralding change. Leaders emerged able to stir the spirits of citizens around the world by talking openly and ardently about what was happening to their environment and what needed to be done to preserve it.

At the core of the world's environmental community is a cadre of remarkable people. The oft-quoted adage of Margaret Meade certainly captures the essence of the more hopeful chapters in the planet's recent ecological history: "Never doubt that a small group of thoughtful committed citizens can change the world. Indeed it is the only thing that ever has!" With the benefit of hindsight, it would seem that it was a relatively modest number of environmentalists who actually changed the world, or perhaps even saved it.

The variegated objectives of the international environmental "movement" reflect the rich diversity of the countries and the cultures on the planet. Yet the global environmental community shares certain common assumptions. Among the most basic is the notion that humans are not treating the earth with sufficient care and it is time to speak out about this.

This book attempts to explore the one universal tool that all green activists and leaders wield at some point in their work: *their voices*. It seemed peculiar to me that, amid the innumerable technical case studies of ecological campaigns published, none attempts to chronicle the actual speeches that accompanied a very real, international revolution. As in every social movement, the "oration" has been a central mechanism for galvanizing change. Yet there appears to have been no systematic effort to collect, edit, analyze, and detail the circumstances surrounding environmentally significant speeches around the world.

Once I decided to embrace such a challenge, I understood why no one had undertaken it. Like environmental change itself, the task was easier said than done. A commitment to wide geographical representation has a price tag, even today after the internet has shrunk the planet so astonishingly. But by the time I realized how complicated the task was, it was too late; I was already fully engaged.

The research began quite ingenuously with what I deemed a most clever "icebreaker," which I brought with me to the World Summit for Sustainable Development in Johannesburg in August 2002. The peculiar status of being a "*nongovernment* representative" for the Israeli *government* delegation conferred on me a most agreeable measure of freedom. I was at liberty to wander the endless halls of the official conference and side events, and to meet a tiny sample of the sixty thousand participants, all of whom had come to South Africa to talk about the state of the planet. I would approach a perfect stranger, size up the name and nationality on the nametag, smile, and say, "Hi, I'm writing a book about great environmental speeches. Can you think of a great speech from your country's ecological heritage that the world should know about?"

To be sure, there were plenty of delegates who responded with decidedly blank stares. But many stopped and took a moment or two to think about an answer. Others tracked me down later to give their response. (I am still waiting for Tanzania's Minister of Environment, who promised to get back to me via email as soon as she mulled over her country's oratorical history.) Most of the speeches in this book are here as a result of these informal consultations.

The selection of individuals and speeches featured in this book therefore, is not the result of an excessively systematic search or the product of formal rules of decision. Nor does the volume purport to contain "the greatest environmental speeches ever made." I am well aware that the *greatest* environmental speeches were probably never written down, as a long-forgotten campaigner extemporaneously and zealously speechified about an intolerable hazard or a healthier way to treat the local land and waters.

At the same time, the selection process was not arbitrary. I did seek out speeches that seemed to have "made a difference" given by people who had "made a difference." I wanted speeches that contained an important ecological message or captured an important environmental moment or impulse. Yet, although supported by the recommendations of experts and peers, the preferences were ultimately personal and intuitive. They reflect the bias of someone who has spent most of his professional career working in environmental advocacy. I believe these to be important speeches by people who made an important contribution to protecting the planet's environment

Sometimes a speech remembered as having great consequence could not be found—apparently never recorded and sadly lost to history. Other "nominees" did not pass the audition. Although nobody had actually seemed to have read it, environmentalists from Vietnam animatedly told me of Ho Chi Minh's wonderful speech in praise of tree planting. After substantial efforts by Tran Hai Hau, the Vietnamese ambassador to New Zealand (efforts including his very gracious English translation services), the speech was found. As it turns out, the revolutionary leader's commitment to afforestation amid the turmoil of Indochina in 1960 is impressive; the speech, however is not.

In spite of significant efforts to be inclusive, the present volume may contain a disproportionate number of speeches from European and English-speaking nations. This reflects to some extent not only my own limitations, but the modern environmental movement. Certainly the three American entries represent diverse pioneering stages of world environmental history, each critical in its own right.

The selection of the actual speeches reprinted in this volume was also not a uniform procedure. The easy cases involved a specific oration that had attained sufficient stature to justify inclusion. In the other cases, it was the individual and her or his environmental contribution that drove the decision. Here I often had to sift through many options and decide which text was most appropriate. This was no simple task; how can one choose "the best" Rachel Carson speech when each has its own literary and substantive merit?

The final choices probably came down to the very definition of what "a speech" is or should be. A review of the literature reveals many definitions for "speeches," my favorite being "a projected conversation." Most emphasize the vernacular or the conversational tone. Many people in the world cannot read. Many more can read, but don't, lacking access or inclination. A speech transcends this barrier and has the power to reach out to everybody present and move the audience.

A year after Johannesburg, while on academic leave in New Zealand, I had time to begin the tedious task of tracking the speeches down and, in a few cases, translating them. (The many "international forums" at which English presentations were given facilitated several original English speeches by non-native speakers of English; in other cases, translations had already been produced, or approved, by the speakers themselves.)

then that the book evolved into something a little more ambitious. understanding the context, it often seemed difficult to fully ap- either the content of a speech or its significance. Accordingly, the brief introductory "bios" grew and became more extensive environmental history vignettes, telling the story of the speaker's environmental challenge and identity.

These sections do not purport to be proper or authorized biographies. But I believe that readers deserve something more gripping than a one-dimensional synopsis of a resume. I also hope to convey some of my personal admiration for the environmental commitment and achievement of the speakers. Clearly, I could have chosen other particulars and anecdotes that would have painted the book's protagonists in a less favorable light. Personally, I have never had much regard for revisionist historians, who seem to take pleasure in highlighting the blemishes and debunking the achievements of sundry cultural champions. Of course, even great environmentalists suffer imperfections; however, I feel strongly that a focus on their talents, accomplishments, and courage offers the fairest representation and most appropriate use of limited space.

The goal of a good environmental speech is not simply to convey information. This would be a lecture. Rather, the objective is to change the way the audience feels about a subject. To be effective, speakers are forced to share some of their personal motives. People come to hear speeches not because they are too lazy to read. Rather, they want to be entertained, stimulated, edified—and this often requires gleaning insights about the speaker. Speeches therefore tend to be far more personal than essays. Mercifully, this also makes them easier to read.

Hence, I looked for speeches where speakers share their experience and convictions about a specific environmental challenge, and also raise (and answer) fundamental questions: Why should we care? How should we think about the issue in question? What needs to be done?

Many of the book's speeches were originally given to friendly listeners and can be disparaged as "preaching to the choir." To this I would respond that even the faithful are often in need of encouragement. And I hope that the dispassionate reader, as well, can relate to the call to arms. Most of all, I believe that regardless of who first heard them, these speeches offer an authentic definition for modern environmentalism. Together, they constitute a patchwork quilt that mirrors the rich and colorful fabrics making up the global environmental movement.

The cast that I finally assembled is motley indeed. Some green activists may wonder how Margaret Thatcher made it onto such an illustrious green team; I would urge them to temporarily suspend any prejudices and listen to what she said. Although I tried to pick high-profile individuals, name recognition carried far less weight than environmental contribution, as a selection criterion.

Although the group is certainly diverse, these individuals and their speeches have in common several characteristics and themes. The common desire for treading more sensitively on this troubled planet is hardly surprising. More interesting to me is that environmental speechmakers *everywhere* seem to ignore the accepted conventions of public speaking.

What constitutes a memorable speech? Ronald Reagan took as much interest in his speeches as did any other modern political leader. He espoused a few axioms about the form a public address should take:

- Never talk longer than twenty minutes;
- Keep your argument to the essentials;
- Don't ramble;
- Start with a joke.

It seems that, with only a few exceptions, this book's environmental speeches break these rules. They tend to be long-winded and frequently go on and on about technical matters, revealing little regard for accommodating a supposed typical audience's attention span. The speakers jump about among tangents, having a connection often only understood by themselves. The speeches are almost never funny. They are full of facts. Frankly, they can often be depressing. And yet they are compelling. Looking back with the benefit of historical hindsight, I find them deeply inspiring.

Perhaps, it is only natural that the "environmental speech" reflects a movement that from the start has eschewed conventional wisdom. Environmental leaders rarely try to win popularity contests. (They are mostly concerned with winning the ecological battle of the moment.) Environmentalists are "paid to worry," although typically the pay is not very good. But they do enjoy one advantage: they invariably are blessed with unshakable conviction and a healthy dose of righteous indignation.

It is this fundamental integrity that makes their speeches interesting, moving, and inspirational. Winston Churchill may have been the greatest orator of modern times. He would often say that "believing in what you are talking about" was the key to great public speaking. Audiences remain unmoved if they do not sense the depth of the speaker's feelings. The people featured in this book were not necessarily spellbinding orators, but they all cared with enormous intensity about rivers, mountains, animals, the ozone layer—and the people affected by our environmental crisis. Theirs was an intensity that forced listeners to stop and think.

I remember when I heard David Brower give a keynote address at the Public Interest Environmental Law Conference in Eugene, Oregon, in 1993. By then, he was over eighty years old, old enough to be a great-grandfather to most of the student audience. Like me, they were spellbound during his talk. I left the hall feeling changed, committed to trying a little harder to tackle the world's environmental problems. I feel privileged to share the text of the "sermon" he gave with readers, who no longer have the privilege of hearing him talk. A written text will never have the impact of his actual presentation, nor can it capture the oratorical passion, the gesticulating hands, the crescendo to a fevered pitch, all the pathos and the integrity that he exuded. But the vision remains.

It is well to preserve such visions. Collectively they represent thousands, if not millions, of other speeches that helped change the way the residents of the world look at the planet. *Speaking of Earth,* then, is ultimately a book that documents the history of the world's environmental movement. It is a movement that seeks to return some of the lost harmony between human beings and this good earth, on which we are so fortunate to live. Like any movement it has its leaders and heroes. There is no better way to understand their environmental vision, than through their spoken words.

Alon Tal
Macabim, Israel

Speaking of Earth

1. Rachel Carson

UNITED STATES OF AMERICA

Photograph courtesy of *Life Magazine*.
Alfred Eisenstaedt/TimeLife Pictures, 1962.

With the end of World War II, a new generation of chemical pesticides was enthusiastically embraced around the world. The magical properties of DDT and other chlorinated hydrocarbons featured low costs and amazing persistence: nothing prepared nature to break down the chemical compounds' chlorine–carbon bonds. With insects and malaria in retreat, in 1948 Paul Muller of Geigy Pharmaceuticals in Switzerland won a Nobel Prize in medicine and physiology for developing, a decade earlier, DDT as an insecticide.

In fact, the enthusiastic and unregulated spraying of chemicals was wreaking havoc on biological systems, but no one seemed to be paying attention to the scale of the damage. Well, almost no one. One perspicacious woman had been paying attention for some time. In 1962, Rachel Carson, an American scientist who wrote books about the sea, spoke out, challenging the underlying premise of the technology's ostensible victory over nature. Relying on extensive scientific documentation, her *Silent Spring*'s grim appraisal of ecological imbalance offered a grave warning: "no civilization can wage relentless war on life without destroying itself." Critics, congressional representatives, and even Supreme Court judges called it the most revolutionary American book since Harriet Beecher Stowe's anti-slavery polemic, *Uncle Tom's Cabin.* This seemingly bombastic description is by now commonplace. Carson is hailed as one of the few authors whose writing not only changed the course of history but jump-started the modern environmental movement.

Rachel Carson was born in 1907 in Springdale, a small town in rural Pennsylvania near the Alleghany river. From a very young age, her mother would take her exploring in the local woods and orchards. This bucolic world would soon give way to a more industrialized morass, a shift that undoubtedly affected Carson's keen sensitivities and opinions. Living in an isolated section of town, Carson would later refer to herself as a "solitary child," with ample time to become an avid reader and resolve to grow up to be a writer.

While she was attending the Pennsylvania College for Women as a scholarship student, however, her passion and talent for biology induced her to change her major. This decision would lead her to complete a master's degree in marine biology at Johns Hopkins University, where her studies initially took her to the marine science research station in Woods Hole. This was her first encounter with the sea, and by all accounts it was love at first sight. Carson thrived in academia, but her family's financial situation and the Great Depression forced her to leave her doctoral studies in 1934 to seek more gainful employment. The U.S. Bureau of Fisheries was committed to producing a fifty-two-part radio series about marine life, called "Romance Under the Waters." With her considerable writing skills, Carson was a natural choice to write the script. This temporary position eventually gave way in 1936 to a full-time civil service position as a "junior aquatic biologist" with the Bureau.

Carson would remain a government biologist for over fifteen years, during which her position gave her unusual access to unique natural settings across the United States. Eventually becoming editor-in-chief for the Fish and Wildlife Bureau, she wrote about nature in America with a lyricism that even government publications could not stifle. Without the burden of a family, she also found time to freelance on a range of natural history topics, at first for newspapers and later for national magazines.

When she integrated a series of articles into *The Sea around Us,* a lyrical summary of developments in oceanography, Oxford Press agreed, in 1951, to print it. The book was serialized in the *New Yorker.* Carson's ability to be at once a psalmist and a scientist made for an exhilarating read. By all objective criteria, the book was a homerun: selected as a National Book of the Month offering, gleaning a front-page review in the *New York Times Book Review,* receiving a film contract, and ultimately winning the

National Book Award for nonfiction. *The Sea around Us* was translated into twenty-eight languages, stayed on the best-seller list for eighty-six weeks, eventually selling over a million copies. Its popularity induced Oxford to re release her 1941 book, *Under the Sea Wind* (which had not been a commercial success) and allowed her the financial resources and independence to leave the constraints of her government job. *The Edge of the Sea,* also a critical and commercial triumph, followed in 1955. But with its publication, her role as a popular and uncontroversial "biographer" of the sea would come to an end.

The profligate use of pesticides in America and the resulting ecological damage had been giving Carson little rest. As early as 1945, she had approached *Reader's Digest* about writing a pesticide piece, but the idea was rejected. Yet she began to collect materials documenting the phenomenon, for a writing project that would come to define her historical identity and, to a certain extent, that of the world's environmental movement. She would later write a friend, "I told you once that if I kept silent, I could never again listen to a veery's song without overwhelming self-reproach." By the late 1950s, Carson was at last free to explore this seemingly arcane and unpopular topic.

It took four years of painstaking research and consultation for her to write *Silent Spring,* a fact reflected in its fifty-five pages of footnotes. The book opens with a "Fable for Tomorrow" in which a hypothetical American town is described where all creatures have been silenced by the spraying of pesticides. The subsequent chapters detail insidious impacts of insecticide and herbicide misuse: damage to non-target natural predators, bioaccumulation, mutations and pest resistance, and of course effects on human health. Although avoiding many of the more turgid and tedious excesses that often burden popular science, *Silent Spring* is hardly a "light read" and requires considerable attention and commitment from readers.

If *The Sea around Us* was a homerun, *Silent Spring* was a grand slam. Following its release on September 27, 1962, the public snapped up one hundred thousand copies in a single week—by nonfiction standards of the period, a veritable *Harry Potter*. The book has stood the test of time, with over ten million copies purchased world-wide; and even today, thirty thousand copies are sold every year. But the magnitude of sales does not begin to characterize the impact of the book. The press and the public awoke to find a very disturbing issue unaddressed in their backyard, and called for change.

Even before the book was released, controversy surrounded its publication. A three-part serialization in the popular magazine *The New Yorker* catapulted DDT abuse onto the national agenda, and President Kennedy was even asked about it at one of his regular press conferences. (The president responded that the Department of Agriculture and the Department of Health Education and Welfare were looking at the issue, "particularly because of Mrs. Carson's book.")

Kennedy's government was uncertain as to how to handle Carson's allegations and not-so-implicit criticism of its public policy. Secretary of Interior Stewart Udall took a deep interest in the book, reading a promotional copy before it was ever published and finding it persuasive. Secretary of Agriculture Orville Freeman asked for a personal briefing on the subject of pesticide abuse; despite pressure from farming advocates to attack the author, he chose a moderate stance, with a decidedly restrained press release: "Miss Carson presents a lucid description of the real and potential dangers of misusing chemical pesticides. We are fully aware of and share this concern." The President's Science Advisory Committee was ultimately ordered to evaluate the book's claims, and its report was supportive of Carson's position. The U.S. Congress was also generally supportive, and Carson was invited to oversee hearings on the issue, where she called for a minimization of aerial sprayings and a phase-out of persistent pesticide use. Her integrity made a great impression on legislators who praised the book. John Lindsay, then a young representative from New York City, contacted Carson to confer about drafting new regulatory legislation.

The chemical industry, however, had no difficulty in formulating its reaction. The best defense was of course an aggressive offensive, and hundreds of thousands of dollars were allocated to that end. Promotional materials were widely distributed decrying the science in *Silent Spring,* as well as Carson's qualifications. Cataclysmic scenarios were painted of a world unprotected by pesticides, decimated by famine, disease, and insects. Attorneys for pesticide companies threatened legal action if the book was printed, and the *New Yorker* was pressured to stop its serialized publication.

Of course, the easiest attacks are always ad hominem. In innumerable forums and in the media, Carson was branded as a charlatan or an alarmist. On occasion, less complimentary epithets like "Communist sympathizer" and "peace nut" were hurled. One critic wrote, "As for insects, isn't it just like a woman to be scared to death of a few little bugs?" Another tactic more systematically used by the industry was to caricaturize her position. For instance, Carson did not advocate a total ban on pesticides, only much tougher regulation and greater caution, but it was easier for the producers to defend against an extremist position. Similarly, the extensive examples of biological pest options discussed in the second half of the book received almost no attention in producers' polemics. Yet the virulence of industry response roomed to backfire, as it both fueled the ongoing public interest in the subject and cemented public perceptions of Carson as a courageous underdog.

The upshot of the controversy was reflected in the ultimate banning of DDT use in the United States (although the chemical is still produced locally and exported to developing countries). More important, the public perception of chemicals and the blind embracing of environmentally disruptive technologies were changed forever. It is a sad irony that, just when her position began to gain the upper hand and to be manifested in public policy proposals, Carson's twenty-year bout with cancer began to enter its final phase and became increasingly incapacitating. She missed key meetings due to radiation treatment, and suffered stoically, taking great care not to divulge her illness publicly.

Although Carson is of course considered first and foremost an "author," by 1951 her enormous literary success made her a highly sought-after speaker. Initially soft-spoken and demure, she quickly developed into a self-assured and compelling orator. Linda Lear, her biographer, writes of the style and mechanics of a Rachel Carson speech:

> Although Carson never enjoyed the prospect of public speaking, she became more confident in her delivery and more rhetorically skillful with each address. Like her other writing, each speech was the product of several longhand drafts. She typed the text onto three-by-five cards, with the first sentence of every paragraph printed in capital letters. . . . Once she began to speak, Carson rarely strayed from her notes or added extemporaneous details. Her delivery was steady, well modulated and authoritative. As she became more relaxed, she included self-deprecating humor, citing personal anecdotes and telling stories from her past.

Silent Spring thrust Carson into the role of environmental crusader, a role she had never sought nor imagined for herself. Reserved by nature, she had never been an especially active leader in America's conservation movement. (She was a long-time member of the Wilderness Society, was elected to Audubon Society's board in 1948, and ultimately bequeathed one-third of her assets to the Sierra Club and one-third to the Nature Conservancy.) But the ferocity of the industry assault could not be ignored, and public speaking became one of Carson's primary weapons in the ensuing debate. Although she spent much of the period suffering from the relentless progress of her disease and its debilitating treatments, she nonetheless managed to give a litany of high-profile addresses. As new examples of pesticide abuse came to her attention, she sharpened and updated her position.

The speech selected for inclusion in this volume was given to the Garden Club of America on January 8, 1963, roughly three months after the publication of *Silent Spring*. Garden clubs throughout the country were especially tuned into the *Silent Spring* debate. Indeed, perhaps Carson's most effective adversary was Dr. Cynthia Wescott, a Ph.D. entomologist who had served as chair of the National Council of State Garden Clubs, edited several books, served on a variety of professional committees, and published a widely circulated column, "The Plant Doctor." Wescott challenged the veracity of Carson's claims of links between pesticides and cancer, appeared on nationally televised garden shows, and wrote scores of articles characterizing Carson as unscientific.

Carson sought the broadest possible support and did not wish to preach only to the converted. The women who joined garden clubs were an important potential constituency, and it was thus important to bring her case directly to them. The speech was by no means her first public defense of *Silent Spring* or among her speeches most publicized in the press. Yet, her agent felt it a blockbuster and urged her to integrate large elements from it into future addresses, which she did. Biographer Lear notes that the speech "opened a new, aggressively political phase" of the pesticide struggle. The presentation provides additional justification for crediting Carson with launching the modern American environmental movement.

Several elements of the text are worthy of note. After succinctly recapitulating the basic themes of *Silent Spring*, the author quickly assumes a much more activist and tactical tone. She appears as a passionate speaker with considerable political savvy, keen to take on the pesticide industry's retaliation with a tough counterattack of her own. She raises new themes that would be critical to the fledgling environmental movement, such as the potential role of the courts in the struggle against chemical abuse. Carson questions the limitations that tax-exempt status imposes on public interest groups in the United States and the unequal playing field that massive industry funding creates. And of course she addresses the virulent disinformation campaign. Although refraining from populist rhetoric, Carson raises questions about the existing bias among agricultural academic researchers and the real reasons behind their prochemical orientation. Most important, she focuses her audience's attention on the need for legislative reform.

Forty years later, most of the pesticides that disturbed Carson are no longer sold in much of the world, and where they are used, they are applied much more carefully. There are still those who argue that she overstated her case and that the world has suffered unnecessarily from the absence of DDT. Yet, nature offers a different testimonial. The eagles and the pelicans, the blue birds and the falcons, and countless of their winged colleagues have made a comeback. There is still plenty of bad news about biodiversity, and chemical abuse in many developing countries remains a scourge. But Carson's faith in the public's ability to grasp scientific information, and her courageous and ever eloquent message brought humility and restraint to the realm of chemical pest control, proving that trend need not be destiny.

"The Publication of *Silent Spring* Was Neither the Beginning Nor the End of That Struggle"

SPEECH TO THE GARDEN CLUB OF AMERICA, NEW YORK, N.Y., JANUARY 8, 1963

I am particularly glad to have this opportunity to speak to you. Ever since, ten years ago, you honored me with your Frances Hutchinson medal, I have felt very close to the Garden Club of America. And I should like to pay tribute to you for the quality of your work and for the aims and aspirations of your organization. Through your interest in plant life, your fostering of beauty, your alignment with constructive conservation causes, you promote that onward flow of life that is the essence of our world.

This is a time when forces of a very different nature too often prevail—forces careless of life or deliberately destructive of it and of the essential web of living relationships. My particular concern, as you know, is with the reckless use of chemicals so unselective in their action that they should more appropriately be called biocides rather than pesticides. Not even their most partisan defenders can claim that their toxic effect is limited to insects or rodents or weeds or whatever the target may be.

The battle for a sane policy for controlling unwanted species will be a long and difficult one. The publication of *Silent Spring* was neither the beginning nor the end of that struggle. I think, however, that it is moving into a new phase, and I would like to assess with you some of the progress that has been made and take a look at the nature of the struggle that lies before us.

We should be very clear about what our cause is. What do we oppose? What do we stand for? If you read some of my industry-oriented reviewers, you will think that I am opposed to efforts to control insects or other organisms. This, of course, is *not* my position and I am sure it is not that of the Garden Club of America. We differ from the promoters of biocides chiefly in the means we advocate, rather than the end to be attained.

It is my conviction that if we automatically call in the spray planes or reach for the aerosol bomb when we have an insect problem we are resorting to crude methods of a rather low scientific order. We are being particularly unscientific when we fail to press forward with research that will give us the new kind of weapons we need. Some such weapons now exist—brilliant and imaginative prototypes of what I trust will be the insect control methods of the future. But we need many more, and we need to make better use of those we have. Research men of the Department of Agriculture have told me privately that some of the measures they have developed and tested and turned over to the insect control branch have been quietly put on the shelf.

I criticize the present heavy reliance upon biocides on several grounds—first, on the grounds of their inefficiency. I have here some comparative figures on the toll taken of our crops by insects before and after the DDT era. During the first half of this century, crop loss due to insect attack has been estimated by a leading entomologist at 10 percent a year. It is startling to find then, that the National Academy of Science last year placed the present crop loss at 25 percent a year. If the percentage of crop loss is increasing at this rate, even as the use of modern insecticides increases, surely something is wrong with the methods used! I would remind you that a nonchemical method gave 100 percent control of the screwworm fly—a degree of success no chemical has ever achieved.

Chemical controls are inefficient also because as now used they promote resistance among insects. The number of insect species resistant to one or more group of insecticides has risen from about a dozen in pre-DDT days to nearly 150 today. This is a very serious problem, threatening, as it does, greatly impaired control.

Another measure of inefficiency is the fact that chemicals often provoke resurgence of the very insect they seek to control, because they have killed off its natural controls. Or they cause some other organism suddenly to rise to nuisance status: spider mites, once relatively innocuous, have become a worldwide pest since the advent of DDT.

Obviously, it will take time to revolutionize our methods of insect and weed control to the point where dangerous chemicals are minimized. Meanwhile, there is much that can be done to bring about some immediate improvement in the situation through better procedures and controls.

In looking at the pesticide situation today, the most hopeful sign is an awakening of strong public interest and concern. People are beginning to ask questions and to insist upon proper answers instead of meekly acquiescing in whatever spraying programs are proposed. This in itself is a wholesome thing.

There is increasing demand for better legislative control of pesticides. The state of Massachusetts has already set up a Pesticide Board with actual authority. This board has taken a very necessary step by requiring the licensing of anyone proposing to carry out aerial spraying. Incredible though it may seem, before this was done anyone who had money to hire an airplane could spray where and when he pleased. I am told that the state of Connecticut is now planning an official investigation of spraying practices. And of course, on a national scale, the president [John F. Kennedy] last summer directed his science advisor to set up a committee of scientists to review the whole matter of the government's activities in this field.

Citizen groups too, are becoming active. For example, the Pennsylvania Federation of Women's Clubs recently set up a program to protect the public from the menace of poisons in the environment—a program based on education and promotion of legislation. The National Audubon Society has advocated a five-point action program involving both state and federal agencies. The North American Wildlife Conference this year will devote an important part of its program to the problem of pesticides. All these developments will serve to keep public attention focused on the problem.

I was amused recently to read a bit of wishful thinking in one of the trade magazines. Industry "can take heart" it said, "from the fact that the main impact of the book (i.e., *Silent Spring*) will occur late in the fall and winter—seasons when consumers are not normally active buyers of insecticides. . . . It is fairly safe to hope that by March or April *Silent Spring* no longer will be an interesting conversational subject."

If the tone of my mail from readers is any guide, and if the movements that have already been launched gain the expected momentum, this is one prediction that will not come true.

This is not to say that we can afford to be complacent. Although the attitude of the public is showing a refreshing change, there is very little evidence of any reform in spraying practices. Very toxic materials are being applied with solemn official assurances that they will harm neither man nor beast. When wildlife losses are later reported, the same officials deny the evidence or declare the animals must have died from "something else."

Exactly this pattern of events is occurring in a number of areas now. For example, a newspaper in East St. Louis, Illinois, describes the death of several hundred rabbits, quail, and song-birds in areas treated with pellets of the insecticide dieldrin. One area involved was, ironically, a "game pre- serve." This was part of a program of Japanese beetle control.

The procedures seem to be the same as those I described in *Silent Spring*, referring to another Illinois community, Sheldon. At Sheldon, the destruction of many birds and small mammals amounted almost to anni- hilation. Yet an Illinois Agriculture official is now quoted as saying dieldrin has no serious effect on animal life.

A significant case history is shaping up now in Norfolk, Virginia. The chemical is the very toxic dieldrin, the target the white-fringed beetle, which attacks some farm crops. This situation has several especially inter- esting features. One is the evident desire of the state agriculture officials to carry out the program with as little advance discussion as possible. When the Outdoor Edition of the *Norfolk Virginian-Pilot* "broke" the story, it reported that officials refused comment on their plans. The Norfolk health officer offered reassuring statements to the public, on the grounds that the method of application guaranteed safety: The poison would be injected into the ground by a machine that drills holes in the soil. "A child would have to eat the roots of the grass to get the poison," he is quoted as saying.

However, alert reporters soon proved these assurances to be without foundation. The actual method of application was to be by seeders, blow- ers, and helicopters: the same type of procedure that in Illinois wiped out robins, brown thrashers, and meadowlarks, killed sheep in the pastures, and contaminated the forage so that cows gave milk containing poison.

Yet, at a hearing of sorts, concerned Norfolk citizens were told merely that the state's Department of Agriculture was committed to the program and that it would therefore be carried out. The fundamental wrong is that authoritarian control has been vested in the agricultural agencies. There are, after all, many different interests involved: there are problems of wa- ter pollution, of soil pollution, of wildlife protection, of public health. Yet the matter is approached as if the agricultural interests were the supreme, or indeed the only, one.

It seems to me clear that all such problems should be resolved by a conference of representatives of all the interests involved.

If we are ever to find our way out of the present deplorable situation, we must remain vigilant, we must continue to challenge and to question, we must insist that the burden of proof is on those who would use these chemicals to prove the procedures are safe.

Above all, we must not be deceived by the enormous stream of propaganda that is issuing from the pesticide manufacturers and from industry-related––although ostensibly independent—organizations. There is already a large volume of handouts openly sponsored by the manufacturers. There are other packets of materials being issued by some of the state agricultural colleges, as well as by certain organizations whose industry connections are concealed behind a scientific front. This material is going to writers, editors, professional people, and other leaders of opinion.

It is characteristic of this material that it deals in generalities, unsupported by documentation. In its claims for safety to human beings, it ignores the fact that we are engaged in a grim experiment never before attempted. We are subjecting whole populations to exposure to chemicals which animal experiments have proved to be extremely poisonous and in many cases cumulative in their effect. These exposures now begin at or before birth. No one knows what the result will be, because we have no previous experience to guide us.

Let us hope it will not take the equivalent of another thalidomide tragedy to shock us into full awareness of the hazard. Indeed, something almost as shocking has already occurred: a few months ago we were all shocked by newspaper accounts of the tragedy of the Turkish children who have developed a horrid disease through use of an agricultural chemical. To be sure, the use was unintended. The poisoning has been continuing over a period of some seven years, unknown to most of us. What made it newsworthy in 1962 was the fact that a scientist gave a public report on it.

A disease known as toxic porphria has turned some five thousand Turkish children into hairy, monkey-faced beings. The skin becomes sensitive to light and is blotched and blistered. Thick hair covers much of the face and arms. The victims have also suffered severe liver damage. Several hundred such cases were noticed in 1955. Five years later, when a South African physician visited Turkey to study the disease, he found five thousand victims. The cause was traced to seed wheat, which had been treated with a chemical fungicide called hexachlorobenzene. The seed, intended for planting, had instead been ground into flour for bread by the hungry people. Recovery of the victims is slow, and indeed worse may be in store for them. Dr. W. C. Hueper, a specialist on environmental cancer, tells me there is a strong likelihood these unfortunate children may ultimately develop liver cancer.

"This could not happen here," you might easily think. It would surprise you, then, to know that the use of poisoned seed in our own country is a matter of present concern by the Food and Drug Administration. In recent years there has been a sharp increase in the treatment of seed with chemical fungicides and insecticides of a highly poisonous nature. Two years ago an official for the Food and Drug Administration told me of that agency's fear that treated grain left over at the end of a growing season was finding its way into food channels.

Now, on last October 27, the Food and Drug Administration proposed that all treated food grain seed be brightly colored so as to be easily distinguishable from untreated seeds or grain intended as food for human beings or livestock . . .

I understood, however, that objection has been made by some segments of the industry and that this very desirable and necessary requirement may be delayed. This is a specific example of the kind of situation requiring public vigilance and public demand for correction of abuses.

The way is not made easy for those who would defend the public interest. In fact, a new obstacle has recently been created, and a new advantage has been given to those who seek to block remedial legislation. I refer to the income tax bill which becomes effective this year. The bill contains a little known provision which permits certain lobbying expenses to be considered a business expense deduction. It means, to cite a specific example, that the chemical industry may now work at bargain rates to thwart future attempts at regulation.

But what of the nonprofit organizations such as the garden clubs, the Audubon Societies, and all other such tax-exempt groups? Under existing laws they stand to lose their tax-exempt status if they devote any "substantial" part of their activities to attempts to influence legislation. The word "substantial" needs to be defined. In practice, even an effort involving less than 5 percent of an organization's activity has been ruled sufficient to cause loss of the tax-exempt status.

What happens then, when the public interest is pitted against large commercial interests? Those organizations wishing to plead for protection of the public interest do so under the peril of losing the tax-exempt status so necessary to their existence. The industry wishing to pursue its course without legal restraint is now actually subsidized in its efforts.

This is a situation which the Garden Club and similar organizations, within their legal limitations, might well attempt to remedy.

There are other disturbing factors, which I can only suggest. One is the growing interrelation between professional organizations and industry, and between science and industry. For example, the American Medical Association, through its newspaper, has referred physicians to a pesticide trade association for information to help them answer patients' questions about the effects of pesticides on man. I would like to see physicians referred to authoritative scientific or medical literature, not to a trade organization whose business is to promote the sale of pesticides.

We see scientific societies acknowledging as "sustaining associates" a dozen or more giants of a related industry. When the scientific organization speaks, whose voice do we hear, that of science or [that] of the sustaining industry? The public assumes it is hearing the voice of science.

Another cause of concern is the increasing size and number of industry grants to the universities. On first thought, such support of education seems desirable, but on reflection we see that this does not make for unbiased research; it does not promote a truly scientific spirit. To an increasing extent, the man who brings the largest grants to his university becomes an untouchable, with whom even the university president and trustees do not argue.

These are large problems and there is no easy solution. But the problems must be faced.

As you listen to the present controversy about pesticides, I recommend that you ask yourself: Who speaks? And Why?

REFERENCES

Carson, Rachel. *Lost Woods.* Ed. Linda Lear. Boston: Beacon Press, 1998.
———. *The Sea around Us.* London: Oxford, 1991.
———. *Silent Spring.* London: Penguin, 2000.
Lear, Linda. *Rachel Carson: The Life of the Author of "Silent Spring."* London: Allen Lane, 1997.
Natural Resources Defense Council. "The Story of *Silent Spring.*" http://www.nrdc.org/health/pesticides/hcarson.asp. 1997.
Tal, Alon. "*Silent Spring* at Forty: Assessing Rachel Carson's Legacy." *Eretz V'Tevah* (November–December, 1999). In Hebrew.
Watson, Bruce. "Sounding the Alarm." *Smithsonian Magazine* (September 2002).

2. Yizhar Smilansky

ISRAEL

The loss of biodiversity on the planet is considered by many environmentalists to be the most critical crisis facing the world. Extinction, after all, is forever. Loss of biodiversity, however, is largely a symptom of a wider phenomenon. There are increasingly few corners of the globe in which the creatures and plants with whom we share the planet can flourish, untouched by the long reach of human resourcefulness. Although there are many formulas for preserving dwindling species and landscapes, the heart of any conservation strategy requires the creation of sanctuaries, reserves, or protected areas. Here, habitats remain intact and the evolutionary process can continue, with the natural world enjoying a measure of respite.

Despite progress and constant campaigns by preservation advocates, these natural havens remain in short supply. Estimates by the World Resources Institute project that only 5.1 percent of the earth's surface (or a meager 1.5 percent of the total surface of the planet) are presently set aside in protected areas. Although the number of nature reserves is, across the planet, growing, optimistic scenarios do not project this number to grow beyond 10 percent of land surface on the planet.

In small countries, a far greater proportion of lands must be preserved if a representative sampling of the natural world is to survive. Israel is an example of such a land, facing particularly daunting challenges in its efforts to reach a healthy equilibrium with nature. And yet, with a relatively early start, its efforts appear to be succeeding. A speech to the country's parliament by one of the nation's most venerated authors, Yizhar Smilansky, is attributed with changing the country's leadership's perceptions about the need for an aggressive policy of preservation. The resultant strategy, and the institutions it spawned, for forty years has stemmed a tide of extinctions that seemed unstoppable during the first half of the century, during British colonial rule.

Because media coverage of Israel's political controversies is so extensive, many people are surprised to discover just how small a country it is. No bigger than New Jersey or Belgium, this thin strip of Holy Land is also the home to an extraordinary variety of landscapes and species. One need only open a Bible to read of the rich flora and fauna that can still largely be found in the country today. For instance, tiny Israel has more bat species than has all of Europe, and almost as many birds. As a meeting ground for the ecological systems of three continents, Israel contains a natural history that the first British high commissioner to Palestine, Herbert Samuel, described as "the diversity of a continent in a land no bigger than a small province." In 1962, however, this ecological legacy was in jeopardy.

The British Mandate's colonial government, which assumed power after defeating the Ottoman Turks in World War I, had been extremely disinterested in regulating the hunting by the local Arab populations. In the middle of the twentieth century, England made an unceremonious departure from Palestine. By then, after having roamed throughout the countryside for thousands of years, many of Israel's large, glamorous animals such as the Syrian Bear, the crocodiles, the cheetahs, the fallow deer, and the ostriches were gone.

Among the very first laws enacted by the newly established State of Israel was stringent hunting legislation. But a more pervasive menace soon became apparent. Massive immigration of Jewish refugees to their newly liberated homeland led to a doubling of the population within ten years and created urgent exigencies for housing and employment. At the same time, Israel's neighbors continued their relentless attack, leaving the government little time or inclination to focus on the ostensible luxuries of conservation, zoning, and preservation procedures. The resulting development, though impressive in its swiftness, was often merciless in its environmental impact.

During the 1950s, a small band of biology teachers, hikers, and kibbutz members organized as the "Society for the Protection of Nature" and began to sound the call for greater sensitivity to the natural world. Although the group was technically a nongovernment organization that criticized official policy, its message was openly patriotic. The unabashed love of the "homeland" and its ancient landscape was consistent enough with the Zionist philosophy of the leaders of all political parties to make the group a powerful force in the national discourse. What the organization lacked, however, was a dedicated representative in the corridors of power. It made sense then that Yizhar Smilansky, one of the country's leading young novelists, should fill this role. For Smilanksy (who wrote under the pen name "S. Yizhar") was not merely a gifted and acclaimed young author—he was also a politician.

Smilanksy was born in 1916 into a family of writers and farmers. He attended the newly established Hebrew University in Jerusalem, began teaching in boarding schools across the country, and published his first book when he was only twenty-two. But his literary career had to wait as the six hundred thousand Jews of Palestine were forced to defend themselves from constant Arab terrorism during the British Mandate and then to stave off an attack launched by five neighboring armies the minute the British departed Palestine in 1948. Like his peers, Smilanksy was forced to bear arms, and the military experience found its way into the novels that he penned soon thereafter. These books capture many of the traumatic moral dilemmas and unavoidable horrors that soldiers face, even when fighting for just causes.

Smilansky's literary works were distinguished by their lengthy and detailed descriptions of the countryside and by his protagonists' angst and agitation, particularly in uncomfortable military situations. Smilanksy's characters are famous for internalizing their landscape, and the effect of the environment on human character became a theme in his successful but often controversial novels. His fans hailed his clear call for decency and compassion to civilians, while his critics assailed him for irresponsible or quixotic moralizing. But the books were not sufficiently controversial to affect his personal popularity. After the country's 1948 War of Independence, Smilansky was elected as a member of the ruling Mapai party into Israel's parliament, the Knesset, and served there for five consecutive terms, until 1967. In a political culture that venerated artists and men of letters, his lyrical and often passionate voice for justice resonated with his party colleagues, especially those holding senior government portfolios.

When the environmental advocates found themselves in the thick of an intense struggle over the form that a new national park system would take, it was only natural to turn to Smilansky for help. The battle was parliamentary in nature, and it appeared to be a losing one. Unlike some controversies over conservation agency authorities, the conflict was not one between the "good" environmentalists and "evil" developers. Not only is Israel blessed with a remarkable natural heritage, but it also is home to an astonishing cultural heritage. The density of its historically significant sites may be unmatched.

The weathered hills and valleys of the Holy Land have seen prophets, pilgrims, conquering armies, and settlers come and go for millennia. Even its most remote corners bear little resemblance to true wilderness. Yet the gnarled Mediterranean trees and ancient undulations hold a beauty and medley of ecosystems that offer inspiration and solace. In 1962 they still were largely free of modern human progress. Little of this was to be protected by the law proposed by the bureaucrats at the Landscape Improvement Department. Theirs was a vision of small fenced-in parks with swimming pools, snack bars, and entrance fees. Nature lovers were appalled that, after a decade of lobbying and waiting for a proper conservation statute, they might be left with a pitiful regulatory framework. But the opposing camp of park proponents was headed by a powerful ex-general, Yan Yanai, and enjoyed the seemingly omnipotent prime minister's office as a base of operations.

Undaunted, Smilansky happily took it upon himself to "hijack" the proposed legislation and turn it into a very different kind of law, one that empowered an independent nature protection agency that might counter the national enthusiasm for development and sprawl. There was little political capital to be made from the fight and no powerful interest group to turn to for support. The farm lobby was decidedly unenthusiastic about ceding potential ground for cultivation. The Jewish National Fund, a development agency involved since the British-Mandate in forestry in Israel, felt threatened by any new institution that might bear a remote similarity and constitute competition for support. And the idea of leaving enormous tracts of land untrammeled as a habitat for nature was some-what alien to the prevailing Zionist ethos of economic growth and immi-grant absorption. But Smilansky enjoyed the benefit of Zionism's visceral devotion to the Land of Israel. For many, preservation was synonymous with patriotism.

It was to this naturalist impulse that Smilansky appealed when he stepped up in a Knesset plenary and seized the rostrum in June 1962, delivering a speech about the issue of preservation and the appropriate role for government. Formally, the debate was a review of national budget, but Smilansky decided that the topics for legitimate debate in this session were wide enough to squeeze in something as esoteric as nature preserva-tion. Most important, "budget skirmishes" were important enough for the government to ensure that an attentive Prime Minister David Ben Gurion would be in attendance, a fact that would prove quite important. So Smilansky took the opening shot in his campaign during the budget deliberations; the speech is translated below.

As is often the case with literature, much of the lyricism of Smilansky's elegant Hebrew is lost in translation. But the essence of the human im-pulse to protect nature is a romantic one far more compelling than the contingent valuation of species diversity or some utilitarian description of ecosystem services. Here, Smilansky's ardor and righteous indignation shine through. For the Israeli lament and ecological misfortune consti-tute an extreme expression of the sense of loss felt around the world. Smilansky's was a cry against the decimation of the very land for which scores of his generation had died. It was inconceivable to him that Jewish stewardship of the land could be as careless and foolhardy as the first decade of Zionist sovereignty implied.

In retrospect, his eloquent appeal proved a triumph. Given his flare for language, a Smilansky speech was always considered a treat; his colleagues came to listen. But this speech was especially gauged to tug at the senti-mental side of the crusty prime minister's heartstrings. And it actually succeeded in entirely changing his view on the issue. This became clear during the subsequent deliberations over the proposed National Parks Law, in December.

Not only did Ben Gurion's surprise presentation in the Knesset break ranks with his own office and reject the original bill submitted; it also adopted many of the revisions that Smilansky sought. The prime minis-ter also went as far as to quote entire sections of the Smilansky Knesset speech that he had heard six months earlier. Ben Gurion qualified his po-sition by stating that he saw grandeur not only in natural creation but also in human artistic, technological, and economic achievements, But, substantively, he embraced the "preservationist" critique that ultimately led to the bureaucratic restructuring and ultimate ecological success of the new legislation.

Rather than establish a single National Park Service, the Smilanksy compromise created the parallel frameworks of a National Parks Authority and a Nature Protection Authority. National Parks were to be landmarks, largely of historical significance, where human presence was allowed and honored. Nature reserves were to be sanctuaries where people were the guests and development was eschewed. The dichotomy was described as analogous to the book of Genesis's call "to work and to preserve" the Garden of Eden. National Parks were to be worked, Nature Reserves preserved. In retrospect, this prescient, seemingly bureaucratic, distinction was responsible for saving dozens of ecologically precious corners of the land of the Bible.

The Nature Reserve Authority quickly came to be the dominant of the two agencies, especially in the magnitude of its land holdings. A full 25 percent of all Israeli lands were designated for preservation as Nature Reserves. Yet, as every wildlife warden knows, even this is hardly a panacea for the challenges of preservation and management in the face of a simmering military conflict as well as staggering population and economic growth. Large portions of protected lands are in the desert, and frequently the Israeli Army uses sections of the reserves for military maneuvers, essentially closing the areas to the public and often pummeling the land, flora, and fauna. As the country continues to fulfill its role of "ingathering the Jewish exiles," Israel's population has increased by one million people every decade. This level of growth invariably takes a harsh ecological toll. After all, people have to live somewhere and the country is so very small.

But the Israeli Nature Reserve system is a critical first step and offers hope. The present network of 373 reserves contains representative samples of the unique landscape that has long served four of the world's major religions (Christianity, Islam, Judaism, and Bahaism) as a "Holy Land." Here, the essential elements of the country's wetlands, mountains, drylands, valleys, and forests remain unchanged. In popular areas, hiking is limited to trails, to contain anthropogenic damage. Not even camping is allowed in reserves. Thus the creatures and plants of the land can still thrive in a country that grows increasingly crowded, segmented, and inhospitable.

The name Yizhar Smilansky today is largely unknown to Israelis (although schools still teach the books of S. Yizhar). For the most part, the environmental movement in Israel is also unaware of the enormous historic contribution to ecological sustainability by this man of letters: that it was his fervent plea to parliament that led to Israel's realization that existing practices were destroying the scenery of the Holy Land and should be discontinued. Smilansky's subsequent work in the legislative corridors and committees also brokered the necessary amendments to catapult an Israeli Nature Reserve system into action, preserving not only scenic lands but endangered species of plants and animals. Forty years later, notwithstanding the violence, development, and turmoil the country has suffered, it has been surprisingly successful in preserving much of the beauty and holiness of its land. Every country that has created effective institutions to protect biodiversity has a unique story to tell. In Israel, it started with a speech.

"A Land without Wildflowers Will Be a Hotel, Not a Homeland"

THE KNESSET (ISRAEL'S PARLIAMENT), JUNE 12, 1962

*M*y Colleagues, Knesset Members:

I have asked for the podium to offer a few comments on a subject that may not be in the sole jurisdiction of the prime minister's office, but they are surely within it. For, while he is not responsible for every solution to all the questions that I might ask, as one involved with these questions (and as others are not available to address them), it is he who ultimately will be required to embrace and implement the task.

I fear that the subject to which I draw your attention will seem inappropriate, and even a bit eccentric, and in spite of this it is no other than: the way our land will look tomorrow. If you wish, the subject is: the destruction of the landscape. If you wish: the development of the land.

After all, this is such a small country that it is enough for two or three gross errors to disfigure its facial profile. These are the mistakes that produce such ruin that they cannot be reversed. And even if such actions were taken in good faith, and these hasty efforts were made with the intention of helping, not only were they devoid of wisdom, but they also hold the risk of defiling the face of the land. And if we do not know how

Speech reprinted by permission of Yizhar Smilansky.

to stop, there is a real danger that an entire generation of young citizens will spring up here without any real affection for the land, and without any direct contact and identification with its appearance.

I in no way refer here to the important efforts to develop various sites in Israel or improve lovely corners for the enjoyment of the country's citizenry and its tourists. Rather I mean the disfiguring of the country's features and the squandering of her beautiful treasures as they are, as they have the power to be, and as nature intended them to be.

Before we can beautify this or that corner of the countryside, the landscape is wasted. Before we can offer an opinion, someone has already stretched out his hand, taken, and "developed" a particular region—developed and destroyed, struck and totally injured. By the time we even get around to cultivating the odd garden, some "planner" or another owner has beaten us to it and decimated the foundations of the land—an entire region, a whole mountain, a spring, or a forest, not to mention plants and wildlife and their fateful extermination. So great is the damage that not only is it difficult to mend, but the repair itself may only extend the spoilage. We must therefore save these natural wonders before some nimble hotel owner comes and buys the land for pennies and the public finds it has been short-changed.

Need I add that for humans it is impossible to live without some open vistas that have not been transformed by the hand of man. It is impossible to exist in a place where everything is organized and planned unto the last detail, until all remnants of the original image, the natural and organic signs of the earth's creation, are erased. It is a necessity for man to have a place to go to shake himself off and refresh himself from the city, from the constructed, from the enclosed, from the delivered. And it is essential to soak up the refreshing connection with the primal, with the exposed, with the "before the coming of mankind." A land where the breeze blows without wildflowers is a place of suffocation. A land where winds cannot blow unobstructed will be a hotel, not a homeland. A land that is all roads and sidewalks and a sense of ultimate construction will devour all good portions in the hearts of its young people.

Every winter, the wild flowers are rudely uprooted. It will not take long until every narcissus and anemone and cyclamen—the most common, prevalent, and characteristic [flowers] of our land—shall disappear and remain only as museum exhibits. Some species of irises have already been decimated. The tulips of the hillsides are continually being destroyed. A city that cuts down the tiara of its trees on one side of the street each year so as not to interfere with the electric lines grows unsightly; we should also not be surprised if its children walk with one elevated shoulder while the other slouches down.

A seventy-year-old tree that is cut can never be replaced by a beneficial building. There is no substitute for the ancient tree. He who uproots this tree destroys human roots. There is no building or electricity that is more important than a wide eucalyptus tree, an old sycamore, and a grove of oaks; they are the roots of humanity. A building can always be constructed here or there. But the hundred-year-old tree has no replacement. It is not just vandalism for the present, but a hazard for the future. And with what insouciance do we uproot? Trees will always be found to bother someone or something: the straight line of the sidewalk or the electric lines or an inconsequential city square that someone initiated in their narrow imagination. After all, such development shows disdain for anything that is not a "revenue item."

There are those who would rationalize such an empty vision and eviscerated heart by citing lack of funds. Every hurried and stingy building project is always breathlessly explained. But the truth is not always lack of funds. Sometimes it is lack of imagination, or lack of heart: not stinginess in financing but a stinginess in humanity or an alienation from the land.

Was it anything but stinginess that led to the stealing of the ancient city of Safed's face and its deformity in bricks of ugliness? And whom might we call to account to ensure that no other such unrepentant "development momentum" recurs? Is there any other Safed? Or a second Mount Meron? Are there two Mount Carmels in this land, that we might take one of them and abandon it as property to any speculator willing to pay cash? Or to the planner, deceived by his own omniscience, who would entirely transform nature into ugly neighborhoods Or the private palaces of the wealthy who pilfer from the public to build themselves a complimentary domain on "their" personal Carmel Mountain? The best of the peaks, the most pleasant of the woods, the sweetest of the hillsides—are they to be turned into real estate, sold by the square acre, while we go through the motions of improving some isolated spring?

Or the seashore? For whom should the coasts in this land be? For the miners of sand that raze our short shoreline with neither mercy nor thoughts of restoration? To private individuals or corporations who close off plot after plot and who perceive the sea as private property and charge an entry tax? Ours is such a short shoreline, and most of it is already closed or destroyed or essentially contaminated for swimming. Does this not displace the feeling of a citizen's freedom, his entitlement to come and go as he pleases and to immerse himself in the sea? To play and frolic on the beach without having to seek permission from a soul? Who is responsible for maintaining safe, swimmable beaches, freely available to all? Is this not among the most basic joys of life that compensate for so many other feelings of dissatisfaction? ...

It would seem that it has become impossible to continue without intervention, without an appropriate law that would limit and prohibit all local aggressors who treat the nature of this land as if it were their own, who would choose to be the sole arbiter in matters that concern the public well into the distant future. The number of authorities that scurry about must be limited, as one contradicts what the other builds. Hasty construction must be stopped. The creations of humanity, powerful though they may be, must never replace the work of the Creator.

But legislation alone will not suffice here. A broad, comprehensive, and fundamental public campaign needs to be initiated in every town and hamlet, and in every educational outlet—schools, the radio, the newspaper, the cinema—through every possible form of appeal. So that no man shall pick a flower without pangs of regret, so that earthwork is unable to destroy, to uproot, and to decimate what a narrow imagination does not perceive, and to spoil with the power of a single bulldozer what has been so gradually fashioned since the advent of time.

This is a small country. Most of it is desolate and scorched by the sun. It may yet develop and grow. If we do not know how to balance our enterprises with caution, with love and foresight, we shall leave after us a deformity that will alienate all who are young of heart. Who would love a land that is not beautiful? A land grown repulsive from impatience, rash planning, and obsessive but unimaginative organization? ...

As this land becomes more crowded, the question of open spaces—wild, innocent havens of quiet that have not been touched by the hand of man—grows more pressing. We must remember that no urban playground, as enhanced as it may be, can be a replacement for open space. We must turn to the very best and most tasteful: painters, poets, architects, scientists, nature lovers, citizens groups, whose hearts are open so that they may assist in finding ways to keep the wild forest on Mount Meron intact in its unblemished form. That an oasis, or a cluster of sands, or a remote stream, will not be obliterated without a sound or notice. That entire regions can continue to exist as they are, regions that can be crossed without tripping over the obstacles of man or the spillover of human transactions, places where nature remains authentic, reflecting what is true in man, where humans can have natural and innocent contact with the animals and the plants in their appropriate habitat.

It is possible that the question that I ask may appear excessively naïve or extremely peripheral. And in spite of this, it appears to me to be the most essential. What will the landscape where humans live look like? What will a man see when he opens his windows in the morning? Will there be a sea breeze blowing on his face? What will be the measure of "the green" in his habitat? What will be his sense of freedom to move and to absorb, as he seeks the ultimate, uninterrupted connection? Where will he be able to be seek refuge, when life in the closed city has consumed everything?

In short: what should the leaders of the nation do if they want the people of this land to love their land?

REFERENCES

Divrei Ha Knesset (*Knesset Proceedings*), Jerusalem, June 12, 1962, p. 2278 (published December 11, 1962).

Gabai, Shoshana. *The Environment in Israel.* Jerusalem: Israel Ministry of Environment, 2002.

Institute for the Translation of Hebrew Literature. "S. Yizhar." *www.ithl.org.il/author_info.* 2004.

Paz, Uzi. "Thus It Began." *Eretz V'Tevah* 264 (1994). In Hebrew.

Seh-Lavan, Yosef. *S. Yizhar: The Man and his Work.* 2d ed. Tel, Aviv: Or-Am, 1990. In Hebrew.

Tal, Alon. *Pollution in a Promised Land: An Environmental History of Israel.* Berkeley and Los Angeles: University of California Press, 2002.

World Resources Institute. *Earth Trends Data Tables.* "Protected Areas." *http://earthtrends.wri.org/pdf_library/data_tables/Bio2_2003.pdf.* 2003.

Yizhar, S. *Jewish Virtual Library. http://www.us-israel.org/jsource/biography/yizhar.html.*

3. Thor Heyerdahl

NORWAY

On March 18, 1967, the *Torrey Canyon,* an oil tanker carrying 117,000 tons of crude oil from Kuwait across the North Sea, had an unanticipated encounter with the Seven Stones Reef near Great Britain's Cornish coastline. Six of the ships' tanks were torn open by the initial impact, giving the world its first experience with a major televised oil spill. The environmental devastation caused by the eight-mile-long slick, captured in images of ghoulishly blackened waterfowl and fish, was an ugly and shocking sight. The subsequent decision to send in the Royal Air Force—which for two days dropped eighty thousand kilograms of explosives, twelve thousand liters of napalm, and innumerable rockets to pulverize the remaining oil—along with the hapless clean-up efforts, made a grave message even clearer. The all-powerful sea had become yet another victim of the growing ecological crisis.

The highly publicized catastrophe was of course only a warning sign alongside a host of less newsworthy, but even more insidious, insults decimating the world's oceans. The ecological pathology has been understood by marine scientists for some time. Then as now, not shipping but, rather, activities on land caused most of the damage to the marine environment. For example, some 44 percent of pollutants in the ocean can be traced to run-off and land-based effluent discharges, while 33 percent involve fall-out from air emissions to the atmosphere. By the time of the *Torrey Canyon* disaster, it was clear that the growing intensity of human actions on land and sea, the toxicity and persistence of chemicals discharged into the waters, along with the new technologies that allowed for expanded human exploitation of marine resources, all contributed to the oceans' vulnerability.

It also was clear that no country's unilateral actions could save the sea. The family of nations would have to establish new forms of cooperation and finally learn to work together. But who had the international stature and commitment to galvanize the growing concern and convince the world to change its way of looking at the planet's oceans, even before modifying the norms for utilizing it? Thor Heyerdahl, certainly the most flamboyant if not most famous anthropologist of the twentieth century, found himself in this role. His theories about ancient migrations led him to the sea. And what he found there led him to the corridors of power, where he tirelessly worked for change.

Perhaps the most remarkable thing about Thor Heyerdahl was that he had no formal training in maritime navigation, marine biology, or even in environmental studies or in anthropology. In fact, when he began sailing around the world in primitive vessels, he claimed he hardly knew how to swim and had almost drowned as a child. Yet, by the end of the 1960s, this Norwegian anthropologist extraordinaire emerged as the world's leading spokesperson on behalf of the world's beleaguered seas.

Born in 1914, in the whaling town of Larvik, Norway, Heyerdahl was raised primarily by his mother, a highly liberated, atheistic museum curator who instilled in him a love for nature and learning. He apparently was born a *natural* showman. While still a wee schoolboy, he opened a one-room animal museum in the deserted outhouse at the brewery that his father ran, and caught specimens to display there. As a youth, he confided to friends his ambition of one day becoming an explorer. Yet Heyerdahl appeared very much on a conventional track when he pursued his university degree in zoology and geography at the University of Oslo. This proved misleading. Subsequent events showed that there was nothing conventional about the man.

Heyerdahl startled his family when, at age twenty-two, he announced that he would marry Liv, a high school acquaintance, and set out on a one-way ticket for field research in the South Pacific. It was the first of many surprises.

Tahiti was certainly a romantic destination for a newlywed couple, who happily embraced life as "Adam and Eve living in a Garden of Eden." Adopted by the island's supreme chief, Teriieroo, Heyerdahl and his wife moved out to a more remote island where they could live in a more traditional Polynesian style. Originally, Heyerdahl planned to focus on the origins and diffusion of local flora and fauna, but it was the Polynesian *people's* history that quickly came to fascinate him, especially after he noticed surprising similarities between the "indigenous" plants with those found in South America. And so it was that, with no formal training to speak of, Heyerdahl left behind his zoological pursuits and became an anthropologist.

Heyerdahl became convinced that the conventional theories of Pacific island settlement were unfounded and that ocean currents from the west had brought the people of these islands from South America eons earlier. He soon published his hypothesis that Polynesia had been settled in two waves by immigrants who came on balsa rafts from Peru and Easter Island. He defended the theory in his encyclopedic (eight-hundred-page) work *American Indians and the Pacific,* but it became the subject of some ridicule within the academic establishment. Heyerdahl's rebuttal was truncated when Nazi Germany brought World War II to peaceful Norway's doorstep. He enlisted in the Free Norwegian Paratrooper Unit and won medals for distinction in the battle to liberate his occupied country.

But, after defending his nation's freedom, Heyerdahl turned his considerable energies to defending his anthropological hypothesis. Skeptics argued that the basic premise of Heyerdahl's ideas was preposterous, if for no other reason than that "primitive" man had no ships for sailing such distances. Heyerdahl would prove them wrong.

He built a simple "aboriginal" balsa raft, which he called the *Kon-Tiki,* took a crew of five with him, and sailed for 101 days—from Peru to the Polynesia. During this time the expedition covered the astonishing distance of eight thousand kilometers. Although this amazing demonstration did not immediately convert the staid scholarly community to Heyerdahl's point of view, it certainly silenced the dismissive claim that such a journey simply could not have been accomplished. It also transformed an arcane academic discussion into a compelling international media event. Heyerdahl's subsequent 1951 book about the experience sold an astonishing 60 million copies worldwide and the film he produced won the Academy Award for best documentary. The showmanship that had so annoyed professors delighted an entire planet, which identified with the intrepid explorer on the sea.

Heyerdahl would take three more journeys in his efforts to explore the prospects of interactions among ancient civilizations. In 1969 he converted twelve tons of papyrus to construct a fifteen-meter vessel, the *Ra,* that left the ancient Phoenician port of Safi in Morocco, and sailed five thousand kilometers to the Caribbean. After storms forced the team to abandon the journey a week before arriving in Barbados, he returned a year later with a smaller boat and completed the journey: 6,100 kilometers in 57 days. The possibility of Mediterranean settlement in the Atlantic, years before Columbus attempted such a trip, was established.

Heyerdahl's favorite adage, "Man hoisted sail before he saddled a horse," supported his almost mystical perception of the sea as a conduit that connected people and cultures rather than divided them. The implicit ancillary message that accompanied his anthropological conjectures was a deeper vision of international harmony. On his last major expedition, his reconstructed Sumerian reed vessel, the *Tigris,* traveled 4,200 miles in 143 days through the Arabian Gulf to ultimately reach the Red Sea. Yet the internecine warfare in the countries along the way (Ethiopians were fighting Eritreans, and Somalia and Yemen were immersed in bloody civil wars) made it impossible to find a place to land. To highlight the madness of these violent conflicts to the world, Heyerdahl and his crew decided to burn the boat when, after five months at sea, they finally came ashore in the newly established nation of Djibouti. After the "peace bonfire," he wrote the secretary general of the United Nations about the situation: "Our planet is bigger than the reed bundles that have carried us across the seas, and yet small enough to run the same risks, unless those of us still alive open our eyes and minds to the desperate need for intelligent collaboration, to save ourselves and our common civilization from what we are about to convert into a sinking ship." This was a moderate response compared to the *environmental* report he sent the U.N. and the campaign he waged after the *Ra* expedition. After suffering daily contact with such copious quantities of oil slicks and chemical spills that he "couldn't find a clean spot in the ocean to rinse his toothbrush," Heyerdahl grew incensed. He was stunned by the magnitude of the increase in contamination since his first voyage twenty years earlier. "We seem to believe the ocean is endless, but we use it like a sewer," he would say. Without any formal organizational infrastructure to back him, he personally assumed the role of lead advocate for addressing the menace that pollution suddenly posed for the world's oceans. Leveraging his international celebrity status, he appealed to governments around the world, pushed the United Nations, and in over twenty-three countries testified about the issue of marine contamination. Among the diverse venues were the U.S. Senate and the Soviet Academy of Sciences.

Although Heyerdahl continued to be a vigorous conservation activist for thirty years, his influence was most apparent during his "celebrity" days of the late 1960s and 1970s. Accordingly, the speech selected for this anthology is one he gave at a satellite event at the Stockholm Conference of 1972, used as a forum to "educate" attending government representatives. An extraordinarily compelling description of the roots and nature of marine pollution problems, Heyerdahl's presentation may well constitute the most eloquent environmental speech ever recorded on the subject.

Before he died of brain cancer in 2002, Heyerdahl lived to see some meaningful achievements in marine pollution prevention. In 1974, the newly formed United Nations Environmental Program (UNEP) established a regional seas program that fostered action plans and treaties to protect thirteen regions, involving 140 nations from the South Pacific to the Caribbean. The International Maritime Organization has emerged as a highly effective forum, with MARPOL (the International Convention for the Prevention of Pollution from Ships) as its central engine for change. Although the United States has not yet ratified the treaty, the Law of the Sea along with its evolving technical annexes became fully functional by 1978 and has been adopted by 127 nations, representing 96 percent of the tonnage transported by sea. Through the corresponding national laws, the world has fundamentally changed the way oil and other hazardous chemicals are shipped, and a new generation of more secure, double-hull tankers are in place. Discharge of oily ballast waters into the sea, an enormous part of the nuisance that so saddened (and annoyed) Heyerdahl, has been virtually eliminated, especially in sensitive "special areas" like the Mediterranean, Baltic, and Red Seas. Many nations, especially those with sufficient economic capacity, have made real progress in stemming the flow of sewage into the oceans.

Some marine indicators, including fish stocks and acidity, are not encouraging. But there is enough progress to maintain that the worst of the past abuses are over, and that humanity may yet establish a more sustainable and caring relationship with the world's oceans. Thor Heyerdahl's call to save the sea has begun to make waves.

"If Man Is to Survive, the Ocean Is Not Dispensable"

MIRROR BALL ROOM, GRAND HOTEL, STOCKHOLM, SWEDEN, JUNE 1972

At least five thousand years ago, man started to rebel against the nature that had bred him and successfully nourished him for perhaps a million years or more. It has been five thousand years of technological progress and a continued series of victories for the human rebel, the only mutineer among the descendants of nature; Nature has yielded, tree by tree, acre by acre, species by species, river by river, while man has triumphed. He has been able to advance by using the brain and the hands nature had given him, to invent and use tools and to create new materials.

One might say that on the seventh day, when God rested, man took over as Creator. He began to redesign the world and mold it to his own liking. Century after century, he has worked without a blueprint to build a man-made world, each inventor throwing in an idea, each mason thrusting in a stone wherever a hand could reach. Only in very recent years have we begun to wonder what we are building. So far it has been taken for granted that any step away from nature was progress for humanity. Quite recently it has become more and more apparent that some of the changes man is imposing on his original environment could be harmful to himself; in fact, they could even lead to global disaster.

New inventions and new products continue to pour into the market, while representatives from nations all over the world are assembled here in Stockholm today to try jointly for the first time to sort out the problem. What are we building and what are we doing to our environment? Can this unorganized rebellion against nature, this global building without plan, continue at its rapidly increasing pace without the haphazard structure collapsing over our heads? Is there something we can do to safeguard our existence in the changing world? Are we on the verge of

Speech reprint rights granted by the Kon-Tiki Museum.

destroying something that we ourselves and our descendants cannot do without?

Indeed, the problem is manifold, since civilization is complex and the world is large. It is my privilege here to raise some questions pertaining to one aspect of the problem: what are we doing to the ocean? As we all know, the ocean covers 71 percent of the surface of our planet. Is it vulnerable? And if so, is the ocean dispensable?

Unless we stop to reflect for a moment, I think most of us have the impression that the ocean is nothing but a big hole in the ground filled with undrinkable salt water, an obstacle to pedestrians and drivers alike, an abyss separating nations. On second thought, we think of it as a conveyer for ships, a source of food, a holiday playground, and, if we remember our school day lessons, we realize that it acts as a filter, receiving dirty river water and returning it to our fields through evaporation, clouds, and rain. It is probably not unreasonable to assume that most people regard the dominant space of the ocean on our planet as more of a disadvantage than an advantage. With less land covered by the ocean, there would be more fields to cultivate, more resources available, and more space for the growing population to expand. The fact, however, is that the proportion of land to ocean is either extremely well planned or a remarkably happy coincidence, since it is this composition which has made life possible, at least in the form we know it, just on this one planet.

Whether we accept the story of the creation in the Bible or the findings of modern science, we all agree that life on earth began in the ocean. Neither God nor nature was able to create man from lifeless volcanic rock. The long and complex evolution toward man began below the surface of the sea when solar energy transformed the gases and minerals from eroded rocks into protoplasm and the first living cells. We do not know precisely how it happened, but after a certain period of time the first single-celled organisms were alive in the sea; the ancestors of all animals floated side by side with the ancestors of all plants. While many of them evolved into larger species, others continued to survive much in their original size and form until the present day, and are part of the marine microorganisms we call plankton. The animal-plankton, termed zooplankton, sustained themselves by feeding on the plant-plankton, or phytoplankton, and the plant-plankton survived by feeding on dead and decomposed plankton of both kinds, and the minerals of the sea. In this process of metabolism, the plant-plankton, and their descendants among the larger algae, began to produce oxygen in increasing quantities as they multiplied and filled the sunny surface layers of the oceans.

So rich became this production of oxygen from the plant life in the sea, that it rose above the surface and into the earth's sterile atmosphere. When the atmospheric content of oxygen was high enough, some shore-stranded algae took hold, and after millions of years developed roots and leaves, becoming the first primitive terrestrial plants. But it was not until the content of oxygen in the atmosphere was approaching the percentage it maintains today that the first lung-breathing species were able to emerge from the sea; animal life on the land and in the air had been impossible for hundreds of millions of years, until plant life in the sea had produced sufficient oxygen. Then the animals of the sea developed into the creatures of the air and of the land. From then on, conditions were ready for the long evolution to the mammals, which terminated with the appearance of man. Man represents the crown of a mighty family tree with all its roots in the ocean. We cannot overlook this biological background.

We of the twentieth century, in spite of our supermarkets and super-jets, have not become supermen who can cut off the umbilical cord to nature and survive alone as an independent species. We must never forget that we are part of a tremendously complicated system, part of a synthesis of biological species ranging from the oxygen-producing plankton of the sea, and forests of the land, to the food-producing soil and water, which can yield their indispensable supplies only through the activities of insects, worms, and bacteria, inconspicuous creatures which man in his ignorance usually disregards and even despises. Not even the invisible Creator, call him God or call him the Force of Evolution, could place man on the surface of the earth, until all other biological species were already there to support him.

Only in recent years have we begun to understand the interaction of the extremely complex ecosystem—where every single biological species has its function in creating living conditions, birth, and continued survival for other species higher up the ladder of evolution. On the very top of this ladder, man is balancing, ready to fall if for some reason he should lose the support of the species that preceded him and paved his road to existence. More than half of the biological pyramid supporting man at its apex is composed of creatures living in the sea. Remove them and the pyramid collapses; there will be no foundation to maintain life on land or in the air.

We are all aware of the fact that an important part of the human food supply comes directly from the sea. In fact, modern economists are counting on a vastly increased output by ocean fisheries if we are to solve the growing problem of feeding the undernourished world of tomorrow. If we kill the plankton, we lose the fish and thus drastically reduce the protein available for human sustenance. Man can limp along with very little in his stomach, but he has to fill his lungs. It takes weeks to die of starvation, days to die of thirst, and seconds to suffocate. If we kill the plankton, we reduce to less than half the supply of oxygen available to men and beasts, and this at a time when forests are becoming scarcer than ever before. We, like all breathing species, will in fact be increasingly dependent on the plants in the ocean, since green landscapes rapidly recede before the spread of urbanization, industry, and the onslaught of modern farming, while asphalt, concrete, and barren sand dunes advance on previously fertile land. Since life on land is so utterly dependent on life in the sea, we can safely deduce that a dead sea means a dead planet.

Let us humbly admit it: if man is to survive, the ocean is not dispensable. If it is not dispensable, a pressing question naturally emerges: "Is the ocean vulnerable?"

If we ask the man in the street, if we ask the decision makers, if we ask ourselves, we are likely to hear the answer: the ocean is not vulnerable; it is too vast to be damaged by little man's activities; it is an enormous self-purifying filter which has taken care of itself for millions of years and will continue to do so forever. We are all familiar with the phrase "a drop in the ocean."

Since the morning of time, thanks to gravity, nothing has dropped off the earth into space— nothing except a few truckloads of gear recently transferred to the moon. Millions of years with natural pollution. Millions of years without human industry, when nature itself was a giant workshop experimenting, inventing, producing, and throwing away waste—waste by incalculable billions and ever more billions of tons of rotting trees, dead flesh, bones, excrement. Whether we measure in weight or in volume, the wastes of all the world's industry amount to nothing during the few decades of our technical era, as compared with the hundreds of millions of years of volcanic eruption, global erosion, and untold generations with death and decay. Man is not the first manufacturer; why should he become the first polluter? Our spaceship is built with an ocean to take care of pollution. So why worry? . . . .

When nature could produce and pollute, why cannot little man? Volcanoes and sandstorms have sent fumes and dust into the air as long as life has existed, while dead fish and plankton have rained toward the bottom of the sea together with the silt from fields and rivers. There has never been any ultimate pollution of the land or of the air: it is all being flushed into the ocean. Of course, the land has been littered with dead leaves, fallen trees, rotting corpses, fermenting dung. But the rain is there to clean the air and to wash the rocks. Bacteria are there to transform death and subsequent decay into life and subsequent lovemaking. And gravity is there to drag the decomposed surplus by way of nature's drains into streams and rivers bound for the earth's ultimate sink: the ocean. Only the ocean has no outlet for solid waste. But silt and filth from the land are received as magic fuel for the billions of tons of plankton, which help to keep the ocean fresh and clean.

So why the fuss about little man's pollutants? Why can't we pollute, when nature can? Simply because the pollutants of modern man have suddenly become basically different from those of nature.

Man has recently created materials which nature wisely avoided because they had no place among the perfectly interlocking cogwheels of the global ecosystem. Through technology, man has begun to throw extra bolts and nuts into a ready-made and smoothly operating machinery. Although it has only begun with our own generation, year by year, day by day, man's production of nontransformable, nondegradable materials has increased in a virtually precipitous curve. Waste and refuse are littered everywhere, and we try to sweep it all into the ocean as if under a carpet. We realize that an increasing quantity of our modern waste is both toxic and nondegradable, but it doesn't matter: the ocean is endless. The ocean is deep.

This is, in fact, the second misconception. For the ocean is not endless and its depth is greatly misleading. Just as we have seen that the age of the ocean is no guarantee of its invulnerability in technological times, in the same way, we shall see that its size is no better guarantee.

Anyone who has drifted from one continent to another on a bundle of reeds or a log raft cannot help being struck by the fact that the ocean is just another big lake. It is enough to place ten Lake Eries end to end, and they will span the Atlantic from Africa to America.

With technical progress, distances have dwindled, dimensions have changed. With the astronauts we begin to see that the ocean has limits like any lake; we begin to see our planet as a lonely spaceship. A spaceship without an exhaust pipe. We have begun to realize that no chimney is tall enough to pierce the atmosphere and send our fumes into space, nor is any sewer long enough to pipe our pollutants beyond the borders of our common sea. For primitive man standing on the beach, the blue ocean ran into the blue sky; for us it curves beyond sight and falls back on us from behind.

Sea and soil, fumes and sewage, all are here to ride with us forever, in some form or another, on the thin crust of our spinning sphere. Even so, the sea is large compared to man. After all, its average depth is 1,500 meters (or about 5,000 feet), running in places down to more than 10,000 meters (or 30,000 feet). If this average depth of 1,500 meters were stretched out along a road, a runner could cover the distance in less than four minutes. And, if we were to represent the world ocean on a topographic globe, it would be impossible to smear on a coat of blue paint thin enough to represent the depth of the ocean in true proportion.

Although the ocean layer, in a global perspective, is thus much thinner than people suppose, only a fraction of this water needs to be polluted to kill all life. Marine life is concentrated near the surface and, again, most of the surface life is concentrated near the shores. Why is only the upper limit of real importance to marine life? Because marine life, directly or indirectly, depends on the plant-plankton as basic food; and plant-plankton can live only where the sunlight can penetrate the water in sufficient quantity to permit photosynthesis. This upper section, in the sunny tropics, is only 80 to 100 meters deep, whereas in the northern latitudes, on a bright summer's day, it has a depth of only 15 to 20 meters. Below this thin layer, life is immediately very restricted, since it depends on the sinking of decomposing plant and animal remains from the sunlit waters above.

Why is most of this already restricted surface life further concentrated near the shores? Because marine plant life, in addition to sunlight, needs mineral nutriments. In the coastal areas, some of these are brought down by rivers and others are returned from the bottom of the sea. The ocean bottom is rich in these nutriments which have rained down from decomposing organisms near the surface, and they can only return to the surface in areas where strong underwater currents and upwellings occur, such as near continental shores. An estimated 90 percent of all marine life is found in shallow coastal areas generally referred to as the continental shelves. These important areas represent only 8 percent of the total surface of the oceans, and, of course, only a fraction of a percent of the total ocean volume. When we speak of farmable land, we refer only to the usable surface soil; we never count the volume of sterile rock beneath, as deep as it may go. Man harvests the sea as he harvests the land; let us therefore not fool ourselves by relying on the depth of the ocean, any more than we rely on the depth of the land. It is, in fact, the very areas where life is concentrated that man pollutes most.

Most pollutants come from the land. How many rivers today have drinkable water at their mouths? In fact, today some rivers would not flow at all without factory and urban effluents. All the polluted rivers and all the sewers of the world empty their toxic refuse directly onto the continental shelves. This is also the nearest and cheapest dumping area for the enormous quantities of unwanted chemical poisons shipped away from the shore. What is so dangerous that we are afraid of storing it on land, we dump overboard, guided by the principle "out of sight, out of mind." As an example, incalculable quantities of poison, including entire shiploads, have both openly and secretly been transported from industrial countries in Europe in recent years to be dumped in the presumably bottomless North Sea. This sea is so shallow that, at certain points, the depth is only thirteen meters, and during the Bronze Age half the North Sea was dry land.

Much has been written for and against the American act, repeated by others, of dumping vast quantities of nuclear waste and obsolete war gases in the Atlantic with the excuse that it was all sealed in special containers. There are already enough examples in shallower waters like the Irish Sea, the English Channel, and the North Sea of similar foolproof containers moving about with bottom currents and cracking open with the result that millions of fish are killed or mutilated. In the shallow Baltic Sea, seven thousand tons of arsenic were dumped, in cement containers, forty years ago. These containers have now started to leak. Their combined contents are three times more than needed to kill the entire population of the earth today. It may be difficult to find means of stopping ocean pollution from seepage and sewers, but deliberate dumping in the sea of material too dangerous to keep in sight should be considered a criminal act. It could easily be forbidden, and the offenders should be most severely punished under international law.

In fact there is no such thing as "national waters." The ocean is in constant movement. Only the solid ocean bottom can be mapped and divided among nations, not the mobile water above it. If you launch a raft off the coast of Peru, it will be carried with the currents to Polynesia. If you set a reed boat afloat off the coast of Morocco, it is carried to tropic America. This illustrates that there is no such thing as territorial waters for more than days at a time. What are territorial waters of Peru today are territorial waters of French Oceania tomorrow. What are territorial waters of Morocco now will shortly become territorial waters of various states around the Caribbean Sea.

Even though it is extremely important to put an immediate end to deliberate ocean dumping, this is only part of the problem. By far the greatest quantity of toxic refuse constantly reaches the sea in a much less spectacular way from agricultural fields and urban and industrial sewers.

To visualize the immense quantities of solid and dissolved waste and fluid chemicals of all kinds which every minute flow into the ocean from the shores of all continents, we should imagine the ocean without water, as a big, empty depression. The fact that every river in the world empties into the sea without causing an overflow makes us subconsciously think of the ocean as a witch's cauldron whose contents never come over the brim, no matter how much is poured in. We are apt to forget that the ocean has its own sort of outlet: the evaporation from its surface which permits only pure water to escape while all our poisons, all our solid and dissolved wastes, are left to accumulate forever in the pot. Visualize, then, the ocean as a dry and empty valley ready to receive only what man is pouring in. The rising level of toxic matter would clearly be visible from all sides. A few examples picked at random will illustrate the input we would witness.

French rivers carry 18,000 million cubic meters of liquid pollution annually into the sea; the city of Paris alone discharges almost 1,200,000 cubic meters of untreated effluent into the Seine every day.

The volume of liquid waste in the Federal Republic of Germany is estimated at over 9,000 million cubic meters per year, or 25.4 million cubic meters per day, not counting cooling water, which amounts to 33.6 million cubic meters per day. Into the Rhine alone, 50,000 tons of waste are discharged daily, including 30,000 tons of sodium chloride from industrial plants.

A report of the United Nations Economic and Social Council states that we have already dumped an estimated billion pounds of DDT into our environment and are adding an estimated 100 million per year. Most of this ultimately finds its way to the ocean, blown away by wind or washed down by rain. The total world production of pesticides is estimated at over 1,300 million pounds annually. The United States alone exports over 100 million pounds per year.

Less conspicuous than the constant flow of poisons from the shores is that even the tallest chimneys in the world send their pollutants into the ocean. The densest city smog and the darkest industrial smoke will slowly be carried away by the wind, only to descend with rain and snow into the ocean. Cities and industries are expanding day by day, and so far, in America alone, waste products in the form of smoke and noxious fumes amount to a total of 390,000 tons of pollutants every day, or 142 million tons every year.

The ocean is the ultimate sink for all pollution disposed of in modern communities—even what we try to send up in smoke. It is common to think of ocean pollution as waste thrown overboard from thousands of ships, or a spectacular accident with an oil drill springing a leak, such as in the Santa Barbara accident, or a supertanker running on a reef, such as the *Torrey Canyon* in the English Channel. It is not the spectacular accidents that hit the headlines that should scare us most, but the daily, intentional, almost inconspicuous discharge of crude oil from navy and merchant ships all over the world, above all the routine cleaning of oil tankers.

The whole world was upset when the *Torrey Canyon* unintentionally spilled 100,000 tons of oil in the English Channel. Every year, more than 100,000 tons are intentionally pumped into the Mediterranean, an almost landlocked sea. The traffic of oil tankers in the Mediterranean is increasing at a tremendous rate and, according to a report made at the University of Trieste, it is estimated that, in the year 1980, 500 million tons of crude oil will be unloaded in Mediterranean ports. A recent study showed that for every square kilometer in the Mediterranean south of Italy there are 500 liters of solidified oil. In recent years, visible pollution has begun to appear even in the largest oceans.

In 1947, when the balsa raft *Kon-Tiki* crossed forty-three hundred miles, or nearly eight thousand kilometers, of the Pacific in 101 days, we on board saw no trace of man until we spotted an old wreck of a sailing ship on the coral reef where we landed. The ocean was clean and crystal clear. In 1969 it was therefore a blow to us on board the raft ship *Ra* to observe from our papyrus bundles that entire stretches of the Atlantic Ocean were polluted. We drifted slowly past plastic containers, nylon, empty bottles, and cans. Yet most conspicuous of all was the oil. First off the African coast, next in midocean, and finally in front of the Caribbean islands, we drifted for days on end through water reminding us more of a city harbor than of the open sea. The surface and as far as we could see through the waves was littered with small clots of solidified black oil, ranging in size from that of a pinhead or a pea to that of a large potato. . . .

The problem of oil pollution is a complex one. Various types of crude oil are toxic in different degrees, but they all have one property in common: they absorb other chemicals, notably insecticides, like blotting paper. Thus, on the surface of the ocean, DDT and other chlorinated hydrocarbons which do not dissolve in water and do not sink are attracted to oil slicks and oil clots, where in some cases they can be concentrated to an even higher percentage than when originally bottled with dissolvents for spraying purposes.

From the *Ra* we observed that larger oil clots were commonly covered with barnacles, marine worms, and small crabs, which did not feed on the tar lumps but used them to hitchhike across the ocean. However, these riders are attractive bait for fish, which swallow the whole cluster. These ever-present oil clots can hardly, even if they are not baited with barnacles, avoid getting into the bodies, gills, and baleen of filter-feeding fish and whales. Their effect naturally depends on their concentration of inherent and acquired toxic matter. In the famous Sargasso Sea, the oil lumps are now so common that recently an expedition of marine biologists had to give up working with dragnets on the surface, since the mesh of their nets was constantly getting plugged up by solidified oil, and their catches literally brought in more oil clots than seaweed.

What happens to all this floating oil? The optimist says that very likely the lumps may gradually disintegrate and sink to the bottom. Perhaps this is true, but certainly not before they have done harm to surface life and the coastal flora and fauna. The tourist industry is concerned about the oil washed up on the beaches, but it is time to get more concerned about the oil washed against the inaccessible rocks. Maybe the oil clots gradually sink, but so far they are certainly only accumulating, disclosing their presence and leaving their effects in an ever more conspicuous way.

Fishermen have already begun to notice a grayish belt, darkening from year to year, just above water level on coastal cliffs and boulders. Particularly in the eastern and southern Mediterranean and on several of the local islands, the yellowish rock is becoming discolored from yellow to gray and even black in a belt six to eight feet wide. In many areas, this belt along the waterline, once covered by seaweeds, clams, mussels, limpets, and all sorts of crustaceans and small fish, is now dead. Completely sterile. Nothing undulates or darts about. The once yellow rock seems like coke, and in many places sizable clots of oil are hammered into the pores like sheets of tarmac. And this is happening in what is the cradle for the bulk of marine life, since most species have to pass one stage of their life cycle on the rocky shores of islands and continents.

We hardly need to be reminded of the fact that even a drop of liquid oil will spread out over a large surface area of water, and the thicker the film of oil, the less is the photosynthesis and the production of oxygen. In spite of all this, it is not the floating oil clots we should fear the most. Their presence shows us that our planet is not endless and that visible human waste is beginning to bridge world oceans. The oil clots in the sea tell a similar story to that of the refuse on the beach. Visible pollution is seen by some as a symptom of welfare. If we want to bless its presence, however, it should be as an eye-opener. Each empty plastic bottle or tube, each can, each oil clot we see along the roadside or on the beach should ring a bell and make us think of invisible pollutants already lost in the soil or the sea: liquids and particles not discernable to the naked eye.

Man does not dispose of empty packing only. It is the lost contents and not the empty containers that should worry us. Where is the spray, the paste, the powder, the liquid no longer inside the empty packing? DDT is now found in Antarctic penguins and Arctic polar bears living far from any area where insects have been sprayed. Even in the blubber of each of twenty whales recently caught by special license for testing in the Arctic current off the Greenland coast, six insecticides, including DDT, were present. These whales, born and raised off the East Greenland glaciers, had never been near the shores of agricultural lands. But the ocean is revolving and with it the pelagic plankton which is eaten by the krill that forms the basic diet of the whale. The plankton, just like the oil, has the property of absorbing, assimilating, and concentrating the insecticides. . . .

In the short period that the United Nations representatives are meeting here in Stockholm to discuss the problems of our environment, an estimated fifty million pounds of additional pesticides will have time to reach the ocean to join what has already accumulated there, not to mention the vast quantities of toxic chemicals pouring in from both industry and household.

I appeal to the multinational representatives in Stockholm to put aside all immediate personal and national interests, and to be aware of the immense responsibility they have toward present and future generations. Let us hope they bear in mind that the ocean currents circulate with no regard for political borderlines, and that nations can divide the land, but the revolving ocean, indispensable and yet vulnerable, will forever remain a common human heritage.

REFERENCES

BBC News. "Explorer Thor Heyerdahl Dies." April 18, 2002.

Blair, Betty. "Thor Heyerdahl in Azerbaijan." *Azerbaijan International* 3, no. 1 (spring 1995).

Clark, R. B., Chris Frid, and Martin Attrill. *Marine Pollution.* Oxford: Clarendon Press, 1997.

Green Cross International. "Dr. Thor Hyerdahl." *www.gci.ch.* 1997.

Heyerdahl, Thor. *The Kon-Tiki Expedition by Raft across the South Sea.* London: Readers Union, 1952.

———. "How Vulnerable is the Ocean?" *Who Speaks for Earth?* Ed. Maurice Strong. New York: W. W. Norton and Company, 1973.

————. *In the Footsteps of Adam: An Autobiography.* London: Little, Brown, and Co., 2000.

Independent World Commission on the Oceans. *The Ocean, Our Future.* Cambridge: Cambridge University Press, 1998.

International Maritime Organization. "International Convention for the Prevention of Pollution from Ships, 1973, as Modified by the Protocol of 1978 Relating Thereto (MARPOL 73/78)." *www.imo.org.*

Loftas, Tony. *The Last Resource: Man's Exploitation of the Sea.* London: Hamish Hamilton, 1969.

Plehsakov, Constantine. "Adventurer's Death Touches Russia's Soul." *Azerbaijan International* 10, no. 2. (summer 2002).

Ralling, Christopher. *The Kon-Tiki Man.* London: BBC Books, 1990.

United Nations Environmental Program (UNEP). "Regional Seas Program." *www.unep.org/water/regseas/regseas.htm.*

4. Maurice Strong

CANADA

The 1972 United Nations Conference on the Human Environment at Stockholm constituted an institutional, legal, and psychological watershed for international environmentalism. This first "Earth Summit" marked the first time that the nations of the world explicitly recognized that, in environmental matters, it was time to begin talking in terms of global governance. Yet not until the final gavel closed the proceedings was there any basis for believing that the meeting would be successful and produce meaningful results.

There had already been more than a few U.N. sponsored conferences on issues concerning the environment, which had led to underwhelming results. Expectations were not much higher for the 1972 conference, considering tensions between former colonial powers and developing nations, as well as the politics surrounding the Cold War (the Soviet Union and the Eastern bloc countries would boycott). Nonetheless, on December 3, 1968, the United Nations General Assembly unanimously approved the organizing of a U.N. Conference on the Human Environment and gave the secretary general four years to iron out the details. Now all that was needed was somebody to produce, choreograph, orchestrate, and conduct what was sure to be a cacophonous ballet. For over a year, no one was appointed to head the initiative and things seemed to founder. It was under these rather unpromising circumstances that Maurice Strong was picked by U.N. Secretary General U Thant to fill the post.

For the fledgling environmental movement, appointing an unknown Canadian oil executive as conference secretary general neither added luster to the already precarious event nor improved its prospects for success. But history would tell otherwise. Despite an understated demeanor that has been characterized by uncharitable journalists as "anticharismatic," Strong knew how to get things done. Riding a rising wave of global concern about massive ecological degradation, Strong proved to be an astonishing "operator," translating his incipient identification with environmentalism into the sustained, activist involvement of the United Nations.

Maurice Strong, it turns out, was no ordinary oil executive. Never would a prosperous business person engender so much suspicion and hostility among conservative capitalist circles. Today, Strong is still controversial. The internet is full of conspiratorial rantings calling Strong everything from a "New Age flake" to "Communist provocateur." (Publicly, at least, he laughs off such critics as extremist, and counters that he wishes he had a "smidgen" of the power and money his critics attribute to him.) Strong often pushed the line of conflicts of interest beyond the comfort level of some colleagues. But it is true that no individual has exhibited greater stamina in the effort to push the nations of the world beyond conventional concepts of sovereignty to embrace the enormity of humanity's global environmental challenges.

The Maurice Strong biography appears as unlikely as a fictional Hollywood script. Born in 1930 to a destitute family in rural Manitoba, Canada, Strong was heavily influenced in childhood, he has said, by the disenfranchisement of the Great Depression, the enchantment of bucolic surroundings, the erudition of his loving but troubled mother, and the liberal social policy positions of his school principle. Having more or less completed the secondary school curriculum, he ran away from home at age fourteen to join the Merchant Marine. Although his father soon dragged him back home from Vancouver, British Columbia, within a year he headed off again, this time to the Arctic to apprentice himself with a fur trader. There, he befriended the indigenous Inuit population as well as the occasional visiting oil company executive.

This ability to forge diversified personal connections would remain Strong's greatest asset, and his uncanny networking capabilities became the subject of some marvel. He was friends with a succession of U.N. secretary generals, and his friendship with George H. W. Bush led to that president's intervention on his behalf in 1992 to maintain the leadership position at the Earth Summit in Rio de Janeiro. Only a few years later, Strong would rely on even stronger ties with a Bush political rival, Al Gore. More recently, he has started to rely on his protegés: when he hired teenager Paul Martin as a hand at an Alberta oil patch, and later as his personal assistant, he may have had a sense of Martin's potential. But he could not have foreseen that Martin would be elected in 2003 as the Canadian Prime Minister.

A characteristically fortuitous discussion at a dinner party with a visiting senior U.N. official in 1947 enabled the eighteen-year-old Strong to secure an entry-level job at the newly established UN Security Department in New York. He stuck with the position for two exciting months. The stint provided Strong with his first meeting with the Rockefeller family, an association that would continue for half a century. More importantly, the experience would cultivate his fascination with the United Nations. Failing to qualify for the Canadian Air Force, Strong settled for a position as an analyst with Dome Petroleum, a Canadian corporation. Marrying within the year, he then traded this excellent career opportunity for a world cruise that left him in Nairobi. There, Strong again took a job for an oil company—CalTex, where he was responsible for finding new gas station sites, allowing him to visit the most exotic corners of Africa for two years. The racist orientation of the crumbling colonial regime in Nairobi would leave him at odds with the local administration, and with an even stronger sense of solidarity with the peoples of the developing world.

It was during this period that Strong became engaged with the YMCA and soon joined its international committee. This would be Strong's first public interest involvement; he has retained leadership positions in nongovernmental organizations (NGOs) ever since. By the age of twenty-five, he had returned to Canada, and resumed his leap up the corporate ladder to secure a vice presidency in Dome Petroleum. Soon after, at age thirty-one he talked his way into the presidency of the Power Corporation of Canada, a major Quebec energy player. But Strong's heart had always been in public service rather than business. Political connections led to his appointment as director general of Canada's International Development Agency, which distributes foreign aid around the world. His creativity in this position was conspicuous enough to attract the attention of Swedish officials, who in turn brought him to U Thant's attention.

When he took on organization of the Stockholm Conference, Strong had no formal experience in environmental affairs. Having spent most of his adult life working for oil interests, he raised suspicion among those bearing excessive ecological passions. But he brought with him superb diplomatic skills and powerful idealism as well as a clear conception of the predicament and needs of developing nations. He also brought his own share of passion on the subject. His intense emotional ties with nature had continued beyond childhood and matured in the savannas of East Africa and as a member of Canada's Alpine Club. And, by all accounts, Maurice Strong was a quick study.

After moving his family to Geneva, Strong began trying to save the ailing conference. He insisted (and got) a senior Soviet scientist on his staff, in a move to bridge Cold War suspicions. He traveled to China and coaxed its leaders into sending a representative. It would be their first attendance at a U.N. function since the Communists took power in 1949. In retrospect, however, most important were his enormous efforts to ensure the participation of the developing world, which was inclined to boycott the entire affair. This included an interview with Indian Prime Minister Indira Gandhi, in which he appealed to her to attend the meeting herself, and guaranteed her a special place on the agenda to present the perspective of the Third World. Strong also convened a panel of twenty-seven scientists in the Swiss mountain village of Founex to find a formula for international action that would take developing countries' concerns into account. The experts' conclusions did little to resolve the conflicting hemispheric perspectives on global environmental issues, conflicts that persist to this day. But, at the time, it gave developing countries a critical sense of involvement.

Hence, despite the conference slogan, "Only One Earth," when the conference finally opened there was considerable disagreement about how to translate amorphous ecological anxiety into operational measures. (A newsletter headline distributed after the first day of the conference quipped "Only 113 Earths.") Of course, the Stockholm Conference itself lacked even minimal delegated authority to make any decisions; even trivial resolutions would require subsequent General Assembly adoption. But this never bothered Strong, who from the outset harbored an ambitious vision of the meeting's potential and never wavered.

Of the 132 countries that were members of the United Nations, 113 sent delegations to Stockholm. Despite the absence of the Soviet Union and the Eastern Bloc countries (on account of East Germany's exclusion from participation), Strong was in daily communication with their local embassies. It has been argued that the Soviet absence may have liberated the meeting from the traditional communist–anticommunist bickering and enabled the forum to focus on north–south tension. Some 85 nations had already submitted national reports, which in retrospect constituted the first serious, systematic attempt to chronicle the ecological state of the world. At the time, Stockholm did not pack the prestige of subsequent Earth Summits. With the exception of Indira Gandhi, who indeed gave a brief and eloquent address, the world's heads of state stayed at home, preferring to send foreign ministers in their stead.

Strong confounded nervous security officials during the Stockholm Conference's festive opening parade by riding a bicycle painted in U.N. white and blue. But things did not roll as smoothly in the sessions, where the usual hairsplitting over diplomatic formulas began to derail the summit. Notwithstanding the intergovernmental advisory committee that had already met four times in two-week sessions to make sure that Strong's script would fly, a final consensus text appeared unattainable. At four in the morning on the last night of the summit, Strong began to see his Summit slipping away and decided it was time to intervene.

He recalls: "I quietly got up from my seat, went over to where I had noticed the interpretation facilities had been plugged into the electricity supply, and surreptitiously pulled the plug. Somehow this seemed to provide just the right jolt to rouse the delegates into getting the process moving again. When even the French, who are normally adamant on the subject, agreed to continue in English, some kind of a breakthrough had been obtained. It was nearly dawn before agreement was reached and the wording settled."

In the end, the years of preparation and his persuasive ebullience paid off; the Stockholm Conference adopted the basic components of Strong's proposals. This included the twenty-six principles of the "Stockholm Declaration," the first enunciation of a global environmental creed. It established key concepts, such as the compatibility of development with environmental stewardship and concern for future generations. (The Declaration's definition of clean air and water as "human rights" reflects the enthusiasm of the participants, but unfortunately has not transformed their legal status internationally.)

Perhaps more important than the Declaration was Stockholm's Action Plan for continuing U.N. activity, and a series of resolutions that included a ban on nuclear weapons testing that released radioactive fallout, the creation of international environmental data banks, and creation of an environmental fund. To the consternation of many government representatives, Strong pleased the many NGOs attending a parallel Stockholm meeting by pushing through a call for a ten-year moratorium on whaling. The International Whaling Commission that convened in London, soon after, reluctantly adopted a partial ban.

But the actual achievements of Stockholm go far beyond any specific documents drafted there. The Conference was a high-profile show that for the first time made global environmental cooperation the world's top news item. Delegates returned home inspired to establish domestic environmental protection agencies in their countries. NGOs became a key part of the scenery in international environmental meetings. And the international community was pushed beyond the point of no return. The United Nations was in the environmental business to stay.

Strong's environmental perspective is clearly expressed in his opening address to the Stockholm Conference. Indeed, one can see the speech as a blueprint for many subsequent global environmental successes and achievements in response to his call: a regional seas program that has stemmed the deterioration in waters around the world; empathy and assistance for developing countries; and a permanent institutional commitment to the environment at the global level, in the form of the United Nations Environmental Program (UNEP).

After Stockholm, Strong served as UNEP's first director general, returning to Nairobi to establish its headquarters. But, two years later, he would move on, returning to Canada to continue his peculiar juggling act of multiple initiatives in both the commercial and the environmental worlds. For example, while chairing Petro-Canada and, later, Hydro-Quebec (the largest utility in the world), he would serve as a board member for the World Wildlife Fund and the World Resources Institute, and eventually head up the 1992 World Summit at Rio de Janeiro. At the same time that he served as Chair of the Earth Council and trumpeted expanded models of environmental governance, Strong happily cut deals with Arab oil sheiks that left him with two hundred thousand acres in Colorado.

Strong's attempts to span both worlds led, inevitably, to inconsistency. Thus, despite his enormous personal wealth, in his 1992 speech opening the Rio Conference Strong sermonized to scores of world leaders, "It is clear that current lifestyles and consumption patterns of the affluent middle class—involving high meat intake, consumption of large amounts of frozen and convenience foods, use of fossil fuels, appliances, home and workplace air conditioners, and suburban housing—are not sustainable."

Critics like to taunt that, in spite of his calls for self-restraint and responsibility for controlling overpopulation, Strong has five children. (They fail
to mention that one is adopted.) However, no one denies that Strong is
consistently effective.

Since 1972, the United Nations sponsors conferences every ten years to
consider the ecological state of the world. It is rather telling that the first
and third of these meetings (Stockholm and Rio de Janeiro) were highly
successful gatherings that set new standards for international environmental cooperation, but the other two, in Nairobi in 1982 and Johannesburg in 2002, did little to forward a global environmental agenda. Strong
was the secretary general for both of the successful summits. Although it is
more than thirty years since he opened the proceedings at Stockholm,
Strong's 1972 assessment of the world's situation still resonates. The surprisingly optimistic view of what can be done continues to offer a compelling
vision for a better future.

"We Do Not Have to Believe in the Inevitability of Environmental Catastrophe to Accept the Possibility of Such a Catastrophe"

STOCKHOLM CONFERENCE ON THE HUMAN
ENVIRONMENT, 1972

Secretary General of the Conference:
We have made a global decision of immeasurable importance to which
this meeting testifies: we have determined that we must control and har-
ness the forces which we have ourselves created. We know that, if these
forces can be effectively controlled, they will provide everything that life
on this planet desires and requires, but if they are permitted to dominate
us, they will have an insatiable and unforgiving appetite.

Our purpose here is to reconcile man's legitimate, immediate ambi-
tions with the rights of others, with respect for all life-supporting systems,
and with the rights of generations yet unborn. Our purpose is the enrich-
ment of mankind in every sense of that phrase. We wish to advance—not
recklessly, ignorantly, selfishly, and perilously, as we have done in the past—

but with greater understanding, wisdom, and vision. We are anxious, and rightly so, to eliminate poverty, hunger, disease, racial prejudice, and the glaring economic inequalities between human beings.

[T]his conference must be the beginning of a whole new approach to the situation. For the environmental crisis points up the need to review our activities, not just in relation to the particular purpose and interest they are designed to serve, but in their overall impact on the whole system of interacting relationships which determines the quality of human life.

What then, is the prospect for Planet Earth? The answer is that nobody knows. There is much difference of opinion in the scientific community over the severity of the environmental problem and whatever doom is imminent or, indeed, inevitable. But we need subscribe to no Doomsday view to be convinced that we cannot—we dare not—wait for all the evidence to be in. Time is no ally here unless we make it one.

We do not have to believe in the *inevitability* of environmental catastrophe to accept the *possibility* of such a catastrophe. Whether the crisis is, in a physical sense, just around the corner, or well over the horizon, cannot obscure the fact that we have a policy crisis on our hands right now. We need only look at the unintended results of past and present decision.

No one decided to poison the Baltic—or any other of our polluted and dying waterways. No one decided to destroy millions of acres of productive soil through erosion, salination, contamination, and the intrusion of deserts. No one decided to dehumanize life in the greatest cities of the world with crowding, pollution, and noise for the more fortunate, and with degrading squalor for the rest.

We did not intend either these or the many other destructive, dangerous, and unhealthy and unaesthetic consequences of our past activities, but these are what we have. Man has been making social decisions on too narrow a base and in too short a time perspective.

It is this that calls for a renewed sense of trusteeship over the resources he has inherited from the long evolution of nature. It is this that makes man's future role as a decision maker qualitatively different from what it has been in the past. The skills that enabled him to master the techniques of providing his food supply and then of producing the wide variety of goods and services required to support his affluent consumer-oriented societies are now needed even more in managing the new ecological society on which the survival of technological civilization depends. Man the agricultural producer and man the industrial producer must become man the societal manager.

We shall not accomplish this compelling new task in a year or a decade. But we can discern a few essential components of the kind of decision making that will help us to foresee the consequences of alternative actions and to clarify our choices. For one thing, we must learn how to bring to bear our vast resources of knowledge in forms and at times most useful to those whose duty it is to make choices and to those who will be affected by them. For another, we must learn how to engage more effectively in the decision-making process those who must live with the consequences of the decisions. . . .

The fate of Planet Earth lies largely in our own hands and in the knowledge and intelligence we bring to bear in the decision-making process. In the final analysis, however, man is unlikely to succeed in managing his relationship with nature unless in the course of it he learns to manage better the relations between man and man. Yet if we use our present standards as an indication of what will be, three decades from now at least half of humanity will still be enduring a life of uncertain work, permanent undernourishment, poor health, poor housing, and illiteracy and insufficient skills.

The balanced use of the world's resources, the priorities for human action within a well-ordered planetary system, the plain facts of deepening poverty, of protein deficiency, of inadequate housing, of festering urban environments, must be at the center of our concern. Our whole work, our whole dedication, is surely towards the idea of a durable and habitable planet. But what we are heading for is an earth in which fewer than half [the] inhabitants will enjoy such conditions. And this poses the key question that all governments must begin to ask—and answer: can the great venture of human destiny be carried safely into a new century if our work is left in this condition? I, for one, do not believe it can.

Our subject is the human environment. Broadly interpreted, the human environment impinges upon the entire condition of man, and cannot be seen in isolation from war and poverty, injustice and discrimination, which remain abiding social ills on Planet Earth.

The draft Declaration on the Human Environment is less than the inspirational and comprehensive code of international conduct for the age of environment that we hope to articulate over time. But it does represent an important, indeed an indispensable, beginning. In particular, it holds that all nations must accept responsibility for the consequences of their own actions on environments outside their borders. In my view, it is essential that this fundamental principle be accepted here if we are to establish a minimum basis for effective international cooperation following this conference.

The proposed Action Plan is designed to further the principles of the Declaration. It consists of two main components: a series of specific recommendations for action at the international level, and a framework into which all such recommendations can be fitted into their functional categories. The three principal categories are

- the global environmental assessment or earthwatch program;
- activities which together comprise an environmental management program; and
- supporting measures.

The Action Plan cannot of course be a comprehensive approach to all problems of the human environment. It does offer, however, a blueprint for a continuing environmental work program in the international community, and a first indication of priorities.

Our major motivation in gathering here is to consider recommendations, which can only be translated into action by international agreement. By far the major part of the burden of environmental management falls, however, upon national governments operating as sovereign national states. This may be more in accord with political reality than with environmental reality. Yet, in working out their national environmental programs, governments and peoples will become increasingly aware of the direct and indirect links between national causes and transnational effects, between global conditions and local well-being, between personal values and the integrity of planetary resources. The inescapable fact that we face a universal problem does not, of course, require a universal response. In nature, the quality and durability of systems is maintained by variety. In human society, we depend upon cultural diversity to produce similar results. . . .

The particulars of the environmental situation, and the priorities to be accorded to environmental action, are most obviously different between industrialized societies and societies in different stages of development. The developing countries are experiencing some of the same problems which first attracted concern in more technologically advanced states, almost before they have begun to reap the accumulated benefits that some two centuries of industrialization have brought to the more industrialized nations.

At the same time, these countries are struggling, with resources that are only a fraction of those available to the more wealthy nations, to bring to their rapidly growing populations the elementary necessities of life. Their natural resources, including the basic environmental resources of water, soil, plant and animal life, are the essential capital base on which they depend to meet these needs; they can ill afford to abuse or waste them. Many of the fundamental environmental problems of the developing countries derive from their very poverty and lack of resources, and in some cases from inappropriate forms of development. They can ill afford to put the needs of an uncertain future ahead of the immediate need for food, shelter, jobs, education, and health care today.

There is no fundamental conflict between development and the environment. Environmental factors must be an integral feature of development strategy, if the aim of human endeavor is to increase the welfare and not merely to increase the gross national product. Indeed, one of the most promising features of the continuing debate on development and environment is the new synthesis that is now emerging.

We are still at the very threshold of the new synthesis and there is still unresolved controversy over the concept of growth. I do not believe we can cease to grow. No-growth is not a viable alternative. People must have access to more, not fewer, opportunities to express their creative drives, but these can only be provided within a total system in which man's activities are in dynamic harmony with the natural order. To achieve this, we must control and redirect our processes of growth. We must rethink our concepts of the basic purposes of growth. We must see it in terms of enriching the lives and enlarging the opportunities of all mankind. And, if this is so, it follows that it is the more wealthy societies, the privileged minority of mankind, which will have to make the most profound, even revolutionary, changes in attitudes and values. . . .

The overall global goal of the United Nations environmental program must be to arrest the deterioration, and begin the enhancement, of the human environment. Subsidiary global goals, such as the provision of decent water supplies for all inhabitants of the earth, will help us to realize that overall objective. The sooner we can assign target dates the better it will be. . . . [T]o stimulate thought, I am prepared to suggest on my own initiative three top priority areas for environmental action. Each is so important that it is not necessary to rank them in any particular order.

Clean water supply. Water is the key to life. But the water available to most of the world's people brings with it death and distress, both from the ancient plagues of water-borne disease and from the poisonous new residues of progress which are accumulating in mounting quantities in water throughout the world. Almost every single national report submitted to the conference secretariat placed high priority on clean water.

An adequate response to this problem would involve a massive mobilization of resources to provide water supply and purification systems, sewage and waste disposal and treatment facilities, and research directed to developing less expensive technologies of water treatment and waste disposal in tropical areas.

Ocean pollution. This is another inescapable top priority, for the oceans cover some 70 percent of the surface of Planet Earth. They are the ultimate sink not only for wastes dumped directly into the seas, but for what is washed out from rivers and bays and estuaries and what is deposited through the atmosphere. Beginning, as they do, beyond all national jurisdictions, the oceans present a compelling and urgent case for global environmental action. The case for regional cooperation is equally compelling, for a large number of effectively enclosed seas such as the Mediterranean, the Baltic, and the Caspian that are deteriorating at a frightening rate.

Urban settlement. The cancerous growth of cities, the desperate shortage of housing, the expanding slums and squatter settlements which are so incompatible with our concept of the dignity of man, and the threatened breakdown of urban institutions are almost universal phenomena that make urbanization one of the gravest problems of the human environment. There is an important potential role for international assistance and cooperation, but this is primarily an area for national action, including the application of national population policies.

There are of course many other candidates for even a first list of top priorities. But these three fresh water supplies, ocean pollution, and urban settlements—belong, in my view, at the top of the list.

I move now to a discussion of another kind of priority, an area for agreement on which all other actions depend, the organizational mechanisms required.

Organization: if we are to achieve our goals, effective organization at the national, regional, or global levels is of crucial importance. In order to achieve effective and farseeing decision making, we require institutional arrangements which reflect this need and assist in providing for it. We require new institutional patterns which provide for collaboration between governments, the scientific community, and international institutions; it is no more than the truth to say that what governments decide to do will be critical to the implementation of the Action Plan and for assuring the ongoing process of environmental action to which I have referred.

A major feature of new organizational arrangements must be creation of a direct working relationship between the intergovernmental community and the community of science and technology. It is essential that policy makers and administrators have ready access to practical scientific guidance and that scientists—and in this category I include social scientists—are actively involved in the decision-making process. We cannot continue with a situation in which these groups operate separately and often in isolation from each other. . . .

We have determined to assert our domination over forces which we ourselves created. Our determination must be to enrich mankind and to advance together. Our power, our demands, our numbers have made our interdependence an inescapable reality. The task now is to convert it into political and moral reality. The United Nations carries a direct and unique responsibility for taking the lead in discerning and acting upon the new environmental imperatives. No one nation or group of nations commands the air and water of this planet. If we are to ensure their survival, we have to act as the whole community of man.

Can there be any doubt of our technical ability to take on, and succeed at, the task of managing our global environment? I have been told it is unrealistic to expect that we will. But is it unrealistic to expect that man will be wise enough to do what he must for his own welfare?

In our relentless pursuit of competitive, material, and national interest, we have constructed self-justifying promises and values which are themselves the source of a kind of unreality. Is it realistic to think that we as nations, or as a species, can continue on our present course?

Is it realistic to think that we can continue to reap the benefits of exploiting our precious planetary heritage while continuing to permit its accelerating desecration?

Is it realistic to assume that a small minority can monopolize the benefits of a technological civilization, which is inherently global in scale and scope of the interdependences it creates, and which requires global cooperation to sustain it?

Is it realistic, in light of this growing interdependence, to tolerate such disparities in the conditions of people?

Surely a sober and objective appraisal of our present conditions and future prospects must say that this cannot be realistic. Surely, too, our sense of a larger realism must lead us to believe that because we *can* change, because we *must* change, we *shall* change. We must not allow the frustrations of our past failures to prevent us from finding a new basis for international cooperation. The world desperately needs hope, and we must build on this hope. If we fail, we will add to the growing divisions of this planet, divisions which threaten to deny the poor and the powerless their opportunity to participate in the decisions and the benefit of our new technological order, and to deny the powerful the confidence and trust they need for their ultimate security and well-being.

In the final analysis, political and social action must be rooted in the attitudes and values of people. If the changes, already discernible in the mood of many of the generation of young people, constitute the beginnings of the revaluation in attitudes and values which the environmental challenge requires, we have indeed an encouraging base on which to build.

The basic task of this conference is to build in the minds of men the new vision of the larger, richer future which our collective will and energies can shape for all mankind, to build a program of concerted action which will make an important first step towards the realization of this vision, to build the new vehicle of international cooperation that will enable us to continue the long journey towards that creative and dynamic harmony between man and nature that will provide the optimum environment for human life on Planet Earth.

The dominant image of the age in which we live is that of the earth rising above the horizon of the moon—a beautiful, solitary, fragile sphere which provides the home and sustains the life of the entire human species. From this perspective, it is impossible to see the boundaries of nations and all the other artificial barriers that divide men. What it brings home to us with dramatic force is the reality that our common dependence on the health of our only one earth, and our common interest in caring for it transcend all our man-made divisions. In the decades ahead, we must learn to conquer our divisions, our greeds, our inhibitions, and our fears. If we do not, they will conquer us.

REFERENCES

Bailey, Ronald. "Who Is Maurice Strong?" *The National Review,* September 1, 1997.

Birnie, Patricia, and Alan Boyle. "International Governance and the Formulation of Environmental Law and Policy." *International Law and the Environment.* 2nd ed. Oxford: Oxford University Press, 2002.

Chadle, Bruce. "Strong Says He'll Give Martin Advice for Free." *CNEWS,* October 28, 2003.

Dewar, Elaine. *Cloak of Green.* Toronto: Lorimar and Co., 1995.

Lamb, Henry. "Maurice Strong: The New Guy in Your Future." *www.citizen reviewonline.org.* August 2002.

Linnér, Björn-Ola, and Henrik Selin. "How It All Began: Global Efforts on Sustainable Development from Stockholm to Rio." Paper presented at the Sixth Nordic Conference on Environmental Social Sciences, Åbo, Finland, June 12–14, 2003.

Strong, Maurice. *Where on Earth Are We Going?* New York: Texere, 2001.

United Nations Environmental Program. *Evolving Environmental Perceptions: From Stockholm to Nairobi.* Ed. Mostafa Kamal Tolba. London: Butterworth's, 1988.

5. Lois Gibbs

UNITED STATES OF AMERICA

WHY HAS THE N.Y.
STATE HEALTH DEPT.
LEARNED NOTHING

Photograph courtesy of Lois Gibbs.

Perhaps the most impressive environmental leaders are ordinary people who never sought ecological battles, but simply woke to find a vexing problem banging at their door. Lois Gibbs may be the most famous such environmentalist. Her transformation from New York housewife to international environmental icon was swift and certainly uninvited. Yet, when long-forgotten toxic wastes at Love Canal, New York, began to affect her children's health, she proved an exceptionally quick and talented study.

The antecedents of the Love Canal disaster are generally well known in environmental circles; the details of her campaign somewhat less so. In the 1890s, an entrepreneur by the name of William T. Love harbored a vision of linking the upper sections of the Niagara River with the lower ones and tapping the energy from the 280-foot drop for the new industries being established on the mouth of Lake Ontario The six-mile channel would also allow ships to bypass the Niagara Falls. Yet, Love's vision never became operational. Only about one kilometer of the canal was ever dug, and for many years it merely served as an informal swimming and boating resource.

All this changed in 1920 when the land was purchased and transformed into a dump that received municipal and chemical wastes. In 1942 the Hooker Chemical plant began to dispose its hazardous residuals there. Hooker's industrial complex, located on the banks of the Niagara River, became the largest chemical production center in New York State and generated prodigious quantities of waste. By 1953, it had filled Love Canal with twenty-two thousand tons of hazardous chemicals, including many of the nastiest substances ever invented: from dioxins and trichloroethane to lindane and benzene. Beyond carcinogens, the list of toxic materials included neurotoxins and teratogens (chemicals that cause birth defects). Their cumulative effect can only be imagined.

The Hooker operation then covered over the canal and sold it to the local board of education for a dollar, stipulating in the deed that the company was not responsible for any subsequent damage caused by the wastes. Of course, no one paid the matter much attention at the time. As early as 1955, a Love Canal neighborhood, located in the southeast LaSalle district of the city of Niagara Falls, New York, began to spring up around the site, and an elementary school was built on top of the canal. The happy homeowners had no idea that their real estate was a toxic time bomb.

Seventeen years later, twenty-six-year-old Lois Gibbs moved to the neighborhood with her family. Oblivious to the canal's existence, much less its contents, she settled into what seemed the American dream: affordable housing in a pleasant semi-suburban setting, a decent, working-class community, and a safe place to raise a family. Yet something went wrong. In the spring of 1978, after a few years of some sporadic government and press attention, environmental neglect came home to roost. The two rings of houses adjacent to the canal were the immediate site of the most conspicuous problems. Chemicals were beginning to leach into basements; yards were beginning to die; pets were growing ill. The local press stepped up its reporting of the complaints.

That year, Gibbs's son began attending kindergarten at the Ninety-ninth Street Elementary School, built right over the zone of most acute contamination. Suddenly he began to develop a variety of health problems, including a urinary tract problem, a low white blood cell count, and epileptic seizures, none of which had ever appeared in Gibbs's or her husband's family. A newspaper article about toxic exposure triggered the connection in Gibbs's mind between her son's symptoms and the school's proximity to the Canal. As her house seemed a safe two blocks from the site, all she really wanted was permission to transfer him to another public school, as her husband's $150 weekly wage precluded private education.

In retrospect, had the superintendent of the Niagara Falls schools been more flexible about school registration, perhaps the world would never have heard further of Love Canal after initial remedial efforts were begun in 1978. Certainly, Lois Gibbs would not have been thrust into the role of environmental crusader and prototype for citizen activists. But, fearing an exodus, the superintendent played the cautious bureaucrat; he was evasive and later recalcitrant. So Gibbs asked her neighbors to sign a petition to the school board demanding it shut the school down because of its dubious location. As she went from door to door, she heard stories in almost every home that made her realize that her seemingly idyllic neighborhood was very sick. Over half the women had miscarried before the end of their pregnancies. During a five-year period, 56 percent of the children had birth defects. Residents described a terrifying menu of diseases that affected all ages, but especially the young. And there were unexplained deaths.

To protect their lifetime investments and their health, the Love Canal Homeowners Association was established by the end of the summer. Lois Gibbs was elected its president. In this capacity, she employed just about every "activist" trick ever invented and concocted several new ones.

Gibbs's 1982 autobiographical *Love Canal—My Story,* was designed as a personal testimonial, but may be the best primer for grassroots environmental activism ever written. Her group began by picketing, petitioning, and reaching out to state and federal public officials and the press. Initially, it looked as if the campaign was successful. But when the New York State governor agreed to buy only the houses closest to the canal as part of a "disaster assistance" package and to relocate only those residents, Gibbs realized that winning the battle would be a question of stamina.

Residents had to find ways to keep the issue in the eye of the media and general public as well as to maintain pressure on the government to evacuate them. Twice, the group launched and leaked its own health surveys, which suggested that problems were far worse than New York State health department officials would admit. Gibbs herself mapped out the different types of illness in her neighborhood, superimposing the pattern over a map indicating hydrological movement near the canal. She suspected a clear exposure pathway that followed the movement of chemicals along the underground streambeds, or swales. While state experts initially scoffed at the amateur findings, eventually Gibbs's analytical insights became the accepted explanation for the health impacts.

To make her point, Gibbs and her homeowner associates carried coffins to Albany, the New York state capital. She went on national talk shows, and from time to time was even arrested. From the start the group worked with an attorney and filed several legal actions, including a class action suit. National and international interest in the case continued to build. Actress Jane Fonda and her husband, politician Tom Hayden, toured the site, and television networks increased coverage of the case. Yet, with the state purchasing the houses adjacent to the Canal and investing in the stabilization of the waste stream, the governor officially regarded the matter as closed or at least hoped that it would go away. But it didn't.

Activities reached a zenith in May 1980, when U.S. Environmental Protection Agency (EPA) officials came to visit the neighborhood to inform eleven of the thirty-six families who had submitted genetic tests to the agency that they had sustained chromosome damage. Despite the bad news, the EPA physician and publicity officer brought no commitment about disaster assistance from the federal government for the remaining residents. Frustrated by two years of fruitless struggle and growing manifestations of disease, the local citizens grew incensed. Spontaneously the Love Canal residents decided to hold the EPA officials as "hostages." National news, already engaged, made it the top item of the day. When FBI agents called to warn Gibbs that they were going to burst through the crowds encircling the Homeowner Association offices and liberate the hostages by force, Gibbs managed to convince her irate colleagues to release the EPA personnel. She did this on the national news, with the proviso that, if the Love Canal residents did not receive an answer from the White House about Love Canal evacuation and compensation for their homes by noon the next day, "What you have seen us do here today will look like a Sesame Street picnic by comparison."

To Gibbs's great relief, the White House (perhaps due to the dynamics of the election year) acquiesced and announced on the morrow that it was willing to evacuate all 810 families of Love Canal, and that the Federal

Disaster Assistance Administration would cover the expenses. Indeed, when President Jimmy Carter came to Niagara Falls on his reelection campaign, he took the time to meet with Gibbs and commend her on her good citizenship. The direct attention of the president to a local environmental problem was testimony to the severity of the Love Canal situation. But even more it was a reflection of the effectiveness of Gibbs's campaign.

Soon thereafter, Gibbs moved to Washington, DC, and established the Citizen's Clearinghouse for Hazardous Waste, to share her experience with other grassroots organizers. The organization, in 1997 renamed the Center for Health, Environment, and Justice, currently maintains contact with some ten thousand organizations. Through its professional assistance, it empowers other communities that face the bewildering array of challenges associated with acute exposure situations. Gibbs continues to appear on television shows, speak to organizations, and advise people about citizen involvement in environmental health. CBS even turned her story into a television movie starring Marsha Mason. Gibbs's advice to citizen activists is not just scientific and tactical, but personal. Among the antidotes she recommends for burn-out and the inevitable conflict between grassroots environmentalists and their family members, is unplugging the telephone at dinner and spending at least two hours every day with the family—without exception.

When one sees this nationally recognized, charismatic, seasoned leader take the podium today, it is hard to imagine that public speaking was anything other than second nature to her. Yet the following description of her first speech from her 1982 book describes the kind of awkwardness that thousands of grassroots leaders have had to face as they went public with their cry for environmental justice:

I was nervous. I had a habit of saying "OK" after everything I said. I would say: "OK?" "I'd like to talk to you. OK?" "I'd like to talk to you about something that is going on OK?" It was a speech habit or maybe I had so little confidence in myself that I was asking people for permission to speak. Wayne [(Gibb's brother-in-law] took it upon himself to cure my habit by sticking his finger up every time I said "OK"—to make me conscious of what I was saying.

I grabbed the microphone. It started to squeal. Someone told me to take my hands off it; that's what was making the microphone squeal. I looked out at the people and said, "OK." Wayne stuck his arm up in the air with one finger showing. I grabbed the microphone again because of Wayne's finger, and it squealed and squeaked. Everyone was getting a little restless. I told them, as they already knew, Commissioner Whalen had discussed an order for pregnant women and children under two to be moved from the area temporarily. He issued the order because they had found an above-normal number of miscarriages and birth defects in the area. Pregnant women and children under two were particularly vulnerable. He also recommended that the Ninety-ninth Street School be closed during construction. Every time I said "OK," Wayne stuck a finger up. I think he got up to six fingers during my speech. I don't know if he missed any, or just ran out of fingers and started again. It could have been sixteen, for all I know.

But Gibbs quickly went on to become one of the most effective speakers in the American environmental movement. The speech included in this volume was given at a time roughly in the middle of the Love Canal campaign. The talk takes the form of testimony that Gibbs gave to a U.S. congressional subcommittee headed by then-Representative Al Gore. It is an important statement for several reasons. It was Gibbs's first foray into national environmental politics and her first opportunity to translate the experience at Love Canal into recommendations that might have relevance for other communities. Her ability to maintain the authenticity of a "local citizen activist," while displaying competency in the science and general jargon of Washington's environmental policy, is remarkable and shows the versatility that is so critical for environmental advocates. It is fairly astounding to think that, only seven months earlier, this same Gibbs for the first time nervously took a microphone to speak before a crowd. Leaders learn quickly in times of crisis.

Indeed, Gibbs was still very new at the environmental advocacy game. Afterwards, she would recall her surprise at having her purse checked for a bomb when she arrived at the Capitol building for her talk, as well as the bells that called the committee members to votes and the somewhat contrived way that congressional aides scripted the results of the hearings in advance. All of these Washington phenomena would become much more familiar to her as she went on to become the leading national advocate for communities facing toxic crises.

Beyond the update on the Love Canal campaign, Gibbs raises several themes in this speech that remain axiomatic to her work today:

- transparency and compassion in government;
- citizen empowerment and technical independence;

- sensitivity to communities that face environmental disasters;
- a respectful but healthy distrust of government bureaucratic interests.

It is important to remember that Gibbs's speech was given at congressional hearings that succeeded in launching critical environmental legislation. By the end of 1980, "CERCLA" (the Comprehensive Environmental Response, Compensation, and Liability Act) was enacted by the U.S. Congress. This law created "Superfund," drawn from a tax on chemical and petroleum industries. The law was designed to allow the federal government to respond expeditiously to releases of hazardous substances, and for remediation of the hundreds of "orphan" hazardous waste facilities around the country. The fund reached $1.6 billion in its first five years Although several nations have since adopted "brownfield renewal policies," the American statute remains unique in terms of the magnitude of corporate liability and the resources dedicated to emergency response clean-up.

The fund paid for a massive clean-up of Love Canal and, after almost ten years, to the ultimate restoration of most abandoned Love Canal homes to the market. When the public was, understandably, unenthusiastic about buying the homes, New York State discounted them some 15 percent below market value. Gibbs and a coalition of environmental organizations tried unsuccessfully to enjoin this move as exploitative of economically weak communities. As the toxic chemicals were neither removed from the Canal nor incinerated, notwithstanding capping efforts, environmentalists still wonder whether the toxic exposures will eventually resurface. But with the exception of dwellings contiguous to the canal—all but two torn down and buried in the early 1980s—Love Canal is being repopulated, and fortunately is undoubtedly cleaner than it was twenty-five years ago.

It is often said that meaningful progress in environmental policy occurs only after a disaster. Love Canal is often used as the proof. The nightmare of this Niagara Falls community was certainly the catalyst for the extraordinary American Superfund legislation and national commitment to toxic waste clean-up. But ultimately, it was neither the egregious pollution nor the enormous human suffering that got the wheels rolling in Washington, but an extraordinarily effective local campaign that Gibbs transmitted to an entire nation.

"We Are the First, but We Are Not Likely to Be the Last"

TESTIMONY PRESENTED TO THE HOUSE SUBCOMMITTEE ON OVERSIGHT AND INVESTIGATIONS, WASHINGTON, D.C., MARCH 21, 1979

*M*y name is Lois Gibbs and I am president of the Love Canal Home-owners Association (LCHA). The LCHA is a citizens group consisting of over one thousand families representing more than 90 percent of the residents in the area. LCHA was formed to deal with the problem of living near the Love Canal chemical dumpsite. I became involved in this situation after discovering that toxic chemicals were buried two blocks from my home and that these chemicals could be aggravating my children's health problems, one of whom attended the Ninety-ninth Street School located in the center of the dump. I started by canvassing the neighborhood to find if other residents had similar problems. I discovered that the majority of residents had what seemed to me an unusually high amount of illnesses. I then worked with residents to form an organization to identify their problems and to help them find solutions.

The LCHA was formed to voice the opinion of residents on the decisions made by state authorities which would affect our lives. We wanted to work with the health department in identifying problems and suggesting solutions to improve the neighborhood. This organization wanted to work with the different agencies by openly communicating and sharing information with them.

At the start, I would like to say that, upon learning of the situation at Love Canal, the state moved quickly to begin health and environmental studies. They also put into effect a remedial construction plan, which would attempt to reduce chemical migration from the canal.

As president and spokesperson for the LCHA, I sit on the Love Canal Task Force and serve as a direct liaison between members of the task force and the residents. Since June 1978, I have taken an active concern in the chemical contamination problems in the neighborhood. I was responsible for the formation of the LCHA on August 4, 1978. On August 9, at the request of William Wilcox, administrator of the Federal Disaster

Assistance Administration, I attended a meeting in Washington, DC, during which possible financial aid for Love Canal was discussed. Upon returning to Niagara Falls, I requested office space in the school building used as a coordinating center for all the government agencies involved in the remedial construction plan. By the 15th of August the association had set up an office to meet the needs of the residents. Since that time I have spent part of every day working with the various government agency representatives. I have had firsthand experience of the daily workings of the different state departments, which include the Department of Health, Department of Environmental Conservation, Department of Transportation, the Red Cross, the Love Canal Task Force, the Niagara County Mental Crisis Center, the Office of Disaster Preparedness, Department of Social Services, and the Federal Disaster Assistance Administration.

I have met with local elected officials to discuss different measures which may be taken to provide assistance to the residents at the local, state, and federal level. Several times, I met with Governor Hugh Carey to discuss possible relocation of families, the proposed construction plan, and in general the needs of the residents.

The most difficult obstacle to relieving the problems at Love Canal has been "being the first." Neither the state nor the federal agencies who could help were responsible for the situation. And neither wanted to take financial responsibility for cleaning it up. Arguing between state and federal authorities over who should pay for what expenses has continued since the first discovery of contamination. In fact, the remedial work for the middle section of the canal, which was supposed to start in mid-March, has just been postponed until midsummer. The reasons given are the construction contract is going from emergency status to an open-bidding process and that the EPA, who was partially funding the work, refuses to review the construction plans until they know who is paying for what proportions. This is especially alarming since, on Friday, March 9th, thick black, oily leachate was found running off the north section of the canal onto the street and into the storm sewers. Remedial work on this section of the canal, which has not begun at all, must now await the decision of the bureaucrats, while residents remain in a contaminated area which is not being remedied.

The state is conducting major studies to define the health problems and the chemical contamination in the area. The outcome of these studies will be the basis of any decisions to relocate families because of chemical contamination resulting in health effects. Twice it has been necessary to relocate people living in different areas around the canal. In each instance, the state had to absorb most of the cost to buy homes or temporarily relocate these families. However, many people with health problems remain, and many questions about the extent of contamination are still being resolved. Meanwhile, the state is conducting a scientific study, the results of which may end up costing the state many millions of dollars, if the results indicate further contamination.

This is especially alarming since continued announcements by state officials have been made that they do not intend to relocate any more families, because of the lack of cause-and-effect linkage between contamination from Love Canal and health effects found in the area. The political and bureaucratic pressures to be "absolutely certain" of the results place great constraints on the objectivity of the scientists working on these studies. The very nature of the uncertainties of determining or establishing the significance of low-level contamination to many chemicals preclude obvious conclusions of cause and effect. Therefore, the health department, in an obvious conflict of interest, must make subjective recommendations to the politicians who will decide what must be done. I want to stress that the objectivity necessary for good science would be near impossible in these circumstances.

The means and capabilities of the state and local resources were—and still are—simply not sufficient to protect the public health and welfare of the residents during such an emergency situation. In fact, the ability of a governmental body to react to public needs is limited by both the laws defining its responsibilities and the appropriations limiting its ability to function. For example, it was necessary to pass special legislation to give the commissioner of health authority and financing to investigate the problems and determine actions to solve them. Five hundred thousand dollars was provided, but it has been estimated that total costs will be at least twenty-two million dollars. The following comments provide examples of necessary actions taken by the state which are very much out of the ordinary:

1. Thousands of blood samples were taken from residents within a matter of a few weeks. The Department of Health does not as a general matter perform laboratory tests on people except for communicable disease or reference work.
2. The large-scale environmental sampling which was undertaken is not a matter of normal operating conditions, especially in testing from soil and dump contamination. The identification of unknown chemicals complicates this limitation even more. When dioxin, one

of the most toxic chemicals known, was found in the canal, the state was not able to determine with any degree of certainty just what areas are contaminated with dioxin. This is because of the expense and difficulty in measuring this chemical.

3. Very little is known about low-level contamination of many chemicals. The health department made its best estimate of what the levels found in the homes may suggest. However, the best minds in the country should have been called in to evaluate what these levels of contamination mean. A large-scale epidemiological effort was implemented to describe the nature of the health problems of the residents. This has only been duplicated in similar major disasters and is not part of the prior experience of the health department.

Although the state reacted to the circumstances as best it could, it was not able to provide the kinds of assistance needed in an emergency situation to protect the health of its residents. Because of the nature of the problem at Love Canal, it was necessary to bring together different professionals to determine how best to solve the problems. Appropriate state professionals were placed in charge of the individual studies; however, a scientific director was not selected to oversee the entire program. Such a director would ensure that similar goals were followed and that each study group received the advantage of the efforts of other groups.

A political appointee is presently in charge. This is not surprising since the state selected people from within their different departments. This has created a great many uncertainties as to who is in charge of what studies, who is doing what work, and who is responsible for planning and follow-up. This has made our communication with the state especially difficult. The major problem that resulted is that no coordinated plan of action, which could systematically define the problems and then select the best available solutions, was established. I certainly understand the constraints of urgency the authorities were under, but this offers little comfort.

In the situation where people are exposed to a threat the magnitude of which no one understands, there are going to be many anxious moments. The residents have been very scared and emotional. And at first the health department was unsure of how great a problem they were facing. Because they had never dealt with such an emergency crisis before, they had no easy method through which to communicate with the residents. Because of the fear of panic, the state did not know how far to involve the residents in the decisions and findings that were made. And officials often did not inspire confidence in the residents, which made matters worse. For example, prior to [the state's] starting the remedial construction work of the south portion of the canal, I received a draft safety plan for the construction. Although it included precautions for the workers, no considerations were provided to protect residents from possible dangers as a result of the construction. I was told at the time that "a good on-site plan was a good off-site plan." Many of the chemicals in the canal were unknown, as was the boundary of the canal. As a result, it was unclear if during construction the workers would disrupt barrels of chemicals. These uncertainties frightened the residents, and we demanded a safety plan and an on-site monitor to help provide protection for the residents in the event of an accident. What resulted was a meeting held by the Office of Disaster Preparedness during which a "total" safety plan was prepared, and later presented to the residents at a public meeting. However, the confidence in this plan was greatly shaken by a statement made by a state spokesman who, when asked to comment on what he would do if toxic vapors were released through the neighborhood, replied: "I wouldn't wait for the bus, I'd run like hell."

Another problem was the flow of information to the residents. A lot of data and information was given to residents without any explanation for what the data meant. Air values of chemicals found in each home were given to the residents without any interpretation of what these values represented. A need to understand the significance of these values was a major concern of the people. Many residents were also given results of blood tests and liver function tests without any idea of the meaning of the results. In some instances, residents were asked to go for repeated tests without any explanation of why. With so many people afraid that their health was at risk, it would have greatly alleviated the fear of the unknown to have someone accessible to the residents who could answer their many questions. All that was really available was a "hot-line" to Albany.

There were also many instances where neither the residents nor our representatives were invited to meetings held by state officials, during which decisions that were affecting the future of the residents were being decided. We were often told that we were not "professionals" and that we would disrupt the ability of people to speak freely. These closed-door meetings fostered mistrust, confusion, and gossip about the concern of the health department for the residents. These feelings were further perpetuated when information on the health and environmental studies were held back from the homeowners and our representatives. This situation has improved, although the Homeowners Association does not receive any routine communications from the state regarding the status of ongoing health and environmental studies. In fact, the only communications that I receive are to announce public meetings or in direct response to a memo or request that I have made. This general insensitivity has greatly polarized the home-owners from the state. It is unfortunate that this situation has developed, because it could have been mostly avoided by better communication and the involvement of people who have had some experience working with people during difficult times.

I would like to provide several examples in detail which demonstrate the nature of the problems just described:

Upon describing the nature of the contamination in the area, state officials concerned themselves mostly with lateral migration directly into homes adjacent to the canal. This was perfectly appropriate as a first mea-sure. However, after reviewing old photographs and consulting materials made available by the state, it became apparent that the nature of the con-tamination might be greatly influenced by the presence of old stream beds, or swales, which existed during the period when the canal was filled with water. Over the years these stream beds were filled with "fill mate-rial" such as garbage, stones, refuse, dirt, or just plain anything that people could find. I went to the University of Buffalo and consulted with Dr. Charles V. Ebert, a soils specialist, who proved to be most helpful in de-scribing and defining the location and characteristics of these streambeds. In mid-September I mentioned what I was finding to state authorities, and they referred to my efforts as "useless housewife data." Working with Dr. Beverly Paigen, a cancer research scientist from Roswell Park Memo-rial Institute, I looked at the nature of the health effects found along the streambeds. The association between the health effects and the locations of the old streams was quite high, so I then looked at the available evidence on chemical contamination along the streambeds. This was not as con-vincing but a positive trend was evident. On November 1, 1978, Dr. Paigen and Steven Lester, a toxicologist who was hired by the New York State to be our on-site monitor and scientific consultant, presented these findings to the Department of Health in Albany. The state representatives listened, then released a statement which read in part that "information presented by the homeowners' consultants was not gathered in a scientific fashion," and commented that they were not persuaded to draw any of the same conclusions.

This position was reaffirmed in statements made during a public meet-ing on November 22. However, on December 20, at a Task Force meeting, the state admitted that contamination was evident outside the first two rows of houses, and that the streambeds may indeed represent an avenue of escape for chemicals from the canal. At a later Task Force meeting on

February 8, 1979, Commissioner of Health Dr. David Axelrod praised the work of Dr. Paigen, commenting that she was responsible for the finding of unusual health effects along the streambeds. Dr. Axelrod then proceeded to recommend the temporary relocation of all pregnant women and children under two years of age who lived in a six-block area, because of the finding of a "small but significant increase in the risk of miscarriages and birth defects." It is striking that it was the homeowners with our limited resources and personnel—not the health department—who initiated these efforts to further define the extent of the health effects and chemical contamination resulting from Love Canal.

The evaluation of the miscarriage data was similarly handled by the state. Since many of the chemicals identified in the canal are toxic to the very young, miscarriages, birth defects, and crib deaths were one of the first indicators to be looked at. The state reviewed the data from their health survey and examined the number of miscarriages on a street-by-street basis. For the homes immediately adjacent to the canal, they found that the number of miscarriages in Ring I was one-and-a-half times what was expected from national averages. This was sufficient to warrant relocating the families in these homes.

They then looked at each row of homes going away from the canal. On October 25, 1978, the health department made, in part, the following comments: "there is no evidence to date indicating that miscarriage rates among women in the reproductive age group who live between 93rd and 103rd Streets exceed expected levels." Using an analysis prepared by our scientific consultants, a memo was given to the state health department on December 20, 1978, describing their analysis of the miscarriage rate, which showed better than a two-fold increase in remaining homes. At this time, the "swale theory" was no longer a theory, and it was becoming apparent that the extent of contamination was beyond the first few rows of houses. Again, it was at the Task Force Meeting of February 8th that the state announced that the "incidence of miscarriages among women living in the former 'wet areas' between 97th and 103rd Streets and Colving Boulevard and Frontier Avenue was about twice as high as that of residents of 'dry' areas in the same neighborhood and that of a control group in a similar study of miscarriage frequency in Toronto."

From the initial decision to relocate families in early August, until early February, the state continuously denied that any evidence of health problems existed outside the first two rows of houses. Again, it was the homeowners with our limited resources and personnel who initiated these efforts to define the extent of the health effects in the area. With our consultants, we analyzed the data and pointed out apparent patterns of disease to the health department. . . .

The distribution of the health questionnaire and blood sampling was a somewhat different situation For the first two rings of houses, two people went door-to-door handing out the questionnaire, answering any questions residents might have. They also took blood samples. However, when it became necessary to give out further questionnaires and take additional blood samples from other area residents, the situation changed. A general public announcement was made to come to the 99th Street School to have a blood sample taken. Hundreds of people showed up at the same time. The four technicians who were present were totally overwhelmed by the situation. No effort was made to separate the people waiting to have their blood drawn from those having it done. Screaming children coupled with high summer temperatures and overcrowded conditions resulted in an unnecessarily unbearable situation. To make matters worse, as people left they were given a health questionnaire and asked to fill it out. Few people cared at all about this questionnaire. A little planning and organization could have avoided this situation. . . .

All of these examples describe in part the difficulties I have experienced. I have tried to limit my comments because the stories could go on forever, as even today is part of still another story. I will now finish my testimony by making several suggestions and recommendations.

First of all, it is apparent that a means for responding to environmental incidents such as Love Canal must be provided by the federal government. A group analogous to the infectious disease response unit of the Center for Disease Control should be set up to respond to environmental emergencies that require immediate action and special expertise. Specialists in the effects of chemicals on skin disease, kidney disorders, urinary infections, and so on could be alerted and called in as needed. This did not happen at Love Canal. We are the first, but we are not likely to be the last. Something must be done.

Such an agency would provide an agency responsible to pick up the costs of the studies needed, and possibly for the remedial construction. It would also provide a mechanism for ensuring that a state agency with limited resources would not be faced with the difficult task of responding to such an emergency. It would also ensure that an outside group of experts, who would not be involved in the situation and would have no real or vested interest in any outcome of the studies, would be involved. This outside group could thus conduct an objective scientific study of existing health problems.

If necessary a special "blue ribbon panel" of experts could be collected and asked to further review the data. However, the identity of such an advisory group should be publicly announced and its findings and recommendations made available immediately if urgency is required. At Love Canal, such a "blue ribbon panel" has been involved, but its members and recommendations have been kept secret. If urgency is not needed, then interim reports should be available, as should minutes of the meetings. In either case, sufficient time should be provided for such a committee to properly complete its task.

We have made many requests for such an outside group to come to Love Canal and review the existing data, or even conduct a new study, which would include a control population. No federal agency has responded to our requests, claiming they have no authority to do so.

Finally, I would like to say that we have faced many problems at Love Canal, some of which have been solved. Yet many others remain. I hope the congressmen and women who are here today have grasped a sense of the awfulness of our situation. Not only has our neighborhood become a test site for scientists, but no authorities or agencies are willing to take a stand and help us. I ask that you do what you can for us and do what you must to prevent what has happened at Love Canal from ever happening again.

REFERENCES

Center for Health, Environment, and Justice. Web site: *http://www.chej.org/*.
Comprehensive Environmental Response, Compensation, and Liability Act. U.S. Title 42, Chapter 103 (1980).
Ecumenical Task Force of the Niagara Frontier. "Background on the Love Canal." Love Canal Collection, State University of New York at Buffalo Archives. *http://ublib.buffalo.edu/libraries/projects/lovecanal/background_lovecanal.html* 1998.
Gibbs, Lois. Testimony Presented to the House Subcommittee on Oversight and Investigations. U.S. Congress. House. March 21, 1979.
———. "Invited Address by a Distinguished Citizen: Lois Gibbs." *American Journal of Community Psychology* 11, no. 2 (1983): 115–125.
Gibbs, Lois, and Murray Levine. *Love Canal: My Story.* Albany: State University of New York Press, 1982.
Hoffman, Andrew. "An Uneasy Rebirth at Love Canal." *Environment* 37 (March 1995): 4.
Levine, Adeline Gordon. *Love Canal: Science, Politics, and People.* Lexington, MA: Lexington Books, 1982.

Redd, Adrienne. "Lois Gibbs, Champion of Love Canal, Working to Rebuild Democracy." In *A Terrible Beauty. http://www.netaxs.com/~adredd/gibbstext .html.* 1997.

U.S. Environmental Protection Agency. "CERCLA Overview." *http://www.epa.gov/ superfund/action/law/cercla.htm.*

6. David Lange

NEW ZEALAND

Photograph used with permission of the Office of the Prime Minister, Wellington, New Zealand.

*I*n 1962, while still a teenager in the Auckland suburb of Otahuhu, David Lange walked home from a bus stop and quite inadvertently witnessed American nuclear testing at Johnston Island in the Pacific. Although thousands of miles away, the one megaton blast transformed the night sky in New Zealand, which pulsated with red and white shafts of light. The eerie experience started a process that twenty-three years later led him as prime minister to become the first world leader in the West to take and implement a bold antinuclear stance. In an internationally televised debate on the issue, his speech convinced his countrymen that New Zealand needed to be "nuclear free." This is the story and the speech.

Beyond fallout from testing, nuclear arms production creates enormous environmental challenges, many of which are poorly addressed. Even today, the weapons plants of the former Soviet Union constitute a substantial environmental hazard in which radiation is measured at perilous levels. A closed plutonium complex in Seversk in Western Siberia, for example, still releases what observers call "staggering" levels of caesium, strontium-90, and other radioactive materials. Even when production is ostensibly more responsible and contained, it poses considerable health hazards. Tritium, a radioactive isotope of hydrogen made by bombarding isotopes of lithium or helium with neutrons, is a gas required for hydrogen bombs. The residuals generated in its formation leave prodigious quantities of nuclear wastes for disposal. The phenomenally long half-life of nuclear wastes immediately raises hard questions of intergenerational justice; the leftover weapons spun off for short-term military deterrence (bombs need to be replaced fairly frequently) become the problem of our progeny for eons to come.

But it is the environmental impacts of nuclear war itself that dominate environmentalists' concerns. Nuclear winter was first hypothesized in 1983 in the TTAPS study (based on the first letters of the names of the researching scientists, R. B. Turco, O. B. Toon, T. P. Ackerman, J. B. Pollack, and C. Sagan.) The terrifying scenario sketched by the researchers was rigorous enough to be printed in the prestigious international journal *Science*. This apocalyptic analysis envisions a chain reaction set off by the enormous fireballs that the exploding nuclear warheads create. The subsequent firestorms over cities and forests loft immense plumes of soot and dust high into the atmosphere, which drift for as long as a year. This might reduce sunlight by as much as 99 percent, driving temperatures down to -40 degrees C. According to the biologists' prediction, a full-blown nuclear winter thus creates conditions similar to those caused by the meteor that ended the dinosaurs' Cretaceous period. Most of the earth's vegetation and animals perish from the low temperatures and the high radiation levels.

By the mid-1980s, a single medium-size nuclear warhead reached levels of 250 kilotons, the power of all the bombs that could be carried by fifty thousand World War II bombers. It became clear that even a limited nuclear engagement might not only kill billions of people but also compromise the entire planet ecologically. Yet in the Cold War dynamics of the period, most nations of the world stood by helplessly (or even with complicity), choosing sides as the nuclear arsenals of the United States and the Soviet Union grew. But in 1984, almost out of the blue, one country, New Zealand, chose to opt out of the madness.

The decision to make the country "nuclear free" came after the victory of the Labor Party in 1984. David Lange at forty-one became the youngest prime minister in the country's history. An articulate, portly lawyer from Auckland, he quickly transformed his Labor Party as leader of the opposition, and, when surprise elections were called, led the party to a decisive victory over the conservative National Party. American warships' nuclear arsenals and their access to New Zealand was one of the hot election issues. Lange's administration is largely remembered for two major policy shifts: deregulation, with the dismantling of the country's socialist economic orientation; and the establishment of New Zealand as a nuclear-free zone. The first was to be the source of the party's fall from power; the second earned Lange a place in New Zealand history as a national hero, indeed as a protagonist in the international arena.

Having come of age in the 1960s, Lange was in touch with the counterculture, and even mentioned in a press conference once that he preferred the music of Dire Straits to that of Debussy. While still in law school, he worked for a firm headed by a "nuclear free" advocate who assisted the country's fledgling, and then still peripheral, "anti-nuke" movement. As a politician Lange was irreverent, clever, and—like most Kiwis—knew how to joke at himself (once telling the press that he was demeaned by people who thought that he was in the job of prime minister because he had missed out on getting the general manager's job at McDonalds.) But Lange took the potential of a nuclear holocaust very seriously.

After 1951 and the signing of the ANZUS treaty, binding Australia, New Zealand, and the United States together as allies, the cornerstone of New Zealand's security policy was its alliance with American firepower. In the initial post-World War II Cold War line-up, this option made sense. After leaving the safety of the British empire, New Zealand would have found the United States about the best patron around. But this dependence exacted a military price. For example, in 1965 New Zealand sent troops to Vietnam to support the United States–South Vietnamese forces. In the mid-1980s the price meant playing host periodically to the small armada of American nuclear ships; this was something that increasingly seemed at odds with both local Kiwi interests and those of humanity.

When Lange began to implement the Labor platform banning nuclear arms and ships, the American response predictably was that of an angry giant. U.S. cabinet secretaries went on the record saying that the policy was a violation of ANZUS, gave comfort to the Communists, and spelled the end of the U.S. commitment to New Zealand security. American congresspersons called for trade sanctions. Public opinion polls in New Zealand at the time showed that some 70 percent of the country felt uncomfortable at losing American protection under ANZAS, even as a majority was unhappy about allowing America's nuclear weapons or nuclear powered vessels into the country. To test Lange's resolve, the Americans formally requested permission to anchor the S.S. Buchanan at a New Zealand military port, but refused to confirm or deny whether it would have nuclear weapons aboard. In January 1985, Lange denied the ship entry into New Zealand waters. The furious American response and the likelihood of grim political and economic consequences left Lange and his government in a shaky position with voters.

In a series of speeches in February and March of 1985, Lange brought his case to the world and the United Nations. Most of the speeches received moderate coverage at best. When Lange was invited to debate his country's nuclear position with Jerry Falwell, the conservative American minister, at the prestigious Oxford Union debating forum in England, the stage was set for a high-profile showdown.

Lange would later describe the confrontation in detail. "Evening arrived and I strapped myself into my dinner suit. The Union building was jammed with people. . . . The old debating chamber had a church hall feel to it. The audience filled the body of the room and the galleries above it." Despite the Virginia preacher's folksy appearance, Falwell is a sophisticated and intelligent man and can be a spellbinding speaker. Prior to his presentation, a Tory member of Parliament backed his views. After enumerating the ills of Communist Russia and the threat it posed, Falwell condescended: "It is the moral code of the West to take care of those who cannot take care of themselves, or who don't wish to."

The debate forum encouraged interruptions from the audience, which occurred frequently during Falwell's address. Then Lange took the floor and immediately stole the show. His arguments were geopolitical and philosophical in nature, only mentioning "nuclear winter" in passing, with an implicit allusion to the unthinkable human and environmental toll that nuclear weapons could bring.

It was audience participation that brought the most memorable moment of the evening, during a typical Lange "improvisation." Lange gave the floor briefly to a Rhodes Scholar visiting from the U.S. Naval Academy, and later recounted: "He asked me, in view of New Zealand's decision to ban nuclear ships, how I could justify our membership of ANZUS. I said I'd give him the answer if he'd hold his breath a moment. 'I can smell the uranium on your breath,' I added."

Lange's speech was well received by the crowd, and at the end of the evening, when the votes were counted, his "affirmative" position won the debate by a vote of 298 to 250. But the real victory was political, a hemisphere away. Lange's willingness to put his country's economy and security on the line and stand up against what he viewed as American nuclear tyranny resonated back home. As his countrymen watched him live, on one of the country's two television channels, a new sense of pride at New Zealand's independent, antinuclear stance became, almost overnight, part of the national ideology. Today the country's antinuclear stance is tantamount to patriotism, and New Zealand has never looked back.

Soon thereafter, the issue exploded into the international news again when the Greenpeace vessel *Rainbow Warrior* arrived at New Zealand in July 1985. The boat was on its way to protest the French nuclear testing at Mururoa, but it never got there. French secret service agents blew it up, killing a crewman as it sat in the Waitemata harbor. A pair of French agents were arrested two days later, jailed, and eventually convicted of manslaughter. Despite initial denials, President Mitterand of France eventually admitted that they had been on a state mission. The debacle not only lionized Lange, enhancing his political popularity, it also fortified the national will to stay *nuclear free*—the title of the book Lange eventually wrote about the period.

Parliament soon passed legislation forbidding nuclear ships to visit New Zealand, and Lange helped spearhead the South Pacific Nuclear-Free Zone convention (a treaty with more symbolic than actual significance). His Labor party would win the 1987 election, but by 1989, tired of infighting within the cabinet over economic reform, Lange resigned as prime minister. Yet even after the party was voted out and replaced by the right-wing National Party in 1990, the antinuclear policies held. (Interestingly, over 10 percent of the votes that year went to a new Green Party, a group that surely leveraged the national pride at being antinuclear.)

There is little doubt that the Oxford Union speech was what crystallized the national antinuclear perspective. Much as Americans can remember where they were on September 11, 2001, Kiwis can almost uniformly recall watching Lange stand up to American pressure live on national TV. Bringing his country's decency and his own perspicacity to bear, the prime minister won a round against the prevailing nuclear insanity of the period.

"Nuclear Weapons Are Morally Indefensible"

TEXT OF THE ARGUMENT FOR THE AFFIRMATIVE DURING THE OXFORD UNION DEBATE AT OXFORD, ENGLAND, MARCH 1, 1985

*T*here is no moral case for nuclear weapons. The best defense which can be made of their existence and the threat of their use is that they are a necessary evil, an abhorrent means to a desirable end.

I hold that the character of nuclear weapons is such that their existence corrupts the best of intentions, that the means in fact perverts the end. I hold that their character is such that they have brought us to the greatest of all perversions, the belief that this evil is necessary when in fact it is not.

I make my case against nuclear weapons the more vigorously because I distinguish between them and all other forms of coercive or deterrent power. I have no case to make against the policeman's truncheon. I accept that the state must arm itself with military force to protect its citizens against aggression or to defend the weak and helpless against aggression.

I do not accept that the state must for those reasons arm itself with nuclear weapons. That is a case I do not easily or lightly make in Europe. Where governments have held it their duty to arm themselves with nuclear weapons, I do not doubt for one moment the quality of the intention which led to that decision.

I freely acknowledge that the nuclear deterrent is maintained in good conscience with the honorable intention of preserving the life and freedom of the people of Western Europe. Those governments are faced with the close presence of an alien and relentlessly oppressive regime, and felt it their duty to prepare for their own defense by membership in a nuclear alliance. That is an assessment I understand and respect. I do not argue here or anywhere else for unilateral disarmament.

If I make that acknowledgment, I must then deal with the argument that it is the intention which determines the moral character of the action. My contention is that the character of nuclear weapons is such that it is demonstrably the case that they subvert the best of intentions.

There is a quality of irrationality about nuclear weapons, which does not sit well with good intentions. A system of defense serves its purpose if it guarantees the security of those it protects. A system of nuclear defense

Speech reprinted by permission of David Lange.

guarantees only insecurity. The means of defense terrorizes as much as the threat of attack. In Europe, it is impossible to be unaware of the intensity of military preparedness. In New Zealand, the visitor must make an effort to find a military instillation, or indeed any sign of military activity, although it exists. There is no imperative in New Zealand to prepare for war; the result is that I feel safer in Wellington than I ever could in London or New York.

Europe and the United States are ringed around with nuclear weapons, and your people have never been more at risk. There is only one thing as terrifying as the nuclear weapon pointed in your direction, and that is the nuclear weapon pointed in your enemy's direction; the outcome of their use would be the same in either case, and that is the annihilation of you and of all of us. That is a defense which is no defense; it is a defense which disturbs far more than it reassures. The intention of those who for honorable motives use nuclear weapons to deter is to enhance security; they succeed only in enhancing insecurity. The machine has perverted the motive; the weapon has installed mass destruction as the objective of the best intentioned.

The weapon has its own relentless logic, and it is inhuman. It is the logic of escalation, the logic of the arms race. Nuclear weapons make us insecure, and to compensate for our insecurity we build and deploy more nuclear weapons. We know that we are seized by irrationality and yet we persist. We all of us know that it is wholly without logic or reason to possess the power to destroy ourselves many times over, and yet in spite of that knowledge the nuclear powers continue to refine their capacity to inflict destruction on each other and all the rest of us. Every new development, whatever its strategic or tactical significance, has only one result, and that is to add to an arsenal which is already beyond reason.

There is an argument in defense of the possession of nuclear weapons which holds that the terror created by the existence of nuclear weapons is in itself the fulfillment of a peaceful purpose: that the fear they inspire will prevent their use. I pass over, here, the preparations which are constantly being made for the winnable or even survivable nuclear war; I would ignore those and wholeheartedly embrace the logic of the unthinkable war, if it could be established that the damage which would result from the collapse of that logic would be confined to the nuclear weapon states. Unfortunately and demonstrably, it would not.

We in New Zealand, you know, used to be able to relax a bit, to be able to think that we would sit comfortably while the rest of the world seared, singed, and withered. We were enraptured. And the fact is that we used to have the reputation of being some kind of an antipodean Noah's Ark, which would, from within its quite isolated preserve, spawn a whole new world of realistic humankind. Now the fact is that we know that that is not achievable. We know that, if the nuclear winter comes, we freeze—we join the rest of you. And that means that there is now a total denouement as far as any argument in favor of moral purpose goes. It is a strange, dubious, and totally unaccepted moral purpose which holds the whole of the world to ransom.

There is another assertion of the good moral character of nuclear weapons, which holds that they are the armor of good against evil. It is the argument of the Crusaders: the evil, which cannot be defeated by persuasion or example, is to be subdued by threat of annihilation. The obvious difficulty here is that evil has declined to be subdued; it will not accept annihilation; every attempt to subdue it strengthens its resolve to arm itself further. The will of the good is corrupted by the terrible force of the weapon into the will of the evil.

All of us everywhere, wherever we are, whatever we believe, live in fear of nuclear weapons. That is a community of interests which binds us all; it is common ground enough for all of us to wish to see the elimination of all nuclear weapons; yet nuclear weapons proliferate. They govern us. Their existence diverts attention from the fact that there are other ways of resolving the difficulties and tensions which will always abound in the world. Nuclear weapons are not needed. All the arguments which can be brought forward in support of this evil come to nothing in the fact of its ultimate irrelevance. I do not make that assertion because I have some simple answer to the existence of nuclear weapons; all of you in Europe know that negotiating an end to nuclear weapons could hardly be more difficult, just as all of you know that we cannot negotiate control of them while nuclear powers embrace the logic of escalation.

In New Zealand, it is easy to accept that there is no need for nuclear weapons. The collisions and confrontations which take place in Europe are very far away from us. New Zealand is remote. It faces no threat; our close neighbors are like-minded states. We have been to war several times in this century, but never because we were attacked. It makes no sense for a country which faces no threat to seek to surround itself with nuclear weapons. It makes no sense for that country to ask its allies to deter enemies which do not yet exist with the threat of nuclear weapons. It makes no sense for a region which is the most stable in the world to allow itself to become a strategic arena for the nuclear powers. Having considered all this, the people of New Zealand reached a straightforward conclusion: the nuclear weapons which defended them caused them more alarm than any which threatened them, and it was accordingly pointless to be defended by them.

In the South Pacific, it is not difficult to achieve the balance of force which allows you cheerfully to dispense with nuclear weapons. If you remove the nuclear weapons of your friends and allies, you put all the nuclear powers on the same footing. The South Pacific is not the North Atlantic. Nuclear weapons cannot be removed from Europe simply by dismantling the NATO arsenal; do that, and the other nuclear arsenal will still be here. But in the South Pacific there is at this moment the chance to turn away from the inhuman logic of nuclear weapons, to stand aside from the irrationality of the arms race and the doctrines of nuclear confrontation.

The government of New Zealand has excluded nuclear weapons from New Zealand; more than that, I hope that it and other governments in the South Pacific will shortly ask all the nuclear powers to honor a South Pacific Nuclear-Free Zone. New Zealand has done that while honoring its longstanding commitment to the conventional defense of the South Pacific, to the economic and social development of the South Pacific, and to the security of Southeast Asia.

What has happened to New Zealand since the Labor Government was elected last year and began to implement its long-established policy is itself a commentary on the way in which nuclear weapons have assumed a moral life of their own.

New Zealand is not and has never been part of the strategic defenses of the West. The nuclear weapons which our allies have in the past brought to New Zealand are tactical weapons. It is our view in New Zealand that being part of somebody else's tactical nuclear battle is as undesirable as being part of somebody else's strategic nuclear battle; but my point is that the decision of the New Zealand government in no way weakened the deterrent power of the Western alliance. Yet, we have been accused of undermining the West and giving comfort to the Soviet bloc. We have been told by officials in the United States administration that our decision is not, as they put it, cost-free, that in fact we are to be made to pay for our action. Not by our enemies, but by our friends. We are to be made an example of; we are to be ostracized and anathematized until we are compelled to resume our seat in the dress circle of the nuclear theater. We have been told that, because others in the West carry the fearful burden of a defense which terrorizes as much as the threat, we too must carry that burden. We are actually told that New Zealanders cannot decide for themselves how to defend New Zealand, but are obliged to adopt the methods which others use to defend themselves.

Lord Carrington, the secretary general of NATO, made a case in Copenhagen recently against the creation of nuclear-weapon-free zones. He argued that, if the people of the United States found themselves bear-ing the burden alone, they would tire of bearing it. That is exactly the point. Genuine agreements about the control of nuclear weapons do not cede the advantage to one side or the other: they enhance security; they do not diminish it. If such arrangements can be made, and such agree-ments reached, then those who remain outside those arrangements might well and truly tire of their insecurity. They will reject the logic of the weapon and assert their essential humanity. They will look for arms control agreements which are real and verifiable.

There is no humanity in the logic which holds that my country must be obliged to play host to nuclear weapons because others in the West are playing host to nuclear weapons. That is the logic which refuses to admit that there is any alternative to nuclear weapons, when plainly there is.

It is self-defeating logic, just as the weapons themselves are self-defeating. To compel an ally to accept nuclear weapons against the wishes of that ally is to take the moral position of totalitarianism, which allows for no self-determination. Any claim to a moral justification for the West's pos-session of nuclear weapons is thereby eliminated. We are no better than they are.

The great strength of the West lies not in force of arms but in its free and democratic systems of governance.

That is why, in spite of all the difficulties New Zealand has got into with our friends and allies, I am not disheartened. I came to Great Britain by way of the United States, where I put my case to the American people through the news media without any kind of hindrance from the United States administration. Members of Her Majesty's government have made it plain to me that they do not hold the views I hold, but nonetheless I am here and I can say freely whatever I please; just as any member of Her Majesty's government would be welcome in New Zealand to expound any line of argument in any forum she cared to use. That is the true strength of the West.

It is a strength which is threatened, not defended, by nuclear weapons. The appalling character of those weapons has robbed us of our right to determine our destiny and has subordinated our humanity to their manic logic. They have subordinated reason to irrationality and placed our very will to live in hostage. Rejecting the logic of nuclear weapons does not mean surrendering to evil; evil must still be guarded against. Rejecting nuclear weapons is to assert what is human over the evil nature of the weapon; It is to restore to humanity the power of decision; it is to allow true moral force to reign supreme.

REFERENCES

Babst, Dean. "Preventing an Accidental Nuclear Winter." *Waging Peace:* Website of the Nuclear Age Peace Foundation., *www.wagingpeace.org.* 2002.

Barber, David. *Gliding on the Limo: The Wit of David Lange.* Auckland: Benton Ross, 1987.

Brockie, Bob. *The Penguin Eyewitness History of New Zealand.* Auckland: Penguin, 2002.

Greenpeace web site. "History." *www.greenpeace.org.*

James, Colin. *The Quiet Revolution: Turbulence and Transition in Contemporary New Zealand.* Wellington: Allen and Unwin, 1986.

Lange, David. *Nuclear Free, the New Zealand Way.* Auckland: Penguin, 1990.

McQueen, Harvey. *The Ninth Floor. Inside the Prime Minister's Office: A Political Experience.* Auckland: Penguin Books, 1991.

New Zealand Ministry of Foreign Affairs. *Information Bulletin* no. 11 (March 1985): 15–21.

Sinclair, Keith. *A History of New Zealand.* Auckland: Penguin, 2000.

Traynor, Ian. "Worst-Ever Radioactive Leaks Found in Siberia: Condemned Weapons Plants Still Spewing Out Poisons, Say Experts." *The Independent,* November 3, 2000.

Turco, R. B., O. B. Toon, T. P. Ackerman, J. B. Pollack, Carl Sagan. "Nuclear Winter: Global Consequences of Multiple Nuclear Explosions." *Science* 222, no. 4630 (1983).

7. Mongosuthu G. Buthulezi

SOUTH AFRICA

When Chief Mongosuthu Buthelezi established the Tembe Elephant Park during the 1980s, he broke a long tradition of estrangement between the black majority of South Africa and the local conservation community. The new Union of South Africa in 1910 enacted numerous laws designed to keep whites and blacks apart, but it was only in 1948, with the election of the right-wing National Party in South Africa, that apartheid or "racial separation" was fully adopted as public policy. The new laws not only banned blacks from sharing most public resources, from public transportation and schools to toilets, but also proscribed interracial marriages or romantic liaisons. National Parks and nature sanctuaries were, of course, the domain of white people, except when "natives" were needed to perform menial tasks.

At the same time, during the twentieth century South Africa's magnificent and diverse wild life not only offered a prime tourist attraction, but also served as a major source of pride and identity for the white minority. Game reserves enjoyed considerable subsidies from the government that made them inaccessible to the black majority. Very quickly, black residents came to associate game viewing and their country's scenic bush as yet another trapping of an oppressive apartheid regime.

In 1958, Dr. Hendrik Verwoerd became prime minister of South Africa, and in 1959 he promulgated the Promotion of Bantu Self-Government Act. The law divided black people into eight ethnic groups and created a system of Bantustans (or "black homelands") in which the local tribes were granted authority for limited self-administration. These semiautonomous states included Bophuthatswana, Cisei, Venda, and KwaZulu. Far from being a magnanimous gesture, the objective was to institutionalize discrimination. As black residents of these homelands became legally disenfranchised from the South African state, they could no longer expect to vote in the country's "democratic elections."

At the beginning of the 1980s, the dramatic 1989 announcement by President de Klerk admitting the failure of apartheid policies, and the ultimate release of Nelson Mandela in 1991, were far off, indeed unimaginable. And so the ongoing alienation of black South Africans from their natural history seemed yet another ineluctable apartheid-associated tragedy. Beyond the enormous cultural loss, there were pernicious ecological implications, with poaching becoming a form of nationalistic expression. It is within this context that Mongosuthu Buthelezi's commitment to conservation was so extraordinary.

Buthulezi was born in 1928 into a royal lineage and assumed the mantle of Zulu chief before the age of thirty. By 1976 he was appointed chief minister of the Bantastan KwaZulu, a position which he held for eighteen years. The establishment of KwaZulu in the northeast corner of South Africa (bordered by the white province of Natal) just south of Mozambique offered a natural geographic base for the Zulu nation, half of whom lived within its borders. Zulus preserved their traditional culture, formed around the Umuzi, or extended homestead, as the basic social unit and around a largely agrarian economy. Their warrior heritage was certainly the source of much pride; even today, Zulus remain among South Africa's most sought-after security guards.

Buthulezi's politics were always firmly anti-apartheid, and he is credited with reviving the "Inkatha," a Zulu cultural initiative, and turning it into an effective framework for challenging the state. The organization would eventually evolve into the anti-apartheid Inkatha Freedom Party. By and by, Buthulezi would publicly disapprove of the economic sanctions as well as the violence that were brought to bear in the effort to end apartheid, on tactical grounds. This tagged him as a leader of moderate leanings. It also hastened the rift between him and the African National Congress (ANC), which once had included him among its primary leadership. Indeed, he brought a tribalist ideology to his political position that advocated greater territorial autonomy. Eventually, he would leave the African National Congress on ideological grounds, in a split frequently manifested by violent clashes. Yet, after the 1994 elections, Buthulezi joined the National Unity Government at Nelson Mandela's invitation. He served in both the Mandela and Mbeki Governments as minister for home affairs, in addition to being deputized as acting president of South Africa during many of Mandela's visits abroad.

It is important to recall therefore that during the 1980s, with the infrastructure of a Bantustan behind him and with growing recognition internationally, Buthelezi was arguably Black South Africa's most prominent, active political leader. His photograph, in the traditional Zulu chief's "leopard skin," was frequently in the news. But, while using his status to promote human liberties, he did not forget his country's other creatures.

Poaching had reached crisis dimensions for many species in South Africa. For example, after fifty white rhino were reintroduced to the area in 1975, their numbers dropped, falling to eight by 1982. Elephants were also in trouble. Throughout Africa between 1980 and 1989 the estimated population was in free fall, dropping from 1.2 million to 600,000. The plight of the last remaining herds of free-ranging elephants in South Africa required a most immediate response. Given KwaZulu's checkerboard geography, which represented only a fraction of the original "historic" Zululand, pressure for land was acute. Yet Buthulezi decided to set aside considerable real estate for the elephants. The resulting Tembe Reserve was declared on a 29,000-hectare (71,000-acre) stretch of land.

Of course, the challenge of saving elephants did not stop there.

The dilemma that elephants pose to wildlife managers is well known. The animals move as a family unit with a matriarch at the core. Only recently has their ability to communicate, using long frequency infra-sounds inaudible to humans, been identified. Not surprisingly, elephants have rather enormous appetites, each animal consuming between 150 to 200 kilograms of leaves per day. The great beasts leave behind a slightly smaller quantity of dung, although this is generally transported underground by dung beetles and termites, enriching the soils. Like humans, they can completely transform landscapes, de-barking and uprooting trees and decimating the composition and structure of natural vegetation. When elephant population density gets too high, decline in plant biodiversity is easily measured.

When elephant populations wander near agricultural communities, conflict is inevitable. Fences, culling, and, in cases of small populations, birth control, can reduce the clash. But generally, without a systematic preservation program, it is the elephants who are the losers.

Tembe Park's establishment was not without some controversy, but relative to other "takings" it was minimal. Advocating a position which today has become the essence of the *biosphere* concept, Buthelezi insisted that Tembe Park's creation be conducted only after consultation with local residents. Buthulezi also never eschewed the hunting of elephants as part of Zulu culture, provided it was within a sustainable context.

Although some moderate dislocation was accepted by the Tembe elders as an unfortunate consequence, there was some subsequent acrimony about the adequacy of the compensation provided. The solar-powered fence in the park also raised the specter of racial seclusion for locals who had previously had free access, with all the traumatic associations of white domination. In retrospect, however, the move proved critical.

The habitat for the last free-ranging indigenous elephant herd was now protected. Many other animals, like the endangered Suni antelope and the other "big five" game, have since found refuge from land mines and poachers amid the park's sand forest. Once the dust settled, tensions between the physically largest elephants in South Africa and the areas' farmers abated. When first established, Tembe Park bordered both a white reserve (Ndumbo) and the Maputo Elephant reserve in Mozambique, setting the stage for the transnational reserve strategy that has recently come of age.

Although the controversy over the legitimacy of ivory trading or culling in general will probably remain a subject for international debate for some time, the participation of a Zulu chief and head of a Bantustan changed the nature of the discourse. Indeed, it can be argued that the participation of an anti-apartheid tribal leader affected the South African conservation movement dramatically, beginning the process of depoliticization and healing. Thus in 1986, when Buthelezi, with his proven record of ecological commitment, agreed to sit as the chair of a predominantly white, animal protection fund, his move was more than just another small step toward the integration of the South African conservation community.

Buthelezi has continued his successful career as a senior minister in the new South African government. But from an environmental perspective, it is his speech from 1986, reprinted below, that remains a particularly remarkable statement. Buthelezi's involvement becomes even more impressive when set against the charged backdrop of South Africa in those troubled days. With international boycotts at a peak, violent resistance by the ANC continuing, and the peaceful transition to democracy still years away, an audience of white South African environmentalists sought the leadership of a Zulu chief. Buthelezi refused to let the animals with whom his people had always shared the land pay the price for the appalling legacy of human persecution and exploitation. As his speech explains, elephants and rhinos were more than recreation or sport—they were part of his people's very identity. The address was an important message not only for conservation, but implicitly for reconciliation.

"I Too Am One of Those Who Cannot Live without Wild Things"

INAUGURATION OF THE RHINO AND ELEPHANT FOUNDATION, EVERARD READ GALLERY, JOHANNESBURG, SOUTH AFRICA, SEPTEMBER 25, 1986

*M*r. Chairman, Distinguished Guests, Ladies and Gentlemen. It is for me a particular pleasure to be with you today on the occasion of the official launch of the Rhino and Elephant Foundation. I am greatly honored to have been asked to become president of this foundation.

The rhino and the elephant have special significance to me, both as a conservationist and because of their importance to the culture and history of my people. To single out any one plant or animal as being of particular cultural significance to the Zulu Nation is not an easy task. Zulu culture is so interwoven with the natural world as to be inseparable from it. One need only look at the mace of the KwaZulu Legislative Assembly to see how true this is. This mace, or, as it is known in Zulu, "induce Yombuso KaZulu" features such items as a grass hut, a clay pot, ostrich feathers, the wood of both the mbondwenyama or russet willow tree, and the mncaka or red ivory tree, as well as the mystical coil or inkatha, which

Speech reprinted with permission of Prince Mangosuthu Buthlezi, M.P.

was woven from thatch plucked from the doorways of all Zulu chiefs' huts.

It is, however, the elephant which has been singled out to be the central figure on the KwaZulu coat of arms, where it represents strength and intelligence. It is because of these qualities too that Zulu kings are praised as ... Indlovu or elephant as an alternative to Ingonyama or lion, while the king's mother is known as the Ndlovukazi or the She-Elephant. So when Zulus salute their king they shout: "Wena Wendlovu, Wena Wendlovu, Bayehte—You of the Elephant, You of the Elephant! Bring to us our enemies for us to stab them."

Royalty in other parts of the world may not be exactly flattered by such titles, but my forefathers who lived close to these grand beasts understood their true courage, loyalty, and dignity. This in itself is one good reason for conserving elephants, so that future generations too may understand the deeper significance of such praise names. I am proud of this because it also indicates the respect that our people have had for the animal kingdom and for certain individual animals.

I have been told also that some of our medicine men also used the elephant's droppings for various charms. This to me indicates the extent to which the elephant was glorified in Zulu society, that even its droppings are attributed with magical charms or medicinal value. Quite often one will see some strands from the tail of the elephant worn on the arm by hunters and others who believe in the luck charms of the elephant's tail.

Before the advent of the white man in Africa, elephant tusks were used in African trade. It was also an appropriate present that royalty exchanged as a valuable gift. When the white man arrived with the gun, more of these poor animals were shot, as their tusks were used for barter and trade in general. It sounds like a legend that elephants were in abundance in KwaZulu until the reign of King Cetshwayo, who is my maternal great-grandfather. The African elephant is different from the Indian or the Eastern elephant. Each one has wonderful attributes, and it is a disgrace that Africa is today very much denuded of elephant life because of the illegal poaching which both black and white have indulged in so excessively because of their human greed. In the writings on the cover of Clive Walker's monumental work on elephants, "Twilight of the Giants," the Endangered Wildlife Trust states, and I wish to quote them:

The extinction of life has been an integral part of evolutionary development since the beginnings of life on earth. Successful forms have survived; the failures have faded into oblivion. As this is a natural and inevitable process, you may wonder why there should be concern at the animal extinctions taking place in the world today. Extinction by man is the antithesis of this natural process, for it impoverishes organic life and leaves only a void. Some species have been wantonly destroyed, often as the result of commercialized exploitation, as with the fur seals and the blue whale. The majority of recent extinctions, however, are attributable to environmental change arising from alteration and degradation of natural habitats. Pastoral and agricultural expansion and extensive deforestation are the principal causes. Areas which, because of their remoteness or inaccessibility were hitherto undisturbed natural sanctuaries, have been thrown open to human intrusion.

Clive Walker himself quotes Aldo Leopold in his monumental work when Leopold says: "Like winds and sunsets, wild things were taken for granted until progress began to do away with them."

To stress once again the importance of elephants in Zulu cultural life, I wish to recall that, in 1925, my late uncle, King Solomon Maphumzana ka Dinuzulu, my mother's full brother and the grandfather of our present king, sent our young people to the Ingwavuma area to hunt for an elephant. He wished to present a pair of beautiful tusks to a royal visitor from Great Britain, Prince Edward of Wales (later King Edward VIII). They returned with the elephant tusks and these were duly presented to his Royal Highness Prince Edward of Wales in Eschowe in June 1925.

The Zulu king has always had the privilege of naming regiments—that is, groups of young men of an age group. The young men who brought the tusks as sent out by the king were then named Uphondo Lwendlovu meaning "elephant tusk." They have been known by that regiment name up to the present day. Most of them have died, but a few are still alive and they are referred to respectfully as Uphondo Lwendlovu of Madaka (if that is his home) to avoid calling them by name. These are people who were born about the time of the Bambatha or the Zulu Rebellion of 1906, who were in their twenties when they went out on this expedition in 1925 to get elephant tusks at the king's command.

The rhino too is not without significance. Even today rhino horn is a much-sought-after commodity. I will not dwell on this, but will pause long enough to observe that one of the objectives of the Rhino and Elephant Foundation, that of "harmoniously blending conservation with utilization," will give new hope to old men. Men throughout the ages have always been fascinated by the lure of anything attributed aphrodisiac properties.

In addition, both the rhino and the elephant feature prominently in the history of conservation in my region. The story of Operation Rhino is well known and is synonymous with the early history of the Natal Parks Board. The first major undertaking of my Bureau of Natural Resources, which I launched in 1982, was the establishment of the Tembe Elephant Park to protect, among other things, the last free-ranging wild elephants in the Natal/KwaZulu region. The Natal Parks Board has adopted the white or square-lipped rhino as their logo, while the officers of the Bureau of Natural Resources are proud to wear an elephant head emblem on their epaulettes and badges. Unfortunately, the symbolism of rhino and elephant does not end there, for these two animals, perhaps more than any other, symbolize the clash of interests between man and animal in Africa.

Both the rhino and the elephant, but particularly the elephant, require extensive areas of true wilderness in order to survive, even larger areas if they are to thrive. Man too requires vast areas of land, particularly in Africa, where the population growth rate has reached 3 percent per annum—the highest in history! The exponential population growth, coupled to insensitive development and a severe and prolonged drought, has plunged much of the continent into chaos. Hunger is frighteningly rampant through the entire continent, and Africa is the only continent which now grows less food per person than it did twenty years ago. Against this background, the prognosis for survival of rhino and elephant is, to say the least, not optimistic. Thus, the significance of this Rhino and Elephant Foundation we are launching here today.

The old Africa is vanishing; indeed, much has already disappeared. If rhino and elephant are to be spared the same fate, then farsighted constructive action must be taken now. It is for this reason that I welcome the formation of the Rhino and Elephant Foundation, particularly as its stated objectives point to a new approach to conservation. This new approach will be vital to the success of this venture. After all, this is not the first time that a trust to save the rhinos and elephants of Africa has been established. It will be necessary to guard against repeating the mistakes of those whose efforts have failed. Conservationists all over the world are acknowledging that conventional conservation strategies have failed. The establishment and protection of relatively small areas of wilderness in which creatures of the wild are protected against the ravages of man, while ignoring the realities of the situation outside these "green islands," will not help save the rhino and elephant or any other of nature's creatures.

I am convinced that conservation can only be practiced successfully when it is practiced holistically. The necessity of establishing the Bureau of Natural Resources in KwaZulu arose out of a growing awareness that classical approaches to conservation in nations with Third World characteristics were incapable of achieving their aims. The Bureau of Natural Resources is still a young organization, but a very vigorous one, and it is grappling with, and has confronted squarely, the massive problems that conservation in underdeveloped areas present. In so doing, a new philosophy of conservation is emerging. This philosophy is centered around three principles, which could very well become the A.B.C. of conservation in developing regions. These principles are: A equals Alternatives; B equals Bottom Line; and C equals Communication. . . .

The people of developing or Third World regions—and this includes all the range of the beasts the Foundation wishes to save—are forced to exploit nature. Their food, firewood, building materials, and many other daily requirements come directly from nature. These people have no choice, they are desperately poor and feel that they must take what they can today without thought for tomorrow. If conservationists wish to prevent these people from further degrading the environment, then they must provide them with an alternative. If conservationists wish to protect the forest habitat of the black or hooked-lipped rhino from those who exploit it for its timber, then they must help establish woodlots. If the aim is to set aside a large area as an elephant reserve, then they must help those outside this area to produce more, new, and better crops on the land they have, so that they do not look with envious eyes towards the sanctuary area. An effective alternative to rhino horn may do much to halt the poaching of these animals; after all, in KwaZulu we are currently experimenting with establishing herb nurseries where endangered plants are grown by traditional healers to remove the need to gather this plant material from the wild.

Secondly, "Bottom Line." I spoke earlier about the need for a holistic approach to conservation. This to me is the "Bottom Line." I firmly believe that conservation cannot be practiced in isolation from the economy of the region in which it is practiced. The people of these regions are entitled to tangible benefits from conservation projects. These benefits can take many forms, and include employment opportunities, levies from fees paid by tourists (in KwaZulu, 25 percent of all revenue earned by conservation projects is paid into tribal coffers), or . . . a harvest of raw materials such as firewood, reeds, thatch, and medicinal plants.

In the Tembe Elephant Park, we allow the harvesting on a sustainable-yield basis of many natural resources, the most important being reeds from the Mosi swamp. In time (once viable populations of antelope have been established), a sustainable harvest of red meat will also be reaped. It is this approach which is gaining support for conservation throughout KwaZulu. So much so, that tribal chiefs are setting aside areas of land as rural resource areas where they themselves are to manage and harvest the resources of the area. The first of these, near Ulundi, is currently being stocked with impala, kudu, giraffe, and zebra.

The third principle I wish to mention is communication. The success or otherwise of conservation projects in developing regions will ultimately depend on the degree of support [from], and often active participation by, the people of the region. It is therefore vital that efficient two-way communication links are established between those who administer or plan conservation projects, and the people of the region. In KwaZulu, we have coined the phrase "conservation by consensus," and actively seek the involvement of local communities in all conservation projects. Many local authorities have appointed conservation liaison officers who act as link men between the Bureau of Natural Resources and the community they represent. Ultimately, it is our intention that liaison officers are appointed to all local authorities. All conservation projects should, ideally be community projects; good communication can make this possible.

I am reminded of the words of Aldo Leopold, who asserted that "There are two kinds of people; those who can live without wild things and those who cannot." I too am one of those who cannot. May the Rhino and Elephant Foundation help ensure that no one need be forced to live in a world without these two magnificent animals.

Thank you.

REFERENCES

"African Elephants—Tembe National Park." *www.tembe.co.za.*
Hunter, David. "Wildlife and Biodiversity." In *International Law and Policy.* Ed. Hunter, Saleman, and Zadke. London: Center for International Environmental Law, 1998.
Magubane, Peter. *Vanishing Cultures of South Africa.* Cape Town: Struik, 1998.
"Mangsuthu Buthelezi." *www.gov.za/profioes/buthelezi.html.* Updated 2001.
Mountain, Alan. *Wild South Africa.* Cape Town: Struik, 1998.
Player, Ian. *Zululand Wilderness, Shadow, and Soul.* Capetown: David Philips, 1998.
———. *The White Rhino Saga.* London: William Collins, 1972.
Schneider, Robert. Personal communication, September 2, 2003.

Stoddard, Ed. "South Africa's National Parks Woo Private Sector." *Reuters*, November 27, 2000.

Walker, Clive. "Elephant—Symbol of Untamed Africa." *Custos: The National Parks Magazine*, Pretoria, August 1993.

Whyte, Ian. "Elephants and their Environment." *Custos: The National Parks Magazine*, Pretoria, August 1993.

8. Mostafa Tolba

EGYPT

The international treaty is a ponderous and generally blunt instrument for solving global environmental problems. The need to reach consensus is frequently a formula for least-common-denominator wording and inaction. Yet there are a few cases that defied the odds, where nations displayed the good sense to meet the challenge of an imminent environmental disaster. Such success stories do not happen without unusual leadership at the highest levels.

In retrospect, the phase-out of chlorofluorocarbons (CFCs) and the accelerated efforts to repair the damage done to the earth's protective ozone layer may be international environmental law's finest hour. With the advantage of hindsight, the alarming projections about grave health impacts and the availability of alternative technologies made a global response easier. But when the issue of ozone depletion in the stratosphere first arose, the science was far more equivocal than it is today, and there were enormous economic and political interests poised against taking any measures in response.

Lacking any formal authority, Dr. Mostafa Tolba, an Egyptian biology professor turned director of the United Nations Environmental Program (UNEP), made a global agreement to address ozone depletion his top priority. Through a creative combination of nimble phraseology, clever compromises, and arm-twisting, Mostafa turned partisan international paralysis into a triumph for global cooperation. In so doing, he also transformed UNEP's image from a marginal player to that of "mover and shaker."

Ozone, an unstable form of oxygen consisting of three bonded atoms, forms naturally high above the earth, in the 15- to-55-kilometer zone meteorologists call the stratosphere. Ozone was never very abundant, even before humans started affecting atmospheric chemistry. The highest stratospheric ozone concentrations never exceed ten parts per million. Yet this is sufficient to screen out significant amounts of the high-energy ultraviolet radiation generated by the sun. When this ozone shield becomes depleted, all life on the earth's surface is vulnerable to the penetrating UV-B radiation. For human beings the health effects range from increases in cataracts to skin cancer. And humans are among the fortunate creatures who can get out of the sun.

Thomas Midgely Jr. enjoys the dubious distinction of being (probably unwittingly) the twentieth century's most innovative environmental villain. Midgely was the chemist who introduced tetraethyl lead's anti-knock properties into gasoline. Then, in 1930, while at Dayton Laboratories, he discovered "chlorofluorocarbons." CFCs, or freons (the familiar DuPont trade name), are a remarkable group of chemicals indeed. They are neither volatile nor flammable; they are not particularly toxic; and they are cheap to make. Most of all, CFCs are extraordinarily effective as refrigerants, as blowing agents to make flexible and rigid foams, and as solvents for high-tech applications. Even today, nothing compares to them for keeping the house cool in the summer and food unspoiled year round. So sure was Midgely of the benign properties of his first CFC, dichlorofluoromethane, that he filled his lungs with the gas before a transfixed audience of the American Chemical Society and walked away unscathed.

It would take another forty years before scientists Mario Molina and Sherwood Rowland would begin to understand the power of CFCs and other halogenated hydrocarbons to decimate stratospheric ozone. They hypothesized that, being ultrastable chemicals, CFCs persist long enough to waft slowly upwards toward the stratosphere. It takes about seven years for them to arrive, but, when they do, the sun's ultraviolet rays react with them, breaking the carbon–halogen bonds into highly reactive free radicals. These in turn react with ozone molecules, reducing them into basic oxygen and additional free radicals. The newly created radicals go on to attack more ozone molecules, thus creating a chain reaction. The net result is that each molecule of CFC can destroy thousands of ozone molecules before the chain is terminated. As quantities of ozone-depleting chemicals reaching the stratosphere mounted, they literally began to erase the protective ozone level.

During the 1970s, the scientific case was sufficiently compelling for the United States, Sweden, Norway, and Canada to adopt policies that banned the use of CFCs as the propellant in nonessential aerosols (e.g., hair sprays). But, as atmospheric chemists continued to debate the seriousness of the phenomenon and industries lobbied against further actions, ozone depletion was still not considered a pressing global threat. Then, in 1985, the British Antarctic survey discovered a "hole" in its ground-based measurements of stratospheric ozone. The ozone depletion was enormous, roughly the size of North America, and far greater than any atmospheric model had predicted previously. The gap was so huge that initially it was thought the data were faulty and new equipment was sent in to remeasure.

Since the problem became apparent in the 1970s, the United Nations had duly held conferences on the scientific issues surrounding stratospheric ozone depletion. During this period, several nations, such as the United States, Sweden, and New Zealand, wanted to see international action on the issue, but this appeared unlikely. With the American cutback on nonessential CFC production, European manufacturers had gained the lion's share of the world's market; they argued that no chemical alternatives were available to replace freons, chilling their negotiators' hopes for a comprehensive phase-out of these chemicals.

The Europeans were already suspicious of the United States on issues surrounding ozone depletion. A decade earlier, American environmentalists had argued that high-flying supersonic jets would damage the ozone layer. (Subsequent analysis suggested that, if they had any impact at all, it would probably be a positive effect.) European politicians and businessmen immediately seized on what they assumed was disingenuous American advocacy to stymie Europe's aircraft industry, and the years had done little to assuage their distrust. Facing more severe crises, developing countries for the most part remained disengaged and largely indifferent to the issue.

The news coming out of Antarctica was, however, sufficiently bad to push negotiators to complete a basic Convention for the Protection of the Ozone Layer. In 1985, only forty-three nations thought an "ozone hole" important enough to even send a delegate to Vienna to negotiate a treaty. In the end, only twenty countries were willing to sign the treaty, which for the most part contained empty slogans about ozone layer restoration and the importance of continuing research and cooperation. The agreement was a framework convention, in that it primarily called for regular meetings to monitor the situation. Even if the convention created no real substantive targets and commitments, it set a process in motion where the nations of the world would meet regularly to consider the state of the ozone layer. This left the door open for adoption of substantive protocols that could mandate more meaningful action. But in 1986, this looked unlikely.

The United States, initially keen on a meaningful treaty, began to slide under the influence of a conservative Reagan administration. The American secretary of the interior publicly suggested that hats and sunglasses were probably a sufficient response. Under pressure from West Germany, the European position softened moderately, but still only envisioned a 10 percent to 20 percent reduction in CFCs ten years hence. Without serious intervention, the international penchant for consensus would once again limit the response to symbolic efforts. It was here that Mostafa Tolba stepped in.

Tolba had been at UNEP from its very inception. His training was scientific, not diplomatic, and he had been a faculty member at Cairo University during the 1960s. His political skills, however, led to an appointment as undersecretary of state for higher education. Tolba's finesse as Egyptian delegation head, and then as committee chair at the Stockholm Conference, made an enormous impression on Maurice Strong, the Stockholm Conference chair. Strong was so impressed that, on his way to Nairobi to establish the offices for the new United Nations Environmental Program, he made a stopover in Cairo. There he met with the Egyptian professor, and cajoled him into taking a job as his deputy. Strong never had any intention of staying at the job for long, and in 1976 Tolba was his natural successor.

By 1987, with over a decade at the top of the international environmental agency, Tolba was the most experienced "environmental diplomat" in the world. UNEP's status was originally limited to that of a lowly U.N.

program (as opposed to an agency), with a mandate to network and educate, but Tolba's growing stature and sense of urgency imbued him and his UNEP colleagues with ambition.

In April, 1987, Tolba attended a negotiating session in Geneva and berated the national representatives: "No longer can those who oppose action to regulate CFC-release hide behind scientific dissent." Even as Europe spoke of a freeze in CFC production and the Americans called for very gradual phase-out, Tolba called for more meaningful measures: a 20 percent reduction every other year beginning in 1990 until a phase-out would essentially be complete, by 2000, with formal scientific review of progress to be elicited every four years. It was a bold vision.

Tolba began meeting secretly with the heads of the most influential delegations, working on an unofficial draft of a treaty that soon gained the nickname "Tolba's personal text." The normally cautious diplomats found Tolba's combination of ebullience and unexpected informality irresistible, and they were able to negotiate with greater flexibility. After all, once they went off the record, they were not committing their governments to anything. The enthusiasm for Tolba's oblique process was so great that the press mistakenly reported that an ozone agreement had been reached. It had not.

And so it was that in September 1987, the stage was set for an unusual international drama at the conference of the parties in Montreal. Sixty nations that had signed the original minimalist treaty, most represented by government ministers, attended the preparatory diplomatic meeting on September 8. Even a week before the ministers were to move the world from declarations to action, it was not at all clear that Tolba's ambitious draft protocol would garner sufficient support and momentum to become international law. Quite to the contrary: disagreement abounded about the range of chemicals to be controlled, the timetable and extent of phase-out, the role of trade restrictions, and of course what to do about the developing countries not inclined to invest in solutions to a problem they had not created.

Tolba opened the formal meeting and compared the treaty to the U.S. Constitution, which had also been the result of considerable horse-trading. His call for pragmatism relied on a quotation from Benjamin Franklin, who explained: "I consent, Sir, to this constitution and expect no better." Aware of the call for even greater dilution, Tolba asked, "Have we compromised so much that we have emasculated the agreement?" After Tolba's speech and that of Austrian diplomat Winifred Lang, who formally chaired the gathering, Tolba chose a risky strategy and had Lang adjourn the session. The idea was to prevent the dozens of ministers from taking the floor, getting bombastic or truculent, and climbing up the proverbial tree, from which it would be difficult to descend and compromise.

For the entire preparatory week and the three days of the conference itself, Tolba worked with the parties in behind-the-scene negotiations, leaving the formal sessions something of a charade. In his recollections of the tension-filled process, Tolba states "The Ministers occupied themselves as best they could in the corridors of the meeting hall, while behind closed doors the informal consultations continued at fever pitch. As time went by, it became very embarrassing that nothing was emerging, even though in fact three of the issues had by the afternoon of the second day been resolved: control measures, new installations, and entry into force. The main problem, the special treatment of the European Community, seemed insoluble."

As time was limited, the issues complicated, and the language highly sensitive, Tolba was forced to keep his marathon of meetings with different delegations into the wee hours of the night. At four in the afternoon on the last day of the meeting, Tolba prevailed on the chief American diplomat and on the director general of the environment for the European Community to reach a compromise that would eventually cut CFC production in half but only modestly limit the production of other chemicals that the Europeans viewed as indispensable to their current levels. Even this arrangement would require the approval of the twelve European delegations. Indeed, it necessitated Tolba's further intervention, going over diplomats' heads directly to more senior officials of three of the hold-out countries, urging them to instruct the attending delegates to accept the compromise. When Tolba made a late appearance at a reception given by the mayor of Montreal on the final evening of the conference, the atmosphere was gloomy. Then he announced that a treaty was indeed at hand — if they could but get the translations and copying done by morning. He describes the response as "amazed disbelief."

Richard Benedick, who headed the American delegation, captures the excitement of the following day in his book *Ozone Diplomacy:*

In the early morning of September 16, the head of the Japanese delegation exultantly waved a last-minute cable that contained his authorization to sign the protocol, a labor of dedication and burning the midnight oil in Tokyo. A young Chinese scientist who had single-handedly and with distinction represented his country for the first time promised the plenary to do his "personal best" to persuade his government to join later. The chief Soviet delegate publicly endorsed the protocol while apologetically explaining that his government could not sign in Montreal because a Russian-language text was not yet ready. The representative of Senegal, attending the ozone negotiations for the first time, confided that he had signed the protocol before actually receiving instructions from Dakar, because "it was the right thing to do." The Venezuelan delegation, which all morning had been suffering through the lengthy roll call of nations while anxiously awaiting word from Caracas, broke into cheers when a breathless messenger finally arrived with the authorizing cable—just in the nick of alphabetical time. And the expressions of weary relief on the faces of American industry observers contrasted with the stunned disbelief of many of their European counterparts.

The agreement called for a 50 percent phase-out of all CFC types by the year 1999, and a freeze on production of halons (a halogenated chemical used in fire extinguishers). Developing countries were given a ten-year delay in compliance, but in return agreed to remain engaged as part of the international effort. When twenty-four nations signed the Montreal Protocol, the act broke an important barrier. For the first time, the nations of the world were willing to regulate an important chemical, involving significant economic disruption on the basis of a global problem, even though the science was not yet fully understood.

It was an important start, and Tolba understood better than anyone that it was still woefully inadequate. More negotiating rounds would be required. Besides accelerating the phase-out schedule, there was the matter of developing countries that needed to be compensated for losses associated with foregoing ozone-depleting chemicals. But the ball was in motion. Three years later, when the delegates reconvened in London, they agreed to what was perhaps Tolba's greatest diplomatic triumph: a special fund was established (appropriately in Montreal) that allowed for wealthier nations to support developing countries' transition away from ozone-depleting chemicals. Between the years 1991 and 2002, the fund disbursed close to $1.5 billion to more than one hundred developing countries to phase out more than half of their CFC consumption. The hackneyed slogan of "common but differentiated responsibilities" between the First and Third World had, for the first time, an operational expression.

Today the ozone layer is still far from healthy. But the first signs of change are beginning to appear. With feasible substitutes available, what began in Montreal as a 50 percent cut in consumption, by 2000 became an astonishing 100 percent phase-out. Global production and consumption of ozone-depleting chemicals overall has fallen by over one million tons (89 percent). Atmospheric concentrations of chlorine peaked in 1994, and are now declining. As for the bottom line, recovery of the stratospheric ozone layer is expected by 2050, assuming the updated Montreal Protocol is fully implemented by all parties. Many millions of cases of eye cataracts and skin cancers will be averted. And these are only the environmental health impacts that we can quantify.

Tolba's strategy as a patient, but activist, scientist had paid off. His speech, given on that heady September 16, 1987 in Montreal at the closing of the "Plenipotentiary meeting" is remarkably free of technical objectives and specifications. It constitutes an uncharacteristically personal expression of his ultimate faith that science and scientists will rise to the challenge posed by technology's power to damage the environment. The day September 16 itself has since been declared by the U.N. General Assembly as "the International Day for Protection of the Ozone Layer." It celebrates one of the community of nation's finest hours, when the world faced a truly global problem, mobilized, and did the right thing.

"The Question Now Is Simply Whether We Control Science or Whether Science Will Control Us"

REMARKS AT THE CLOSING OF THE PLENIPOTENTIARY
MEETING ON OZONE, MONTREAL, CANADA,
SEPTEMBER 16, 1987

A hundred and fifty years ago, Mary Shelley sat down to write a book. She called it The New Prometheus, recalling the Greek legend in which man receives fire from heaven but is then destroyed by his discovery. In her book, a well-meaning scientist, a certain Dr. Frankenstein, creates a new human being. Frankenstein's monster is science at its worst: life without soul, knowledge without purpose, skill without wisdom.

This is the negative view of human nature. This is the view that assumes that science is the rope with which man will hang himself, that knowledge is the beginning of destruction. It is an old view. The Bible, the

Speech reprinted by permission of Dr. Mostafa Tolba.

Koran, and the Torah begin with the story of man and woman in the garden of innocence. There they are tempted by knowledge, and after that time they are doomed to sin and to death. From Adam to Orwell, the idea has had a powerful grip on the imagination. We have the ability to create but not to control. We are the sorcerer's apprentice, too clever for our own good.

There is a positive view. Anthropologist Jacob Bronowski once declared that knowledge is man's destiny. Knowledge, in this view, is an end in its own right, the goal to which man is ascending. And from knowledge comes a new human being, a human being governed by understanding and freed from material want. The twentieth century has given both schools of thought ample room to express themselves.

The optimists point to incredible progress. More people are alive. More people live longer. More people eat more. More people know more than ever before. Even the mushroom cloud has a silver lining. The Damocles sword of nuclear arms has brought a degree of stability in a century of conflict and doubt. A generation has grown up and is growing old without ever having seen the great powers at war. Science has given us more than we would dare to gamble in war.

Pessimists, however, point to the grim side. More people are hungry now than at almost any time in history. More species have been destroyed in the twentieth century than at any time since the end of the dinosaurs. The nuclear peace is a chimera. Deterrence is a fantasy. We are like the man who has jumped off the Empire State Building: we have plunged to the height of the fiftieth floor and we feel great: nice breeze, good view, no reason to worry.

There is merit in both cases. Both cases, I would guess, are somewhat exaggerated, but both points of view stress an argument that is more debated outside of the scientific community than inside it. That is the question of how we use science.

Are we using science responsibly? Can we do more to bend the resources of science to the needs of society? These are not new issues, but they take on a new urgency in the context of the late-twentieth-century environment. Economic development is definitely accelerating in many countries. Whether that development will benefit the people who need it most, and whether that development can be maintained for future generations, will depend on sustainable development. If sustainable development is the framework for progress, then we have reason for optimism. It is up to scientists to show the sponsors of science that sustainable development can work, does work, must work.

I am aware that this is much easier said than done. I am aware it entails major adjustments in thinking, action, and above all, styles of life. For sure, this also means an important change in the way scientists see their work. Truth has traditionally been the ethical focus for scientific enquiry. To that, we must now add a concern for social, economic, and even spiritual development.

Scientists of the old guard will argue that we are taking science out of the world of pure reason and into the world of politics and economics. But, ladies and gentlemen, that has already happened. We are already being shaped by science as never before. The question now is simply whether we control science or whether science will control us. As the guardians of technical knowledge, scientists can be doing more to direct their tools and to shape the future.

Scientists have, in the large majority of cases, seen themselves as being at the mercy of grant-givers. That is partially true. It is easier to get grants for military research or industrial research than for desert research or tropical forest programs. That is largely beyond the control of scientists. Scientists can—and often do—claim that it is not their fault if science is misused by politicians and economists. This is the easy line: Don't blame me, I just work here.

The fact of the matter, however, is that there is a large margin of error in this assumption. It is based on the consideration that science is above the world of human affairs. Here, I am not theorizing, I am speaking from experience—three decades of experience in the natural sciences. Scientists are an important and potentially influential group of people. But too often they stay above the fray. And by staying above the fray, they become a party to the abuse of science.

Scientists run the risk of becoming cynical. At the end of his life, someone asked Albert Einstein what he thought would be the ultimate weapon of World War III. He said he didn't know, but that he thought the ultimate weapon of World War IV would be the club.

I say that it is the scientist's job to make sure that is not the case. When, from time to time, scientists do climb down from the ivory tower, they can surprise even themselves. One recent example is very close to my heart as the head of the U.N. Environment Program; that is the example of ozone.

Almost fifteen years ago, two American scientists postulated that stratospheric ozone was modified by the emission of chlorofluorocarbons, or CFCs, the chemicals used in aerosols, solvents, propellants, and refrigerators. It was an interesting exercise. For the next decade and more, scientists debated the effects of a CFC build-up. By the early 1980s, scientists were in basic agreement that CFCs did modify stratospheric ozone, and that even a relatively minor depletion could have a major effect on environment and human health, particularly on the incidence of skin cancer. The scientists had said their piece and had been largely ignored.

The mid-1980s widened the argument. Scientists agreed that chemicals known as halons also had the capacity to disrupt the ozone layer. And CFCs turned out to be intimately linked to another issue of environmental significance, the greenhouse effect. Still, not much happened.

Some time ago, UNEP decided that the case against CFCs was strong enough, and that the risk was great enough, that the international community would be wise to restrict CFC emissions. The government of the United States had already banned the use of CFCs as aerosols, but other, primarily industrial, uses were increasing sharply. Other governments, however, were slow to act. They had CFC industries to protect. Why jeopardize jobs and economy at a time of high unemployment and slow economic growth? Why deprive those long deprived of decent refrigeration, especially in the developing countries?

UNEP has great sympathy with these arguments. We are in favor of an agreement that would promote the development of non-ozone-depleting substitutes. We are in favor of phased regulations that would allow substitute plants to come on-stream before the closure of old plants. We are in favor of allowing low-consumption countries, basically developing countries, a grace period to adjust. But we are not willing to turn a blind eye to the fact that millions of lives are being put at risk.

Those who perceived themselves as being threatened by CFC regulation looked at the debate within the scientific community (the normal academic debate that we see all the time), and said that "the scientists couldn't agree."

So the debate dragged on and eventually the scientific fraternity decided to put its foot down. Earlier this year, a group of the world's major ozone modelers came together at Wurzburg in the Federal Republic of Germany. They compared their models using various different scenarios of CFC modification. Once and for all they showed that there was no meaningful difference of opinion within their community. All of them believed that it would be irrational to let ozone-depleting emissions go unchecked.

The press took their views to the public. UNEP convened a meeting of technical and legal experts on the ozone layer. There, the scientific community repeated its stance, and presented, in terms meaningful to politicians, the case against CFCs.

What has been the result? The result has been that we are now on the brink of an international agreement to freeze and reduce the emission of ozone-depleting chemicals. If it can be done once, it can be done a hundred times. If it can be done in one field, it can be done in other fields. Indeed, there are signs, here and there, that scientists are bending their efforts towards sustainable development. . . .

I will finish by recalling the story of Galileo. About four hundred years ago, Galileo let it be known that he thought the world was round, and that Earth revolved around the sun. It was a dangerous belief in sixteenth century Italy. The Pope's inquisitors told him that he could die for a heresy like that. He would either have to recant or face trial. For Galileo, the choice was easy. He would recant: after all, whatever he said, the world would be no rounder, the earth's orbit no different. Galileo could honestly say that his work made almost no difference to the world of human affairs. We have inherited some measure of Galileo's ethereal view of science, but we have not inherited a world in which science does not matter. We have inherited a world that cannot even feed itself without the help of advanced science.

Science is closer to our lives now than it was in Galileo's day. The work of scientists shapes not only the way we think, but the way we live and indeed whether we live at all. Science must play a role in controlling what it creates. Scientists must have a say in the fate of their brainchildren. You can help correct the path. Look at your gathering today. You are coming from every corner of the globe. A message that goes to the world from this and similar gatherings will be listened to. As a group, the scientific community has weight and influence. Use that to ensure a better life for everybody, to ensure that science is used to build and not to destroy, to ensure that the interdependence between nations is a fact not a slogan, and finally to prove that we scientists understand and respect and are determined to fulfill our responsibility towards the generations to come.

REFERENCES

Anderson, Stephen, and K. Madhava Sarma. *Protecting the Ozone Layer: The United Nations History.* London: Earthscan Publications, 2002.

Benedick, Richard Elliot. *Ozone Diplomacy: New Directions in Safeguarding the Planet.* Cambridge, MA: Harvard University Press, 1998.

Climate Institute. "Ozone Depletion." *www.climate.org/topics/ozone.* 2003.

Farman, Joseph, Brian Gardiner, and Jonathan Shanklin. "Large Losses of Total Ozone in Antarctica Reveal Seasonal Clox/Nox Interaction." *Nature* 315 (1985): 207.

Kiss, Alexandre, and Dinah Shelton. *International Environmental Law*. Ardsley, NY: Transnational Publishers, 2000.

Ling, Bing. "Developing Countries and Ozone Layer Protection: Issues, Principles, and Implications." *Tulane Environmental Law Journal* 6 (1992): 91.

Mokhijani, Arjun, and Kevin R. Gurney. *Mending the Ozone Hole: Science, Technology, and Policy*. Cambridge, MA: MIT Press, 1995.

Molina, Mario, and F. Sherwood Rowland. "Stratospheric Sink for Chlorofluromethanes: Chlorine Atomic Catalyzed Destruction of Ozone." *Nature* 249 (1974): 810.

National Institute of Standards and Technology. "NIST industrial impact: Air-Conditioning and Refrigeration." *http://www.nist.gov/public_affairs/fact sheet/cfc.htm*. 1994.

Scott, Gary, Geoffrey Reynolds, and Anthony Lott. "Success and Failure Components of Global Environmental Cooperation: The Making of International Environmental Law." *Journal of International and Comparative Law* 2 (1995): 23.

Tolba, Mostafa K., with Iwona Rummel-Bulska. *Global Environmental Diplomacy: Negotiating Environmental Agreements for the World, 1973–1992*. Cambridge, MA: MIT Press, 1998.

9. *Chico Mendes*

BRAZIL

Photograph courtesy of Antonio Scorza/AFP/Getty Images.

Even before he was assassinated, Chico Mendes enjoyed the greatest name recognition of any environmentalist in South America. In retrospect, what made Mendes unique was not only his effectiveness but his authenticity. Born as Francisco Alves Mendes Filho, he was known to every one as Chico. His perspective on deforestation was entirely different from the prevailing view of the Amazonian rain forest among Western ecologists. The forest he fought and ultimately died trying to save was first and foremost linked to his identity as a rubber tapper. Quite simply, the Amazon provided him, his family, and his community with their livelihood. And, despite its seemingly immeasurably vast size, the Amazon was rapidly being destroyed.

The Amazon is the largest tropical rain forest in the world. The basin itself covers 3.6 million miles. (This is twice the area of India.) The river, for most of its route, is more of a flood basin than a narrow channel. The width from bank to bank can run as wide as five miles. It takes a lot of water to fill such a massive conduit, but this is hardly a problem. As one would expect in the world's most massive jungle, there is a great deal of rain in the Amazon basin, over 120 inches per year (that is, more than 3 meters of water per year!) Filled with silt, the river takes an opaque, turbid form as it rolls across the continent. It also spawns the richest botanical garden in the world in its wake. Tens of thousands of tree and plant species live there. So much of the Amazon remains remote and uncharted that no one really knows the magnitude of the biological diversity it supports.

This biological opulence is not born of rich soil. Eons of relentless rains have eroded the land, leaving it deficient in many nutrients. Consequently, unlike temperate forests that derive their nutrition form the soil, the trees in the tropical forest find their nutrients in the tissues of living organisms, including animals, plants, and microorganisms. Almost miraculously, the forest retains these elements, so that runoff is actually quite clear. And among the most miraculous trees of all are the *seringueiras*—the rubber trees. Their ability to regularly churn out latex makes them the biological equivalent of a small factory.

Rubber tappers (or *serigueiros*) therefore bear little resemblance to their preservationist allies who decry the deforestation of Amazonia. For almost two centuries they have been extracting rubber from the trees that grow there, to supply the world's burgeoning appetite for rubber. The forest to them is a mine for a valuable raw material; a rubber tree can be tapped sustainably only because it is a renewable resource.

Contrary to widespread perceptions, it was not timbering but cattle that drove much of the destruction of the Amazon. Nor is the conception correct that ranching in the Amazon—the beef born of "slash and burn" ranchers—sates the fast-food hamburger habits of the American public: this is true of many Central American forests, but not of Brazil's. Rather, it was the desire of the Brazilian government to provide inexpensive meat to the local population that drove much of the clearing of the land that contained countless natural rubber tree stands.

It was in the Acre region of Brazil that Chico Mendes was born, into this unique rubber tapper milieu whose very livelihood would soon be threatened by domestic meat production. Within the community, his father was considered particularly well educated, as he was able to read, and he taught his son the rudiments of literacy. But far more important to Mendes's worldview were the lessons he picked up in the forest. From the age of nine, Mendes would rise before dawn and join his father in the forest to make their rounds. Rubber tapping is a complex process. Young Chico had to learn how to select the appropriate trees, capable of being pierced but not too weak to tap. The knife had to be inserted so as to drain the white latex but leave the tree intact. Then the optimal spot had to be found to set down the cup to collect the dripping fluid. Then it's on to the next tree. Once the latex was collected and dragged home, the rubber was cured through a smoking process to prevent degradation and transform the material into an optimal form, with its attendant higher prices.

Rubber trees were only part of the family's economy. Collecting Brazil nuts was an important additional income source. And then there was hunting—preferably the tapir, a large Amazon mammal, but monkeys were also fair game. It was an exhausting routine. With an average distance between the trees of up to a hundred meters, a daily quota of two hundred trees required a ten-kilometer walk. And this was only the morning shift; in the afternoon, rubber tappers retraced their steps and picked up the cans by then filled with latex.

It was certainly a sufficiently exhausting routine to leave little opportunity for such frivolities as education. By age eleven, Mendes was working full time. At age eighteen, he knew the forest intimately, but had never seen a newspaper.

Although the outdoor lifestyle may seem romantic to some, the rubber tapper's life was in fact economically grim. Loans from traders left the families constantly in debt to the local economic barons. Although Brazil nuts could be collected by the ton and sold for over a dollar a pound in export markets, the rubber tappers were only given a few cents per pound. Subsistence farming around the house provided much of the family's corn, beans, and other crops. Most rubber tappers lived and died without setting foot in a city, much less leaving the borders of Brazil. It was a narrow existence by modern standards, but a chance meeting led to the rapid opening of Mendes's horizons.

When Chico Mendes described the influences in his life, he always attributed considerable influence to Euclides Tavora. Tavora was a former officer in the army who had participated in an unsuccessful popular uprising. On the lam, he hid out among the rubber tappers. It was then that he met Mendes among the local youth and recognized his unique qualities. He wasted little time in introducing him to the rudiments of socialist, populist principles. It was with Tavora that Mendes began to listen to international radio broadcasts and gain a picture of a world beyond his remote home. In 1975, Chico heard that labor unions had arrived in the

Acre region. With his newly attained class-consciousness and the passion of youth, he was naturally inclined to join them.

In 1976, Mendes and his colleagues organized the first *empate*—an action generally translated as "standoff." According to his account, seventy men and women marched into the forest. There they heard that a hundred-man crew, supported by armed gunmen, were clear-cutting. The rubber tappers joined hands to create a human wall that would physically block them. It was a spontaneous exercise in civil disobedience, but it set the tone for Mendes's subsequent direct actions: nonviolent, yet far more aggressive than polite protest. The demonstrators were simply determined to stop the cutting.

The empates were effective. Women and children were integrated into the ranks of protesters, which chilled local police willingness to fire into the crowed. Although the rubber tappers were invariably dragged away and beaten, there were far too many for the local jail's capacity, and soon after the intervention they would all return home. The tappers would talk to the loggers, usually local acquaintances who had more in common with them than with their rancher bosses. The protestors would point out that, once the trees were cut, the loggers would be no less out of a job than would the tappers. The alternative was to join the local movement to conserve the trees and remove only the renewable latex from the forest.

As he emerged as the leading spokesperson and organizer of Brazil's rubber tappers, Mendes' work began to consume him. His wife estimates that, between 1986 and 1988, she spent only eight full days with him. But the results of the popular uprising were extraordinary. According to Mendes's own estimate, by 1989 some three million acres were saved by these direct actions. One critical move of great tactical importance that Mendes managed to engineer was the forging of a pact between the local Indian population and the rubber tappers. These two groups had a long history of rivalry and enmity, but, faced with the prospect of losing their indigenous habitat and their means of production, the rival populations were able to bury their hostile pasts.

Substantively, Chico Mendes expanded the nature of the rubber tappers' agenda. In the past, labor unions had focused on pay conditions from the rubber barons. As more lands were swallowed by ranchers, and larger swatches of forest scorched, erasing rubber production grounds forever, the campaign expanded to embrace agrarian reform. The scope of public participation also widened. According to one estimate, between 1985 and 1987, the number of people involved in land conflicts leaped from one-half million to over 1.3 million, with the amount of land disputed increasing from 23 million to over 50 million acres.

Tactically, it was not enough to merely stop the logging. That would leave the rubber tappers in a permanently defensive mode, sticking finger after finger in new holes in the proverbial dike. Mendes established a new strategic objective: "extractive reserves." Here, trees would not be cut, but people would be allowed to utilize their products sustainably. The Amazon could continue to serve as a "rubber factory," providing livelihood to the tappers as well as a home to the countless creatures of the forest. In October 1988, the Acre government agreed to establish the first of these sanctuaries. Located near Mendes's village of Xapuri, the 66,000 acre tract was not large relative to the lands in controversy. But the declaration was an enormous victory and marked a key turning point.

With a great deal of money and their own life style at stake, the ranch owners struck back. Forming their own union (the UDR) they launched a campaign under the guise of "protecting free enterprise." The fact that the ranching industry enjoyed enormous state subsidies was conveniently overlooked.

In the subsequent controversy, Mendes set an independent course. Earlier "understandings" with ranchers were abandoned, as were the tappers' ties with the church. Mendes's widow, Ilsemar, cites external intervention from environmental groups and rainforest activists around the world for pushing her late husband in this direction. Even though this determination undoubtedly enhanced Mendes's international stature, it may have weakened his local power base. It undoubtedly put him in harm's way.

The absence of meaningful police presence in the periphery, as well as the economic might of the wealthy cattle interests, created a fearful level of lawlessness in the remote corners of Acre. On July 21, 1980, Wilson Pinheiro, another rubber tapper leader, was assassinated. When the police did nothing to apprehend the culprits, the rubber tappers took matters into their own hands, conducted a summary trial, and shot one of the landowners believed to be behind the murder. Suddenly aroused, the police arrested hundreds of tappers, tortured them, and sent a message as to who held the balance of power in the forest.

Among the more insidious of the ranchers were the Alves brothers. Twenty years earlier, Darly and Alvorino Alves had been implicated in a "hit" that was part of the violent coffee wars of the time. When the Alves brothers bought land with the intention of clear-cutting in Acre, the rubber tappers were ready for them.

Brazilian law at the time actually required a permit for clear-cutting. The Alves bothers had none. The tappers staged a sit-in at the offices of the government forestry representative in May 1988. Their implicit demand was for an extractive reserve to be declared on these lands. The brothers were disinclined to cede their property rights and were certain that, if they could eliminate the chief tapper, the resistance would quickly fade away.

Word reached Chico Mendes that the Alves brothers' father had boasted about the price they had put on his head. But the police were unimpressed, and Mendes's two bodyguards were not enough. In 1989, after a very busy trip across Brazil, Mendes had decided to come home for Christmas. Christmas is a hot time of year in the southern hemisphere of the Amazon. Leaving a dominoes game with his bodyguards in his kitchen to go splash some water on himself at his outhouse, Mendes never got past his back porch. A round of shotguns went off that sent him back into the house, bleeding profusely. The gunmen were apprehended, but Mendes would not survive the attack.

In retrospect, the assassination had been anticipated by Mendes and his followers. Perhaps his most famous "quote" that posthumously circulated inside Brazil expressed his resignation to a violent end: "I don't want flowers at my funeral because they would be taken from the jungle. Rather, I wish that my murder might serve to end the impunity of the gunmen that are being protected by the Federal Police of Acre. If a messenger would descend from heaven and would guarantee that my death would help to strengthen our fight, then it would be worth it. Experience shows us the opposite. It is not with big funerals and support rallies that we are going to save the Amazonian region. I want to live."

As a union leader, Mendes was constantly speechifying and exhorting his colleagues to persevere. Yet surprisingly few of his speeches were ever recorded, and, until the present publication, none were ever translated into English. The speech selected for this book was made by Mendes less than a month before he was killed. Given at a national forum about protection of the Amazon, the address reflects an experienced, pragmatic leader who has greater interest in tactics than in rhetoric. The fact that the rubber tappers and their campaign had managed to produce a major conference in a national venue was a tribute to the rubber tappers' success. But though the movement that Mendes spawned may have slowed the loss of rainforest, it could not stop the enormous wave of the forest's decimation.

Ultimately, Mendes's sober assessment about the limited impact of his death was prescient. It certainly did not serve as a turning point in the battle to save the Amazon. According to local activists, over 570,000 square kilometers of the rain forest have been lost from recent human activities. This is equivalent to an area the size of France. Destruction actually reached a peak after Mendes's assassination, in 1994 with almost 30,000 square kilometers lost in a single year, although subsequently loss of forest cover has tapered down and averages roughly 17,000 square kilometers per year (still an astonishingly large area, almost the size of New Jersey).

Only 29 percent of the Brazilian Amazon is designated as a protected forest, park, indigenous reservation, or extractive reserve. Yet the political calculus is changing. In Mendes's home region, Jorge Viana was elected governor of Acre in 1998 and brought his commitment to preservation to the job. The national government is committed to increasing the Amazon's percentage of protected lands to roughly 40 percent by 2010.

The "extractive reserve" system—perhaps Mendes's most lasting innovation—is also expanding. Concessions are made to associations of inhabitants who live in the reserve. The association then allocates specific sections to families for their rubber tapping activities. With the drop in international prices for rubber, the long-term economic feasibility of the model is uncertain. Yet, in the interim, a sustainable symbiosis between humans and the world's richest biological treasure chest continues in the extractive reserves. The largest of these appropriately bears the name of Chico Mendes.

"The Destruction of Our Rain Forest Affects Not Only the Brazilian People, but in Fact All the People of the Planet"

FORUM FOR DEFENSE AND DEVELOPMENT OF THE AMAZON, NOVEMBER 30, 1988

*I*n the first place, I wish to thank the National Campaign for the Defense and Development of the Amazon for running this forum for the whole of Brazil, mainly in the Amazon Region. I also thank the speakers that came with the objective of helping and contributing with their ideas. As a member of the National Council of the Seringueiros, I would like to emphasize some aspects that I consider of the highest importance.

The matter of the Amazon Region consists of the defense of the people of the jungle. We consider the matter of the Amazon Region a serious problem that has to be dealt with, not through speeches but with facts that we have to develop from now on. The Amazon region is inhabited. In every corner there are Indians, there are working people, extracting rubber and at the same time fighting for the conservation of nature. It is this reality that we want to show here. We want to support a policy that guarantees the future of these workers, who have been living for centuries in the Amazon and have made it productive at the same time.

When one looks at the question of the defense of the Amazon, it does not mean that the *seringueiros* and the Indians want to conserve it as an untouched sanctuary. As long as there are Indians and seringueiros in the Amazonian jungle, there is hope for saving it. We hope that the people who fight for the defense of the Amazonas can carry through with their work, and that in fact they will bring hope. I believe that each one of us has a mission and a very important commitment concerning the defense of this region. This fight does not belong only to the workers: it belongs to all of Brazilian society.

We have been highly criticized, even by the entrepreneurial sector and the landlords that say that we want to internationalize the Amazon, or to deliver the region to the foreigners. In fact, the real threat is that of the great lumber companies, financed by foreign corporations and by the multinationals who seek, in any way, the destruction of our jungle.

We are, indeed, seeking support at the international level, as is being done by the National Council of the Seringueiros and other entities. We are doing this because, unfortunately, in our society support is very small. According to scientists, the problem of the destruction of our rain forest does not only affect the Brazilian people but, in fact, all the people of the planet. We find that this is a question that concerns the entire Brazilian society and the international community.

Today, the National Council of the Seringueiros still fights for the creation of the extractive reserves, which is a way to defend the jungle. This is our proposal to justify this fight. In the twelfth national meeting of the seringueiros, carried out in Brasilia, in October 1985, the idea of forming extractive reserves emerged, which is a way to guarantee the future of the Amazonia. We do not want to be landowners. The seringueiros want the rain forest to be controlled by the union so that those whose livelihood relies on extraction can continue to do so.

One of the alternatives so that this can continue is to solve the economic problem of those that live within the boundaries of the rain forest. One strategy used by the dominating powers is to leave the man of the jungle in a miserable situation in order to compel him to leave the bush.

We are starting to mobilize through the creation of the first Agro-Extractive Cooperative, in Xapuri. Our objective is to reach all the areas of extractive reserves and, later, those that are not yet protected. Thus, we are beginning to demonstrate that it is possible to guarantee the future and the preservation of the Amazonas, and at the same time make it economically productive. So far we have not received help from anybody.

We have already had great expectations. We created this cooperative alone with our own resources, with only the help of the seringueiros. It has been proven that we can improve the production and the economic situation of our fellow workers. We can transform the Amazonas into an important region for the country as well as for the world.

The chestnut, for example, is a product of great importance, as we know. One kilo of this fruit costs from six to seven dollars on the international market. In São Paulo, it is being sold at twenty-five hundred cruzeiros. Therefore, we defend the production of chestnuts as well as rubber processing. We know there is a plan to destabilize rubber production. For this reason, the man of the rain forest is being harassed in the hope of justifying the attempts of the landlords to destroy the Amazon. . . . We believe that our power lies in the support by Brazilian society and the international communities, primarily the scientific ones. We need to show this reality to the Brazilian authorities.

The chestnut, rubber, and other extractive products have great value for our country. But, in order for them to continue, we need to preserve the rainforest. . . . We know there is a policy of destabilizing the rubber production for export. Our objective is to defend not only the rubber, but all the vegetative products that exist in the Amazon rain forest that have thus far escaped the process of predatory industrialization.

We are in favor of a policy of industrialization for export, as part of a preservation process. We have some products of great value and a great variety of resources that still need to be researched—research that has not been conducted so far. We want this to be done, and want it to take into account the extractive reserves. There are many people betting on the failure of these reserves so as to expedite the process of land speculation, and to take care of the interests of the large landowners.

I do not want to extend myself too far, because we are giving the word to Professor Valverde, who has made an enormous contribution to the fight for the preservation of the Amazonian jungle. We are also going to hear the exposition of Dr. Otília, who is responsible for the policy of the MIRAD. It would be very important if the MIRAD released some areas that would be extractive reserves. We call attention to the fact that millions have been invested in projects that are harmful to the Amazon as well as to thousand of workers. We criticize the performance of the MIRAD when it implements a policy that does not benefit the workers.

Many times, the MIRAD has expropriated lands from owners who want precisely this, because the value of the land is insignificant and they are rewarded money in compensation. It happens that this is paid for by public funds, money that is generated by the workers. The seringueiros gain nothing from this, although it is we who made this land productive for centuries—and, before us, the Indians. A person claims he is owner of the land. The government possesses it and pays an enormous amount that comes from the public money. . . . We believe that the government must pay for improvements made on these properties and nothing more.

In the south of Pará, for example, the chestnut fields have been destroyed and later the lands have been nationalized. How is the National Council of Seringueiros going to protect an extractive reserve in the south of Pará, when the chestnut fields have been destroyed? All this is part of a policy of land speculation that has benefited the large land owners and the great multinational companies.

I consider this meeting of the highest importance and I hope that these subjects are discussed with the participation of all.

REFERENCES

"Brazil's Forests in Brief." *http://www.globalforestwatch.org/english/brazil/*.

Cardoso, Catarina. "Extractive Reserves in Acre Brazilian Amazonia." World Bank Case Studies. *http://srdis.ciesin.org/cases/brazil-003.html.* 1998.

Hecht, Susanna, and Alexander Cockburn. *The Fate of the Forest: Developers, Destroyers, and Defenders of the Amazon.* London: Penguin, 1990.

National Forum on Debates over the Amazonian Region. The Brazilian Amazon Region in Focus. CNDDA no. 18, 89/90 (1990). In Portuguese.

Neto, Paolo. "Extractive Reserves, an Initiative of Great Social and Environmental Importance." *www.environmentaldefense.org.article/cfm.* 2000.

Revkin, Andrew. *The Burning Season: The Murder of Chico Mendes and the Fight for the Amazon Rain Forest.* Boston: Houghton Mifflin Company, 1990.

"Ten Years without Chico." *World Rainforest Movement Bulletin* no. 18 (December 1998).

10. *Margaret Thatcher*

UNITED KINGDOM

Many environmentalists may wonder how Margaret Thatcher finds a place in an environmental anthology. Hardly associated with any "green agenda," throughout her political career she was consistently an avid advocate of nuclear power, and as British prime minister opposed several European environmental initiatives. Yet, if leaders are to be judged by their achievements in the area of global atmospheric politics, her contribution eclipses that of any other head of state.

Alarmed by the growing evidence of ozone depletion, Thatcher through her personal involvement caused an acceleration of the CFC chemical phase-out. The two consecutive diplomatic gatherings in London in 1989 and 1990 that she initiated and hosted seem, in retrospect, perhaps the most successful meetings in the history of international environmental negotiations. The London amendments not only expanded the scope of the chemicals regulated under the Montreal Protocol and toughened its deadlines to protect the ozone layer; they also created a fund to assist developing countries in expediting the attendant environmental commitments, a fund that remains a model to this day. It took arm-twisting, overruling her own environmental ministry, and calls to the White House to finalize the deal. This alone constitutes an unusual level of intervention by a national leader, especially when little if any political capital could have been anticipated from her particular constituents. Yet it is in the area of climate change that Thatcher's positions were most radical and her message most profound.

Whether or not the world was getting warmer as a result of greenhouse gas emissions was the subject of considerable scientific uncertainty for some time. Indeed, during the 1970s, the associated confusion led several leading experts, some with the most formidable of environmental credentials, to postulate that pollution was hastening an Ice Age. By the mid-1980s, however, evidence of global warming was beginning to accumulate. Carbon dioxide concentrations in the atmosphere had increased roughly 30 percent since before the industrial revolution. Average temperatures on the planet had risen by about two degrees Celsius during the twentieth century. The weather was changing perceptibly, with a rise in the frequency of floods and droughts.

The existence of a "greenhouse effect" has been apprehended by humans almost as long as windows allowed them to raise plants and flowers indoors. Solar radiation beams right through glass, and, similarly, through the earth's atmosphere. Once this infrared, long-wave radiation hits the earth, it is converted into short-wave-length radiation. This form of energy has a harder time bouncing back across the "pane;" it is this trapped energy that heats the adjacent area. As it turns out, even minute concentrations of certain gases in the atmosphere (most notably carbon dioxide and methane) function as thicker glass, blocking short-wave radiation and metaphorically serving as a greenhouse for the planet. The phenomenon has always been critical to ensuring a hospitable climate on earth. But recent human activities—in particular, combustion—created a new and possibly disastrous balance in the atmosphere.

In theory, the higher the concentration of these gases, the more heat will be trapped. The ramifications of the resulting temperature increase are still not well understood. The more cataclysmic visions include massive melting of glaciers, rise in sea level and inundation of low-lying lands and islands, floods, droughts, spread of tropical diseases, and species decimation for starters. Other models are less alarmist, but global warming is an experiment that nobody wants to attempt.

By the 1980s, the implications for remediation were bemusing. For years, engineers had aspired to scrub and filter the emissions from factories and automobiles so that they would only release carbon dioxide. Carbon dioxide was the "solution." Now it seemed, however, that carbon dioxide emissions were actually a problem, and threatened to transform the climate of the planet.

In fact there are gases, like perfluorocarbons, that are much more efficient "greenhouse gases" than carbon dioxide. (Their "global warming potential" may be fifty thousand times stronger than that of CO_2.) But the overwhelming prevalence of the CO_2 makes it the dominant cause of global warming, accounting for 80 percent of the problem. Methane (CH_4), produced when bacteria breaks down organic material without air, is a distant second, contributing about 8 percent of the warming. But here again, the rice, coal, and cattle production associated with the precipitous increase in methane releases make reduction a challenge for almost all of humanity.

International efforts to restore the ozone layer were starting, but many perceived them as irrelevant. To phase out a small class of chemicals, while hardly a simple task, was certainly a conceivable one; transforming the energy infrastructure of modern transportation, and switching the fuel base and agricultural practices of modern civilization, seemed a challenge of quite another order. Little wonder, then, that most world leaders preferred either to ignore the problem or to hide behind the considerable number of scientists who continued to find uncertainties in the data and flaws in the elaborate computer simulation models of weather systems.

But Prime Minister Margaret Thatcher was not inclined to evade the issue. Never one to take much notice of what other people thought, she had an intellectual honesty and concern about the planet's future that launched her on a mission. By 1988, long before panels of scientific experts were able to offer consensus endorsements of the existence and severity of global warming, she found the evidence not only plausible but overwhelming. The fact that the most quintessentially "conservative" head of state in the world called for dramatic measures to address the climate change crisis changed the political dynamics of the issue in the international arena.

By then, Thatcher was a remarkable political figure on the world stage. She was the United Kingdom's first woman prime minister. Elected in 1979,

she maintained power for eleven years, making her tenure as prime minister the longest continuous run in well over a century. More important
than her ability to hold onto power was her ability to wield it to reshape
the role of government and her country's economy. No other prime ministers in British history have a political ideology attached to their name:
"Thatcherism" became synonymous with—depending on the point of
view—either callous, selfish capitalism or individual liberty, lower taxes,
and reduced government intervention.

Born in 1925, Margaret Thatcher hardly came from down-trodden or
even working class stock (unlike the myth of the impecunious "grocer's
daughter" who overcame humble origins to make good). Her father,
Alfred Roberts, not only ran a highly successful grocery, in the days before
supermarkets, but was also a passionate politician who eventually became
mayor of Grantham, Thatcher's humble English hometown. Although he
may have belonged to the middle class, Roberts preached the austere and
self-reliant gospel of the Methodist church, choosing not to install a toilet
inside his house until after World War II. His influence on his daughter's
political ideas and aspirations was profound.

As a schoolgirl, Margaret was remembered mostly for her seriousness.
Thatcher's Oxford's tutors do not remember her distinguishing herself as
a chemistry student, and eventually she would return to sit for law. But her
conservative political views in a generally liberal, academic milieu, along
with her political acumen, were somewhat more conspicuous. In 1943,
only eighteen years of age, Thatcher became the first woman president of
the Oxford University Conservative Association.

After running unsuccessfully for Parliament a few times, she took a
break in 1951 to get married and have twins. Her husband Denis, already
an affluent executive in the chemical industry, would be her lifelong soul
mate and partner. In 1959, Thatcher was finally elected to Parliament, and
within two years, still just thirty-four years of age, became a junior minister
at the Ministry of Pensions. When Edward Heath became prime minister,
he appointed her minister for education.

Thatcher's free-market views included canceling free milk entitlements,
sparking public outrage and a characterization as "the most unpopular
woman in Britain." But she didn't blink. Thus a decade before she became
known as the "Iron Lady," she suffered the somewhat less complimentary
epithet of "Thatcher the milk snatcher." When Heath lost the 1974 elections, Thatcher was ready to "snatch" her battered party from his control,
and then tightened its platform to reflect her personal displeasure with
socialism, public expenditures, and regulation. Five years later, Thatcher

would lead the Conservative Party to a solid victory and a majority in the House of Commons of forty-four seats.

Thatcher once quipped that she was not a "consensus" politician but a "conviction" politician. Her rule was characterized by any number of bold, controversial initiatives:

- high interest rates and high unemployment, as a bitter antidote for the high inflation rates she inherited;
- wholesale privatization of state-owned industries, and unconditional victory over the unions during the year-long miners' strike;
- the decision to send the Royal Navy to take back the Falkland Islands from invading Argentina;
- a stubborn unwillingness to negotiate with convicted IRA terrorists.

Thus reads a standard, if abbreviated, inventory of her achievements in office. Few biographers would include "environment" on their short-list of Thatcher accomplishments.

Indeed, in her central autobiographic work from the period, *The Downing Street Years,* Thatcher herself devotes only 3 out of 862 pages to environmental issues, and these are shared with recollections about her science policy. But Thatcher was never indifferent to environmental affairs. Her growing commitment to ecological harmony was so surprising precisely because it seemed incompatible with her steadfast commitment to free-market capitalism. In the United States, for example, the anti-environmental positions of her chief ally and ideological partner, President Ronald Reagan, were the stuff of legend and indignation. Although every bit as much a capitalist, Thatcher developed a broader view than Reagan of national economic interests. Citing domestic progress in improving air quality, and Thames river restoration, she explained: "Even though this kind of action may cost a lot, I believe it to be money well and necessarily spent because the health of the economy and the health of our environment are totally dependent upon each other. Stable prosperity can be achieved throughout the world provided the environment is nurtured and safeguarded."

Thatcher made a clear distinction between England's domestic environmental issues and the global ones with which she needed to be concerned. Although her sense of order was repeatedly appalled by the litter-strewn streets of London, and though she was proud of the restoration and return of fish stock to a number of British rivers, for Thatcher these ultimately remained second-tier, local issues. It was global atmospheric problems that she needed, as prime minister, to tackle personally.

Thatcher seemed to enjoy invoking her credentials as a chemist, and always maintained an unusual respect for the opinion of scientists. Undoubtedly the perspective of Sir Crispin Tickell, her U.N. ambassador, influenced her thinking on the significance of global warming as an international issue. But it was only after hearing the country's top scientists present the evidence that Thatcher embraced the controversy. She first and foremost advocated strengthening the scientific underpinnings of global climate policy, and England took responsibility for the Intergovernmental Panel on Climate Change (IPCC) that emerged as the definitive international voice on the state of the science.

Meteorologist Sir John Houghton served as cochair of the Science Assessment working group for the IPCC and was known to give the prime minister climate-change "teach-ins." He describes the seriousness with which Thatcher forced her entire cabinet to consider an early IPCC scientific report: "I presented a preview of it to the then British Prime Minister, Mrs. Margaret Thatcher, and members of her Cabinet at 10 Downing Street in London. I had been led to expect many interruptions and questions during my presentation. But the thirty or so Cabinet members and officials in the historic Cabinet room heard me in silence. They were clearly very interested in the report, and the questions and discussion sifters demonstrated a large degree of concern for the world's environmental problems."

In Thatcher's characteristic style, once she latched onto a topic, she quickly came to master the smallest related technical details. More important, she could not seem to rest until sending the most cumbersome and inert systems into motion. The prime minister went public with her new atmospheric passion in a speech to the Royal Scientific Society on 27 September 1988. Ever serious, she worked on early drafts for two weekends with her science policy advisor. In her memoirs, she still records her disappointment that the television did not bother to send cameras, something she had relied on for lighting in the "gloom of Fishmongers' Hall." But her words were sufficiently passionate to resonate throughout the entire nation and transform environmental policy not only in the United Kingdom but eventually throughout the world: "For generations, we have assumed that the efforts of mankind would leave the fundamental equilibrium of the world's systems and atmosphere stable. But it is possible that with all these enormous changes (population, agricultural, use of fossil fuels) concentrated into such a short period of time, we have unwittingly begun a massive experiment with the system of this planet itself. . . . Protecting this balance of nature is therefore one of the great challenges of the late twentieth century and one in which I am sure your advice will be repeatedly sought."

Thatcher's subsequent intervention led to the establishment of a national center for climate prediction. Basing her view on her own domestic energy policy, in international forums she strongly advocated a global shift from coal to natural gas, combustion of which produces lower greenhouse gas emissions.

But it was her relentless advocacy for immediate international action that changed the tenor of debate. When she appeared in front of the United Nations in 1989, she limited her comments to environmental matters, primarily global warming. Her absolute commitment to a treaty that would control greenhouse gases, along with the passion with which she preached global responsibility to address climate change, caught attending world leaders off guard. The text, printed below, demonstrates Thatcher's characteristic erudition and integration of science, politics, British national heritage, and concern for the planet's future. A year later, in one of her final international appearances as prime minister, she participated in the second world climate conference in Geneva. Thatcher's presence (and ongoing call for a climate-change treaty) at once gave the meeting a much needed boost in stature for the climate-change control advocates struggling with a U.S. administration recalcitrant about the issue.

Environmentalists credit Thatcher (and skeptics of global warning blame her) as a *causa sine qua non* for the 1992 climate-change treaty, ultimately signed at the United Nations Conference on Environment and Development in Rio de Janeiro. By the time of the signing, Thatcher was no longer prime minister, but she had promoted the issue enough, and her influence on President George H. W. Bush was sufficient, to guarantee the launch of an international response. The actual implementation has proved just as thorny as she had predicted in her U.N. speech. But the community of nations had finally acknowledged that a problem existed that it was obliged to address. When the United Nations Environmental Program awarded her a Global 500 award, she joined the elite ranks of the planet's most distinguished environmentalists. A decade later, U.K. Prime Minister Tony Blair broke ranks with President Bush's son over the issue of global warming. As the British government announced the planet's most ambitious program to reduce greenhouse gas emissions to date, the press was quick to cite a Thatcher environmental legacy.

"The Prospect of Climate Change Is a New Factor in Human Affairs"

SPEECH TO THE UNITED NATIONS GENERAL ASSEMBLY,
NEW YORK, 8 NOVEMBER 1989

*M*r. President, it gives me great pleasure to return to the podium of this assembly. When I last spoke here four years ago, on the fortieth anniversary of the United Nations, the message that I and others like me gave was one of encouragement to the organization to play the great role allotted to it.

Of all the challenges faced by the world community in those four years, one has grown clearer than any other in both urgency and importance—I refer to the threat to our global environment. I shall take the opportunity of addressing the general assembly to speak on that subject alone.

During his historic voyage through the south seas on the Beagle, Charles Darwin landed one November morning in 1835 on the shore of Western Tahiti. After breakfast, he climbed a nearby hill to find a vantage point to survey the surrounding Pacific. The sight seemed to him like "a framed engraving" with blue sky, blue lagoon, and white breakers crashing against the encircling coral reef. As he looked out from that hillside, he began to form his theory of the evolution of coral; 154 years after Darwin's visit to Tahiti, we have added little to what he discovered then.

What if Charles Darwin had been able, not just to climb a foothill, but to soar through the heavens in one of the orbiting space shuttles? What would he have learned as he surveyed our planet from that altitude? From a moon's-eye view of that strange and beautiful anomaly in our solar system that is the earth?

Of course, we have learned much detail about our environment as we have looked back at it from space, but nothing has made a more profound impact on us than these two facts.

First, as the British scientist Fred Hoyle wrote long before space travel was a reality, . . . "once a photograph of the earth taken from the outside is available . . . a new idea as powerful as any other in history will be let loose." That powerful idea is the recognition of our shared inheritance on this planet. We know more clearly than ever before that we carry common

Speech reprinted by permission of the Margaret Thatcher Foundation.

burdens, face common problems, and must respond with common action.

And, second, as we travel through space, as we pass one dead planet after another, we look back on our earth, a speck of life in an infinite void. It is life itself, incomparably precious, that distinguishes us from the other planets. It is life itself—human life, the innumerable species of our planet—that we wantonly destroy. It is life itself that we must battle to preserve.

For over forty years, that has been the main task of this United Nations.

To bring peace where there was war.
Comfort where there was misery.
Life where there was death.

The struggle has not always been successful. There have been years of failure. But recent events have brought the promise of a new dawn, of new hope. Relations between the Western nations and the Soviet Union and her allies, long frozen in suspicion and hostility, have begun to thaw. In Europe, this year, freedom has been on the march. In Southern Africa— Namibia and Angola—the United Nations has succeeded in holding out better prospects for an end to war and for the beginning of prosperity. And in Southeast Asia, too, we can dare to hope for the restoration of peace after decades of fighting.

While the conventional, political dangers—the threat of global annihilation, the fact of regional war—appear to be receding, we have all recently become aware of another insidious danger. It is as menacing in its way as those more accustomed perils with which international diplomacy has concerned itself for centuries.

It is the prospect of irretrievable damage to the atmosphere, to the oceans, to earth itself. Of course major changes in the earth's climate and the environment have taken place in earlier centuries when the world's population was a fraction of its present size. The causes are to be found in nature itself—changes in the earth's orbit, changes in the amount of radiation given off by the sun, the consequential effects on the plankton in the ocean, and in volcanic processes.

All these we can observe, and some we may be able to predict. But we do not have the power to prevent or control them. What we are now doing to the world, by degrading the land surfaces, by polluting the waters and by adding greenhouse gases to the air at an unprecedented rate—all this is new in the experience of the earth. It is mankind and his activities which are changing the environment of our planet in damaging and dangerous ways.

We can find examples in the past. Indeed, we may well conclude that it was the silting up of the River Euphrates which drove man out of the Garden of Eden. We also have the example of the tragedy of Easter Island, where people arrived by boat to find a primeval forest. In time, the population increased to over nine thousand souls and the demand placed upon the environment resulted in its eventual destruction as people cut down the trees. This in turn led to warfare over the scarce remaining resources, and the population crashed to a few hundred people without even enough wood to make boats to escape.

The difference now is in the scale of the damage we are doing. We are seeing a vast increase in the amount of carbon dioxide reaching the atmosphere. The annual increase is three billion tons: and half the carbon emitted since the Industrial Revolution still remains in the atmosphere.

At the same time as this is happening, we are seeing the destruction on a vast scale of tropical forests which are uniquely able to remove carbon dioxide from the air. Every year, an area of forest equal to the whole surface of the United Kingdom is destroyed. At present rates of clearance we shall, by the year 2000, have removed 65 percent of forests in the humid tropical zones. The consequences of this become clearer when one remembers that tropical forests fix more than ten times as much carbon as do forests in the temperate zones.

We now know, too, that great damage is being done to the ozone layer by the production of halons and chlorofluorocarbons. But at least we have recognized that reducing and eventually stopping the emission of CFCs is one positive thing we can do about the menacing accumulation of greenhouse gases.

It is of course true that none of us would be here but for the greenhouse effect. It gives us the moist atmosphere which sustains life on earth. We need the greenhouse effect—but only in the right proportions. More than anything, our environment is threatened by the sheer numbers of people and the plants and animals which go with them. When I was born, the world's population was some two billion people. My grandson will grow up in a world of more than six billion people.

Put in its bluntest form: the main threat to our environment is more and more people, and their activities:

- The land they cultivate ever more intensively;
- The forests they cut down and burn;

- The mountainsides they lay bare;
- The fossil fuels they burn;
- The rivers and the seas they pollute.

The result is that change in the future is likely to be more fundamental and more widespread than anything we have known hitherto. Change to the sea around us, change to the atmosphere above, leading in turn to change in the world's climate, which could alter the way we live in the most fundamental way of all.

That prospect is a new factor in human affairs. It is comparable in its implications to the discovery of how to split the atom. Indeed, its results could be even more far-reaching.

We are constantly learning more about these changes affecting our environment, and scientists from the Polar Institute in Cambridge and the British Antarctic Survey have been at the leading edge of research in both the Arctic and the Antarctic, warning us of the greater dangers that lie ahead. Let me quote from a letter I received only two weeks ago, from a British scientist on board a ship in the Antarctic Ocean. He wrote: "In the Polar Regions today, we are seeing what may be early signs of man-induced climatic change. . . . Our data confirm that the first-year ice, which forms the bulk of sea ice cover, is remarkably thin and so is probably unable to sustain significant atmospheric warming without melting. Sea ice separates the ocean from the atmosphere over an area of more than thirty million square kilometers. It reflects most of the solar radiation falling on it, helping to cool the earth's surface. If this area were reduced, the warming of earth would be accelerated due to the extra absorption of radiation by the ocean." He goes on, "The lesson of these Polar processes is that an environmental or climatic change produced by man may take on a self-sustaining or 'runaway' quality . . . and may be irreversible." That is from the scientists who are doing work on the ship that is presently considering these matters.

These are sobering indications of what may happen, and they led my correspondent to put forward the interesting idea of a World Polar Watch, amongst other initiatives, which will observe the world's climate system and allow us to understand how it works.

We also have new scientific evidence from an entirely different area, the tropical forests. Through their capacity to evaporate vast volumes of water vapor, and of gases and particles which assist the formation of clouds, the forests serve to keep their regions cool and moist by weaving a sunshade of white reflecting clouds and by bringing the rain that sustains them.

A recent study by our British Meteorological Office on the Amazon rainforest shows that large-scale deforestation may reduce rainfall and thus affect the climate directly. Past experience shows us that without trees there is no rain, and without rain there are no trees.

Mr. President, the evidence is there. The damage is being done. What do we, the international community, do about it?

In some areas, the action required is primarily for individual nations or groups of nations to take.

I am thinking for example of action to deal with pollution of rivers—and many of us now see the fish back in rivers from which they had disappeared. I am thinking of action to improve agricultural methods—good husbandry which ploughs back nourishment into the soil rather than the cut-and-burn which has damaged and degraded so much land in some parts of the world. And I am thinking of the use of nuclear power which, despite the attitude of so-called greens, is the most environmentally safe form of energy.

But the problem of global climate change is one that affects us all, and action will only be effective if it is taken at the international level. It is no good squabbling over who is responsible or who should pay. Whole areas of our planet could be subject to drought and starvation if the pattern of rains and monsoons were to change as a result of the destruction of forests and the accumulation of greenhouse gases.

We have to look forward, not backward, and we shall only succeed in dealing with the problems through a vast international, cooperative effort. Before we act, we need the best possible scientific assessment; otherwise, we risk making matters worse. We must use science to cast a light ahead, so that we can move step by step in the right direction.

The United Kingdom has agreed to take on the task of coordinating such an assessment within the Intergovernmental Panel on Climate Change, an assessment which will be available to everyone by the time of the Second World Climate Conference next year.

But that will take us only so far. The report will not be able to tell us where the hurricanes will be striking, who will be flooded, or how often and how severe the droughts will be. Yet we will need to know these things if we are to adapt to future climate change, and that means we must expand our capacity to model and predict climate change. We can test our skills and methods by seeing whether they would have successfully predicted past climate change for which historical records exist. . . .

But, as well as the science, we need to get the economics right. That means first we must have continued economic growth in order to generate the wealth required to pay for the protection of the environment. But it must be growth which does not plunder the planet today and leave our children to deal with the consequences tomorrow.

And second, we must resist the simplistic tendency to blame modern multinational industry for the damage which is being done to the environment. Far from being the villains, it is on them that we rely to do the research and find the solutions. It is industry which will develop safe alternative chemicals for refrigerators and air-conditioning. It is industry which will devise biodegradable plastics. It is industry which will find the means to treat pollutants and make nuclear waste safe—and many companies, as you know, already have massive research programs. The multinationals have to take the long view. There will be no profit or satisfaction for anyone if pollution continues to destroy our planet.

As people's consciousness of environmental needs rises, they are turning increasingly to ozone-friendly and other environmentally safe products. The market itself acts as a corrective; the new products sell and those which caused environmental damage are disappearing from the shelves. And by making these new products widely available, industry will make it possible for developing countries to avoid many of the mistakes which we older industrialized countries have made.

We should always remember that free markets are a means to an end. They would defeat their object if by their output they did more damage to the quality of life through pollution than the well-being they achieve by the production of goods and services.

On the basis, then, of sound science and sound economics, we need to build a strong framework for international action. It is not new institutions that we need. Rather, we need to strengthen and improve those which already exist: in particular, the World Meteorological Organization and the United Nations Environment Programme. . . .

The United Kingdom has recently more than doubled its contribution to UNEP and we urge others, who have not done so and who can afford it, to do the same. And the central organs of the United Nations, like this General Assembly, must also be seized of a problem which reaches into virtually all aspects of their work and will do so still more in the future.

The most pressing task which faces us at the international level is to negotiate a framework convention on climate change—a sort of good conduct guide for all nations. Fortunately, we have a model in the action already taken to protect the ozone layer. The Vienna Convention in 1985 and the Montreal Protocol in 1987 established landmarks in international law. They aim to prevent, rather than just cure, a global environmental problem.

I believe we should aim to have a convention on global climate change ready by the time the World Conference on Environment and Development meets in 1992. That will be among the most important conferences the United Nations has ever held. I hope that we shall all accept a responsibility to meet this timetable. . . .

But a framework is not enough. It will need to be filled out with specific undertakings—or protocols, in diplomatic language—on the different aspects of climate change. These protocols must be binding, and there must be effective regimes to supervise and monitor their application. Otherwise, those nations which accept and abide by environmental agreements, thus adding to their industrial costs, will lose out competitively to those who do not.

The negotiation of some of these protocols will undoubtedly be difficult. And no issue will be more contentious than the need to control emissions of carbon dioxide, the major contributor—apart from water vapor—to the greenhouse effect.

We can't just do nothing. But the measures we take must be based on sound scientific analysis of the effect of the different gases and the ways in which these can be reduced. In the past, there has been a tendency to solve one problem at the expense of making others worse.

The United Kingdom therefore proposes that we prolong the role of the Inter-governmental Panel on Climate Change after it submits its report next year, so that it can provide an authoritative scientific base for the negotiation of this and other protocols. We can then agree to targets to reduce the greenhouse gases, and how much individual countries should contribute to their achievement. We think it important that this should be done in a way which enables all our economies to continue to grow and develop.

The challenge for our negotiators on matters like this is as great as for any disarmament treaty. The Intergovernmental Panel's work must remain on target, and we must not allow ourselves to be diverted into fruitless and divisive argument. Time is too short for that.

Mr. President, the environmental challenge which confronts the whole world demands an equivalent response from the whole world. Every country will be affected and no one can opt out. We should work through this great organization and its agencies to secure world-wide agreements on ways to cope with the effects of climate change, the thinning of the ozone layer, and the loss of precious species.

We need a realistic program of action and an equally realistic timetable. Each country has to contribute, and those countries who are industrialized must contribute more to help those who are not. The work ahead will be long and exacting. We should embark on it hopeful of success, not fearful of failure.

I began with Charles Darwin and his work on the theory of evolution and the origin of species. Darwin's voyages were among the high points of scientific discovery. They were undertaken at a time when men and women felt growing confidence that we could not only understand the natural world but we could master it, too.

Today, we have learned rather more humility and respect for the balance of nature. But another of the beliefs of Darwin's era should help to see us through, the belief in reason and the scientific method. Reason is humanity's special gift. It allows us to understand the structure of the nucleus. It enables us to explore the heavens. It helps us to conquer disease. Now we must use our reason to find a way in which we can live with nature, and not dominate nature.

At the end of a book which has helped many young people to shape their own sense of stewardship for our planet, its American author quotes one of our greatest English poems, Milton's "Paradise Lost." When Adam in that poem asks about the movements of the heavens, Raphael the Archangel refuses to answer. "Let it speak," he says,

The Maker's high magnificence, who built
So spacious, and his line stretcht out so far,
That Man may know he dwells not in his own; An edifice too large
    for him to fill,
Lodg'd in a small partition, and the rest
Ordain'd for uses to his Lord best known.

We need our reason to teach us today that we are not, that we must not try to be, the lords of all we survey. We are not the lords, we are the Lord's creatures, the trustees of this planet, charged today with preserving life itself—preserving life with all its mystery and all its wonder.

May we all be equal to that task.
Thank you, Mr. President.

REFERENCES

International Panel on Climate Change. *Third Assessment Report: Summary for Policy Makers.* World Meteorological Organization, UNEP, 2001. Available at http://www.ipec.ch.

Jenkins, Peter. *Mrs. Thatcher's Revolution: The Ending of the Socialist Era.* Cambridge, MA: Harvard University Press, 1988.

Kiss, Alexandre, and Dinah Shelton. *International Environmental Law.* Ardsley, NY: Transnational Publishers, 2000.

Oppenheimer, Michael. "Declare Warm on Global Warming." *International Herald Tribune,* April 8, 2003.

Ponte, Lowell. *The Cooling.* Englewood Cliffs, NJ: Prentice Hall, 1974.

Scott, Gary, Geoffrey Reynolds, and Anthony Lott. "Success and Failure Components of Global Environmental Cooperation: The Making of International Environmental Law." *Journal of International and Comparative Law* 2 (1995): 23.

Thatcher, Margaret. *The Downing Street Years.* New York: Harper Collins, 1993.

———. Speech to the United Nations General Assembly, November 8, 1989.

Young, Hugo. *The Iron Lady: A Biography of Margaret Thatcher.* New York: Farrar Straus and Giroux, 1989.

Young, Hugo, and Anne Sloman. *The Thatcher Phenomenon.* London: BBC Press, 1986.

11. Petra Kelly

GERMANY

*I*n the late 1970s, a motley coalition of feminists, peace activists, anarchists, communists, and, of course, environmentalists, launched "Die Grünen," the German Green Party. Despite their diverse outlooks, the party founders shared a common history as citizen activists who had operated largely outside the political arena. They all agreed that the time had come to change tactics. In 1979, "The Greens" exploded onto the German political landscape, winning a million votes in the European elections and placing candidates in the Bremen district parliament. The reverberations were soon heard across Europe and as far away as Tasmania and Canada. With a sunflower and the simple inscription "Die Grünen" emblazoned on their green flag, they waved a banner for radical changes in German society: decentralization, referenda, disengagement from NATO, unilateral nuclear disarmament, women's rights, and an economic system sensitive to social justice.

The party's environmental agenda went far beyond any narrow technical pollution standard or conservation program. After thirty years of complacency produced by Germany's astonishing 5 percent annual growth in its post-war boom, the voices of ecological discontent resonating around the world had only begun to penetrate German society. The Greens heard the call, and dismissed the traditional view that perceived economic growth as synonymous with progress. The party called for ecological and social objectives to drive public policy. The Greens also rejected the accepted norms of German politics. Half the Green candidates were women. All of its institutions and meetings remained open to the press. Elected officials were to rotate on a regular basis. And civil disobedience was not only countenanced but encouraged.

In the 1983 elections, the Green candidates received 5.2 percent of the vote (enough to catapult them into the federal Bundestag) and, by 1987, the party managed to garner an impressive 8.3 percent. Tactical errors, infighting, and poor posturing over reunification issues led to loss of electoral support in 1990, but this was only a temporary setback. The Greens soon returned to claim forty-seven seats in parliament, enough to make it, since 1998, a coalition partner in the German government. The profile of Green constituents has from the start been consistent: young, highly educated, urban, and nonreligious—liberal people who had traditionally supported Germany's Social Democrats but were won over by the authenticity, idealism, and originality of the self-proclaimed "anti-party party." That defining phrase was coined by Petra Kelly. As the first female head of a German political party, and its spokesperson during its critical early years, she came to symbolize Die Grünen's unique vision and spirit.

Like her politics, Petra Kelly's personal path departed from any typical Germany route, and in fact contained a substantial American detour. In 1960, Kelly was just another bright thirteen-year old girl, studying in a conservative Catholic boarding school in Gunzburg, Bavaria. (Kelly would often mention the town's dubious distinction as home to the notorious Auschwitz doctor, Mengele.) When her mother remarried a lieutenant colonel in the U.S. Army, however, she took her daughter along to the American South. While still learning English, the adolescent plunged head first into the simmering civil rights movement in Athens, Georgia, helping black children in a variety of civic projects. It was the first of countless battles for social justice.

Despite her involvement in antiwar campus protests at American University in Washington, D.C., and a lucrative job as national student coordinator for Robert Kennedy's 1968 presidential campaign, Kelly managed to complete her degree on time, cum laude. The experience left her with an axiomatic belief in nonviolent activism, along with the American environmental and feminist consciousness of the time. These she brought back to Europe, where she sailed through a master's degree in political science, in Amsterdam. For the duration of the 1970s, Kelly worked as a civil servant for the European Community's Economic and Social Committee, where she quickly developed an expertise about a full menu of European policy issues.

The job left her ample time for involvement in German civil society. She signed on with the West German Federal Association of Citizens for Environmental Protection, eventually becoming a board member and spokesperson for this umbrella organization for German environmental citizen groups. She also became active in the ruling Social Democratic Party. A loyal fan of Prime Minister Willy Brandt, Kelly became increasingly disenchanted with his successor's leadership and sought an alternative model for political involvement. And so, with a couple dozen friends and colleagues, she founded Die Grünen and began campaigning. In 1979, with Kelly at the head of an unknown national list, the new anti-party party took 3.2 percent of the vote in Germany's European Parliament elections. Apparently, a Green constituency existed.

Kelly's subsequent crusade was focused on her opposition to the stationing of nuclear-headed missiles in Germany. Along with Gert Bastian, a former German major general turned peace activist, she started a petition drive. Five million people signed the petition. Kelly became chairperson of the fledgling party and, despite disappointment in the 1980 elections where the Greens fell short of the 5 percent support required for entering the Bundestag, she knew it was only a matter of time. Two years later, Kelly took a year-long leave of absence from her job at the European Community to devote her energies to the national elections. During that year, she appeared at 450 meetings, talks, and rallies. Over two million Germans identified with her message and, along with twenty-six other Green candidates, Petra Kelly had a seat in parliament.

There she joined the Bundestag's Foreign Relations Committee (where she was the sole female member) and became a political spokesperson for her parliamentary delegation. As an opposition politician, she did not forget her previous nongovernmental affinities and tactics. Hence, her colorful and courageous extra-parliamentary activities thrust her into the national and international spotlight. Kelly held a mock trial for the war crimes of five nations for their nuclear arsenals (the trial included both the United States *and* the Soviet Union). She crossed into East Germany and Moscow, and staged pro-peace demonstrations there. She blockaded American military bases. Along with other Green parliamentarians, she occupied the German embassy in Pretoria to protest Germany's economic activities with the apartheid regime in South Africa. She was often arrested for these activities, and fined. But her antics kept her party's message in the headlines and helped slow its ossification and slide into political irrelevance. Kelly always insisted that the Greens were more of a movement than a party, and her initiatives were designed to reinforce this contention.

In practically all of her projects, domestic and international, she was accompanied by Bastian, who had long since left his wife. The two were certainly an odd couple. He was twenty-five years older than her, a career military man who had actually fought as a Nazi soldier in World War II. But they were totally devoted to each other, and Kelly constantly referred to him with obvious gratitude as her "soul mate" and "mentor." Kelly's eloquence in English, good looks, and exuberance made her a charismatic celebrity on the international environmental circuit. She toured the globe, with Bastian (himself a member of the Bundestag) increasingly in the role of what the Germans derisively called "baggage-carrier."

Of course many of her colleagues in the party took umbrage at Kelly's media attention, and not all identified with her tactical gimmicks. The infighting within the party became a growing source of despondency for her and, as she coached other nations' Green Parties during their start-up phases, she would often talk about the importance of preserving an ingenuous collegiality in party culture. Thus she told the 1987 International Green Congress in Stockholm: "We ourselves must become more peaceful, just, and tolerant with one another within our own ranks. The hurt, the hypocrisy, the intolerance, the mean-hearted spirits, and the attitude of always 'controlling' and not 'trusting' each other within the Greens at home has been a strong disappointment to many of us. Such ways have minimized our appeal, our chances, and our concrete results."

Yet it was inevitable that, once successful, Germany's Green Party would face "growing pains." The extremely diverse coalition of actors had never really agreed about what the party stood for, or appropriate strategy once they became a political player. The two areas that engendered the most acrimonious internal debate involved economics and coalition tactics. The majority of party members intuitively were uncomfortable with the rigid constraints of a leftist-socialist orthodoxy. Evading specifics, they relied on slogans like "We are neither left nor right—we are in front of them all." At the same time, a small but militant Marxist-Leninist faction had helped found the party, and pushed for the Greens to amalgamate a new, leftist coalition. Rather than reject this group's ideas outright, the other party founders decided to leave resolution to a new culture of internal dialogue intended to transcend old intellectual divisions.

It didn't. Although party platforms called for the replacement of industrial capitalism with an economic system that was "ecological, social, and grassroots democratic," such generalities could not eliminate this chronic source of tension.

Then there was the longstanding tactical debate that tore the party apart. The "Realo" (or "realists," who urged the embracing of power through coalitions) squared off against the "Fundi" (or "fundamentalists," who saw the perils of pragmatism). Kelly herself was wary of the ethical and cultural price that politically motivated compromises brought. The former approach, which preferred action to dogma, certainly was more popular among voters, and eventually became the dominant position within the party. In the interim, the sides bludgeoned each other mercilessly, a clash that the Green Party's axiomatic transparency broadcast to the entire nation.

Yet there were clear achievements that the Greens could claim during their first decade as a Parliamentary political force. Plans to introduce over a hundred nuclear power plants to the country were derailed, apparently for good, by the passionate Green opposition. They pushed the government and managed to stymie considerable industrialization along the North Sea coast and stop runaway highway construction. Die Grünen's success inspired environmentalists and other activists to organize Green parties across the planet, with a network stretching from Australia to Israel. Indeed, the Green parties in countries like Finland and Belgium soon outstripped the German original.

Kelly used her parliamentary pulpit to address international issues and reach out to the world's weak and disenfranchised. She organized the first parliamentary hearings in the world about the situation in Tibet. She met with Australian aborigines and Chinese student dissidents. And, of course, she established ties and fought on behalf of Green colleagues in East Germany. Kelly also found time to continue her charitable activities.

There are many reasons postulated for the 1990 election results that left the Greens just shy of the minimum 5 percent required to return to Parliament. Clearly, the internal bickering did not help Die Grunen's image. Some claim that other parties had begun to adopt many of the basic environmental postures that had distinguished the Greens. Yet unpopular positions and a foolish campaign offer the best explanation. At a time when the country was obsessed with the dream of reunification with East Germany, the Greens supported maintaining two separate, democratic Germanies, with the logic that European unification was ultimately more important. The election slogan's allusion to global warming, "They are all speaking about the nation, we are speaking about the weather," bombed with voters, and Kelly and her colleagues were suddenly unemployed.

Not that Kelly was short on things to do. She wrote extensively during this period—books about Tibet, childhood cancer, and Green Politics. In January 1992 she began to host a television program about global environmental affairs. And she traveled the world, sharing her ideas about politics. The speech included here, from a 1991 conference in Mexico City, did not appear in her anthology *Nonviolence Speaks to Power,* but is her most thoughtful and spirited from this period. It offers key insights into her intellectual tenacity and the internationalization of her vision for the Green Party's responsibilities. Kelly's tendency to bounce back and forth among her environmental, peace, and feminist passions reflects the complete synthesis of these ideologies in her "Green" world outlook. Moreover, her original convictions appear as strong as ever; she had lost none of her idealism nor sense of urgency in a decade of rough and tumble in her idiosyncratic party. As Kelly once told her Green colleagues: "We, the generation that faces the next century, can add the solemn injunction: If we don't do the impossible, we shall be faced with the unthinkable."

After the 1990 disappointment, Kelly primarily planned for the future, predicting a Green comeback in the next election, and her own assumption of a role in the European Parliament. But she never got the chance.

In October 1992, police were summoned to her home in Bonn, where they found her decomposing body. Three weeks earlier, she had been shot point-blank in the temple. Gert Bastian's body lay in a similar state, but with a pistol in his hand. Police investigation confirmed that Bastion, Kelly's partner for so many years, had powder burns and had pulled the trigger two times. Endless press speculations about whether it was a murder/suicide or a consensual death pact were particularly unfortunate, because it left Kelly's final legacy a lurid, anomalous spectacle.

Although just forty-four at the time of her death, Petra Kelly had managed to define a new manifestation of modern environmentalism. Her version of green politics bore little resemblance to the male-dominated sleaze and backroom deals of traditional parties. No other individual made a stronger case for both the imperatives of Green political organizing and the necessity of preserving an alternative, party culture. And as Kelly showed, environmental principles needed to fuse with a broader agenda of human rights, nonviolence, social equity, and grassroots democracy to seize the imagination of a national electorate and truly transform society.

"If We Want to Transform Society in an Ecological Way, We Must Transform Ourselves"

ADDRESS TO THE MORELIA ECOLOGY CONFERENCE, MORELIA, MEXICO, SEPTEMBER 2, 1991

I am very happy to be able to be here in Mexico—my very first visit here—and to be able to share my thoughts with so many other friends in spirit and action. I am here first of all to learn from you, because we of the Western, industrialized, Eurocentric countries need to listen and to learn from others, more than most of us want to admit.

Let me share with you what I have learned and experienced, not only while working on green and social issues within the European Community in Brussels over ten years, but what I have learned from twenty-three years of grassroots work in the ecology, peace, and women's movements in Eastern and Western Europe and in eight years of parliamentary work for the German Green Party in the national parliament.

First of all—though this view has made me rather lonely in the Green Party—I believe that, if we want to transform society in an ecological way, we must transform ourselves profoundly first. I am more and more convinced that the kind of personal transformation I am talking about is, in itself, a very political act, or as we would term it, "anti-politics"! One important ingredient, I believe, must be humility, and I have met very few politicians in the world who have that special quality of humility.

When we understand the interconnectedness of everything in nature, we realize that countless beings walk within us, that nature is our inexhaustible mirror, that humanness is a function of a wider system. To realize this is to begin to let go of the familiar individual self or ego, and to experience a sense of identification with wider circles of life. Genuinely to experience "falling in love outward," as the poet Robinson Jeffers put it, is to experience a profound personal transformation.

What is needed in present-day politics is a change from both form and content, a vision of holism rather than separation and compartmentalization. To heal the planet earth, we, especially in the West, must end fragmentary problem-solving. And we must, of course, change our daily

Speech credit: Heinrich Boell Foundation, Petra Kelly Archives, File No. 569

consciousness about our own lifestyles and our own attitudes. We must be acutely aware of our own habits and behavior and the ways in which our personal actions can contribute to the perpetuation of the present system.

I have, at the founding of the German Green Party over eleven years ago, coined the term "anti-party party," trying to express with that word a new type of power, a new type of political party. When we speak about the power of nonviolent change and nonviolent transformation, we do not mean the power *over,* but we mean the power common to all, to be used by all and for all. Power *over* is to be replaced by shared power, by the power to do things, by the discovery of our own strength as opposed to a passive receiving of power exercised by others, often in our name. The Green Party has tried to be a political lobby for those who have no voice, for those who are not represented, including the whales, the elephants, the dolphins, the plants and flowers on this planet.

Since those eleven years have gone by, I have also learned how quickly the same old power that we meant to transform has in fact changed us, or large parts of the Green Party who now see all salvation coming from joining regional governmental coalitions with the Social Democrats, at times almost at any price. But how can you, in fact, make nonviolent politics, if there are only one or two Green ministers in a cabinet of ten others who oppose you? What happens when Green governmental partners in a coalition have to vote to increase the police forces and equip them with better water tanks that are used against nonviolent protesters? And what happens when you have promised your grassroots movements not to build a test road for Daimler Benz and then you go ahead and build it anyway? Or when the Greens are forced to make compromises that touch life-and-death issues?

For me, there cannot be a little bit of cancer or a little bit of deterrence or a little bit of dioxin or a little bit of plutonium. There are some ecological issues where you do not make any compromises, where you cannot repair irreparable damages. I have learned that foremost from my sister Grace, who died at the age of ten-and-a-half from cancer, and from many other cancer-ill children that I have gotten to know. And I believe we should be very cautious about getting into power-sharing at governmental levels, unless we are very clear ourselves about when and where to compromise and when and where not to.

In fact, we must get away from the idea of "repairing," or of being able to repair all that we first destroy, because some things in nature cannot be repaired that we have damaged and have injured.

It was Mahatma Gandhi who spoke about not believing in the doctrine of the greatest good for the greatest number. Instead he believed the only real dignified human doctrine is the *greatest good for all.* The Brundtland Commission has expressed the dilemma in the following way: "The Earth is one but the world is not. We all depend on one biosphere for sustaining our lives. Yet each community, each country, strives for survival and prosperity with little regard for its impact on others."

As the German writer Siegfried Lenz put it, "A gravestone for our dying age could well bear the inscription: 'Everyone wanted the best—for themselves.'"

So this brings us right back to the interconnectedness of everything around us, in us, acting locally and thinking globally. Whatever we do to the earth, we do to ourselves! Learning that we are not outside of nature, but a part of it—that is the essence of ecological politics, but this is also a very spiritual statement.

The next point I would like to stress is the great misunderstandings that had existed between those who come from Green movements in the West (movements that grew out of the seemingly unstoppable Western economic growth, and movements that have been concerned about the wasteful destruction of nature) and those in the so-called Third World countries, who rightly . . . asked us not to ignore the questions of economic injustice and exploitation of the poor by the rich.

Thinking on both sides has changed, and now it is understood that nurturing the environment is also central to tackling the grave problems of poverty. The transformation of forests into deserts or fertile earth into sun-baked concrete, of running rivers into silted flood-waters, all proved that only through the care of the environment can the livelihoods of those most dependent on it be sustained.

Behind every environmental drama—and this can be seen right here in Mexico—there are in turn harsh realities of rural poverty, of landless villagers having to destroy nature to eat and drink, and of governments pursuing economic growth at any cost to the environment (encouraged by Western companies and banks). Of course, we must also speak about demilitarization—demilitarizing societies as radically as possible, and of course beginning right at home in the North.

For it is the North which is exporting those high amounts of weapons and military materials to the South. If we are to have a chance at all, we must also tackle this problem of global militarization. We should not forget that superpower rivalry has brought even the most remote regions into the realm of military strategists. Whether in the Arctic homeland of the Inuit or the Dreaming Paths of the Aboriginals of Central Australia, military installations are now in place that continue to be the key targets in the event of even a regional nuclear war (if there is such a thing as a regional nuclear war).

In the industrialized countries, traditional indigenous lands have been misused for bases and military test sites, and the developing countries have often become the killing ground. Let me just quote one figure: although 80 percent of military expenditure is accounted for by NATO and the Warsaw Pact, spending on arms and weapons in the developing world doubled between 1978 and 1988. It doubled, of course, also because we, the Western countries, have exported those weapons and have given the Third World countries the impression that you can only be an important member of this world community if you have enough weapons to deter others.

Within the green parties and movements, we believe that hope does not usually come from governments. Hope, in fact, comes from the many grassroots efforts, from the people working at grassroots levels, and from their strength and their imagination, eager to create a world without fear and without war. What we need more than ever before is the meeting of the minds (like right here at this conference in Morelia) and building new alliances. The rape of the planet earth cannot be halted simply by imposing environmental conservation or green rules on all areas of the world. It must be remembered over and over again: the seedbed of ecological destructions is the *global divisions* between *rich and poor!*

As Ben Jackson wrote: "A series of 'Keep Out' signs around the world's forest would not only be morally unacceptable, with the poor still hungry outside, it just would not work!"

If we finally have linked poverty, inequality, and environmental degradation, then we must also form new alliances—groups concerned with ecology, human rights, peace, alternative production, world poverty, etc. In 1988, for example, over sixty thousand people from all walks of life came to Berlin to protest against the impact of the International Monetary Fund and the World Bank on poor countries and their environment, while the two institutions met there. This is one important step in our strategy of building new alliances. I believe that we can have ecologically based economies and socially useful, nondamaging investment, if only there is the political will.

Of course, we must also reach the progressive people inside the trade union movements. To me, one of the most powerful movements in the trade union area has been the Australian Green Ban movement in the late

sixties and early seventies, a movement that needs to be revived and extended in every country. In the Green Ban movement in Australia, trade
unionists had refused to work on environmentally damaging projects
and, in fact, were imprisoned for their clear choice of conscience.

No official economic policy to date has taken the global damage
resulting from human activity into consideration. The opposite, in fact, is
true. Considerable parts of our natural base have already been destroyed
for economic gain. In the end, the economic system will pull the rug out
from underneath its own feet. We feel that what is ecologically necessary
is also economically sound.

Vandana Shiva puts it right to the point, when she states that Amazonia
is disappearing not because of the local inhabitants but to supply cheap
beef to northern consumers and to supply charcoal for smelting iron for
export. Southeast Asia's forests are disappearing to supply tropical hardwood to Japanese and European markets. And, as commodity prices
fall and the debt burdens spiral, the Third World is increasingly trapped
in the vicious circle of exporting more to earn less. It is as if the sick and
dying are giving blood transfusions to the healthy and rich.

Let me add here that we must speak far louder than ever before about
the connections between debts and environment. Indebted countries
have not just borrowed money; they have mortgaged the future. Nature,
as Susan George writes, puts up the collateral. National economies, both
state socialist and capitalist, proceeded as if there were no long-term costs
for anything. They deny "limits of growth," or they do not even figure
pollution and ecological destruction in their equation. We must expose
the debt–environment connection: First, borrowing to finance ecologically destructive projects, and, second, paying for them by cashing in natural resources. It is one vicious circle.

Many of the megaprojects that helped put Third World countries
on the debt treadmill to begin with, are environmental disasters in their
own right (large dams, hydroprojects, nuclear power plants, etc.). The
U.S. Natural Resources Defense Council stated: "Hydroelectric projects
approved by the World Bank between 1979 and 1983 resulted in the
voluntary resettlement [as they call it] of at least 450,000 people on four
continents."

Massive deforestation, we all know, will change the whole world's
weather for the worse, and it carries heavy economic penalties—the forests, aside from harboring untold numbers of animal and vegetable species, being the habitat of native peoples. Deforestation is simply criminal,
when we realize that rainforests are destroyed merely to extract the fifteen

to twenty kinds of commercially valuable trees they contain. Frequently 90 percent to 95 percent of the trees are left unused when an area of rainforest is logged. And even now the World Bank admits that some 15 to 20 percent of the world's estimated five to ten million plant and animal species will become extinct by the year 2000. Again, a tropical forest is a seamless web, and all its components are necessary or in time it will become as barren as a desert. And yet forests are sold, then loans are given to reforest and repair the damages—to pay *then,* for which more forest is cut, while the banks and landing countries acquire interest payments, export orders, and political and economic power, and the environment is simply ruined. . . .

The next point I would like to raise is that we ourselves must find new criteria for so-called development models, because I believe that democratic, nonviolent, and ecological development is possible. But this means of course that the North must de-develop. The debt crisis is a symptom of a polarized world (the Iron curtain is now between North and South), organized for the benefit of a minority that will stop at nothing to maintain and strengthen its control and privilege. Just look at the so-called New World Order, Pax Americana, and the concepts of low-intensity warfare being discussed at the Pentagon. Even repression technology is being improved.

In the North, there are many of us now working outside of the old development model. Many popular movements, for example, are working against the financial developers. And in the South, we are learning from the courageous indigenous movements, from the courageous women of the Chipko movement, and many others.

If we try to light a candle, let us look at the proposals of the South Commission, issued in Caracas in 1981, with its development strategy of self-reliance; its recognition that no country can be "developed" by outsiders; its determination to see people, their skills, creativity, and wisdom as the instruments as well as the ends of development. One small candle we can light could be the setting up of an alternative credit system to the International Monetary Fund and . . . the World Bank. Perhaps a South Bank that a hundred or so countries of the South could devise as their own alternative. We can call this new idea counter-development, which means disengaging from the single, damaging, present world system.

Our own contribution in the North could be an ecological economy and lifestyle, as the German Green Party declared in 1983: "A lifestyle and methods of production which rely on an endless supply of raw materials, and use those raw materials lavishly, also furnish the motive for the violent appropriation of raw materials from other countries. In contrast, a responsible use of raw materials, as part of an ecologically sound lifestyle and economy, reduces the risk that policies of violence will be pursued in our name. The pursuance of ecologically responsible policies within a society provides the preconditions for a reduction in tensions and increases our ability to achieve peace in the world."

For the West, sustainable development requires a completely new paradigm. We cannot have both growth at any price and sustainable development. As long as we put economic considerations before ecological values, we are going to risk the latter.

Let me quickly turn to another development that is very worrying: Arrogant as we have been in the North, we are calling upon the struggling countries of the Third World to reduce their carbon dioxide emissions, while the big polluters in the North refuse to do so. And yet it is we, the industrialized nations in the North, who are to blame for the threat to our planet. We have caused 90 percent of the greenhouse gas emissions to date and we have to be responsible for the cleaning up of them. It is of course far too late to undo the damage that we have already done to our atmosphere. Let me only remind you that every five years of delay in cutting pollution will lead to a 10 percent increase in global warming. The United States, the Soviet Union, China, West Germany, Japan, and the United Kingdom are the largest emitters of carbon dioxide. Between them they produce almost two thirds of the world's CO_2.

One other issue that is very urgent today is how the changes in Eastern Europe affect the South. Vandana Shiva uses an African proverb: "When elephants make war, the grass gets trampled. When elephants make love, the grass gets trampled."

The Third World environment and the Third World communities are the ones that have paid the highest price for the superpower rivalry of the past. The Cold War in Europe had always been translated into real and burning wars in the Third World, for example in Central America, in Central Asia, and in the horn of Africa. Since 1945, two hundred wars have been fought in the Third World. And, as the industrialized world now moves from an over-armed peace to a disarmed one, the military producers and traders merely find alternative markets in the Third World.

New ecological transformation and reconstruction in Eastern Europe is of course fundamental to societal transformation toward a civil society. We must not forget—and this is one of the most important points, I believe— that it is again the Third World that will have to bear the ecological cost of the new industrialism and consumerism in the North, including the cost of cleaning up Eastern Europe. Eastern and Western Europe will increasingly use the Third World as a dump for hazards and wastes. This is, of course, garbage imperialism. And when the transport routes are too long to the Third World, then the West will use its own backyard, Eastern Europe, for its dumping ground. We call this the Latin Americanization of Eastern Europe.

We must not forget that the old repressive communistic system in Eastern Europe had paralyzed so many people, and that the soft and gentle revolutions that came over night have given us much hope but have also left many of us in a state of shock. Communism had institutionalized the surrender of individual decision-making and problem-solving capabilities to state control. Now that the authoritarian powers have stepped down, how can, in fact, individuals unravel their cultural conditioning and become free agents again? The West, in fact, has never given Eastern European society since the revolution a chance at all. No chance to think and rethink about what type of society they would now like to build. Eastern Europe has to create almost a new economic, financial, social, and ecological infrastructure, and we are asking them to do it in a way in which they can avoid our mistakes.

But how will that be possible, if Western banks and financial institutions dictate what they are to produce, what they are to export, and how they are to live in the coming months and years? As the Iron Curtain opened during the months of 1989, it revealed a land laid waste by industrial pollution. Under the assault of air pollution and acid deposition, Eastern Europe's medieval cities are blackened and are crumbling; entire hillsides are deforested. Life expectancies in the dirtiest parts of these regions are as much as five years shorter, and rates of childhood cancer, reproductive problems, and other illnesses are far higher, than in other areas.

Restoring Eastern Europe's environment will be a most massive undertaking, but it cannot be done at the cost of exploiting the Third World once again. Eastern Europe, I believe, has a unique opportunity to leapfrog the West by implementing only those successful, ecological Western strategies, and sidestepping those that did not work with us. Additionally, as obsolete factories in Eastern Europe are closed down, they can be replaced by ecologically safe and socially useful industries and production. But, unfortunately, at the moment, this is not happening at all. The shift to Western market-oriented economies in Eastern Europe has had little regard for clean industries. For we in Western Europe are sending our old reactors and our old dirty industries to Eastern European countries and to our own backyard, East Germany.

While concluding my remarks, I would like to add two more points that will be perhaps a small candle of hope:

Number one, we must learn in the North that we must begin as critical consumers to reduce our consumption of goods to levels where we do not provide a market for big business. We can reduce our consumption to where we will use only our share of the world's resources and not take what belongs to someone else. This is for me just one very small aspect of nonviolence and the ultimate dimension of noncooperation with corrupt and inhuman practices. We are part of the problem, and thus we together are also part of the solution. The actual danger as well as the potential solutions are not somewhere "out there"; both lie within us. And taking responsibility for our own personal behavior every single day is the only thing in this world over which we have one hundred percent control.

Number two [is the] feminization of power: Feminism and the power of nonviolence are to me very essential concepts of Green politics. Male-led revolutions so often and so tragically have been mere power exchanges in a basically unaltered structure, leaving behind dramatic accounts of crisis and heroism (the siege of the Winter Palace or the taking of the Bastille). These revolutions were often based on the concept of dying for a cause; feminist-conceived transformation is all the more about daring *to live for a cause!*

Women represent half the global population and over one-third of the labor force, and yet we women receive only one-tenth of the world's income and own less than one percent of world prosperity. We are also responsible for two-thirds of all working hours. Not only are females most of the poor, the starving, and the illiterate, but women and children constitute more than 90 percent of all refugee populations.

Toxic pesticides, herbicides, chemical pollution, leakage from nuclear wastes, acid rain, etc. usually take their first toll as a rise in cancers of the female reproductive system, and in miscarriages, stillbirths, and congenital deformities. Furthermore, it is women's work which must compensate for the destruction of the ecological balance.

The overlooked factor in the power of women as a world political force is, I believe, the magnitude of suffering combined with the magnitude of women: women do not constitute an oppressed minority, but a majority of almost all national populations and of the entire human species. I truly believe that we can feminize power, and that we can, in fact, transcend patriarchal power. We can and must elect more ecological feminists to public offices, and we must together dare new transnational political and bold initiatives. I believe we must begin to do this with our Mexican sisters right here in Mexico. If there is a future, I believe, it will be Green and feminist.

Thank you.

REFERENCES

Frankland, E. Gene. *Between Protest and Power: The Green Party in Germany.* Boulder, CO: Westview Press, 1992.

Heertsgaard, Mark. "Who Killed Petra Kelly?" *Mother Jones,* January/February 1993.

Kelly, Petra K. *Nonviolence Speaks to Power.* Ed. Glenn D. Paige and Sarah Gilliatt. Hawaii: Center for Global Nonviolence, 2001.

Lipelet, Helmut. "The Green Case—Die Grunen: Short History—Basic Ideas." Paper presented to the Conference on Ecological Movement and Sustainable Development in Latin America and Europe, University of London, November 1991.

Parkin, Sara. *The Life and Death of Petra Kelly.* London: Pandora, 1994.

Pulzer, Peter. *German Politics, 1945–1995.* Oxford: Oxford University Press, 1995.

12. The Dalai Lama

TIBET

Photograph by Sonam Zoksang.

*T*he subjugation of Tibet is by now greeted with resignation by an international community that hardly intervened to stop one of the great injustices of the twentieth century. The mystique of this scenic land and its exceptional civilization have long been admired, along with its stature as a center for a uniquely gentle, Buddhist tradition. To be sure, there is a tendency to idealize traditional Tibetan culture, which also included a feudal caste system, corruption, discrimination against women, and an astonishingly high incidence of disease. Tibetan monks acknowledge that, for the first half of the twentieth century, materially the country was so "backwards" that there was not even production of matches and most people relied on flint for fire.

But it was a place like no other. The de facto sovereignty of an independent Tibet during the first half of the twentieth century is internationally recognized, even as this autonomy was supported by its isolation and rugged terrain, rather than by any military capability. All this changed in 1950 when the new Communist Chinese army seized the country in a cruel occupation that the Chinese justified by historic claims.

The new Communist regime wasted little time in imposing its oppressive ideology, and sporadic local acts of rebellion only engendered increasingly vicious retribution. Execution, torture, and even forced abortions and sterilization of women have been documented. Sources associated with the Tibetan government in exile suggest that 1.5 million Tibetans have died directly at the hands of the Chinese authorities. During the Chinese Cultural Revolution in the 1960s, the chaos and cruelty reached new heights. More than six thousand monasteries were systematically destroyed and, with them, an immeasurable treasure of literature and artifacts; only twelve operational monasteries remain. Alexander Solzhenitsyn characterized Chinese rule of Tibet as "more brutal and inhumane than any other communist regime in the world." And as early as 1960, the International Commission of Jurists went as far as characterizing the Chinese policies as genocidal, ruling that the Chinese were attempting "to destroy Tibetans as a religious group."

Sadly, this unspeakable crime continues to this day. The military assault was soon followed by a demographic invasion. The Chinese government, through a variety of incentive programs, has repopulated Tibet with some 7.5 million ethnic Chinese who now dominate the 6.5 million indigenous Tibetans; more are on the way. And yet, despite such horrifying travails, more than ever the indigenous people and religion of Tibet serve as a beacon of peacefulness and spiritual inspiration to the world.

No individual has come to represent the fate and spirit of his or her nation in modern times more than the fourteenth Dalai Lama. *Lama* is the Tibetan title for "guru" and *Dalai* means "ocean" in Mongolian—thus, "ocean of wisdom." According to Tibetan tradition, the Dalai Lamas are the human embodiment of the deity of compassion, who returns to the earth to serve humanity. One is not elected or appointed but born into the position; each is the reincarnation of the previous Dalai Lama, in an unbroken chain starting from the thirteenth century. In his autobiography, the Dalai lama acknowledges a "spiritual connection" to his thirteen predecessors, but is predictably more modest: "I myself am just a human being and incidentally a Tibetan who chooses to be a Buddhist monk."

The present Dalai Lama was born Lhamo Thondup (or "Wish-Fulfilling Goddess") to a poor peasant family in Takster village in eastern Tibet. The death of the thirteenth Dalai Lama that year was followed by the customary search parties. Three years later, the traditional reappearance was identified in the form of this three-year-old toddler, who showed the uncanny ability to distinguish items belonging to the previous Dalai Lama and, unprompted, called them his own. The young boy was issued into a local monastery and later traveled to Lhaso, Tibet's capital, and the great Potala Palace. There, in 1910, his hair was shorn, he was given an ambitious new name (Jamphel Ngawang Lobsang Yeshe Tenzin Gyatso) and separated from his parents, and his status as Dalai Lama was declared.

His studies at the Potala Palace commenced immediately. Although Dalai Lamas may enjoy a special spiritual inheritance, wisdom must be gained anew through rigorous studies. From the age of six, the Dalai Lama underwent an intensive educational program. The young boy's irrepressible penchant for taking apart all contraptions, from cars to watches, has become the stuff of Tibetan legend. His naturally mischievous predilections were also a bit incongruous with his status as a divine child, and he gleefully recalls an endless litany of tricks and naughtiness that must have exasperated his team of tutors. But his intelligence did not disappoint them. The Dalai Lama soon reached the highest level of scholarship in Buddhist metaphysics, only granted after grueling public examination and disputations in front of thousands of monks and scholars at three monastic universities over several years.

Beyond the spiritual status, the position of Dalai Lama also confers political powers. Although a regent sat in during the transitional period of his youth, in 1950 the Dalai Lama, at the age of sixteen, assumed political control of his people and began to address the crisis associated with the invasion by Communist Chinese forces. As the Tibetan army was hardly a force to be reckoned with, and the Dalai Lama was committed to passive resistance, negotiations seemed the only option open to the country.

So in 1954 the Dalai Lama traveled to Beijing to negotiate with Chairman Mao Tse Dung and the Communist leadership, who insisted that the country accept the yolk of Chinese domination willingly (including a position for him in the official hierarchy) in exchange for the Communists' willingness to respect the local "minority" culture. Subsequent visits to India did little to engender support for the cause of Tibetan independence. Given the cultural mismatch, tensions were unavoidable. In 1959, the people of Tibet somewhat spontaneously rebelled in a valiant but futile uprising that led to the Dalai Lama's fleeing over the Himalayas into exile in India. There he established a government in exile, which now contains fifty-three refugee settlements. He continues to work tirelessly, touring the globe, and raising awareness about the need to preserve Tibetan culture and liberate his homeland through nonviolent means. In 1989, the Dalai Lama was awarded the Nobel Peace Prize.

Alongside the political and cultural tragedy of Tibet is an ecological one. The record of exploitation rivals any Western colonial abuse. Prior to invasion, the absence of any industry in Tibet, along with the pervasive Buddhist ethos of moderation, limited human impact on the land. Hunting and fishing were nonexistent and, as part of their dogma, the thousands of monks agreed to cut neither trees nor grass, lest it damage the surrounding ecosystem.

But all that has changed. Reports suggest that the Chinese stockpile nuclear arms in Tibet and recklessly dispose of nuclear wastes there. Some 68 percent of the country's forests have been clear-cut and transported back to China. With its habitat vanishing, wildlife was soon to follow. The herds of deer and flocks of ducks and geese, once such an integral part of the landscape, are largely gone, as are the rare snow leopard and the wild blue sheep. Deforestation, of course, exacerbates floods. When Chinese prospectors discovered dozens of minerals, the government immediately set out to mine them, with little regard to the consequent environmental damage. Many of the rivers of Asia (such as the Yellow, Yangtse, and Mekong) originating in the high Tibetan watersheds now start their flows with contaminated waters.

When he addressed the U.S. Congress in 1987, the Dalai Lama set forth a *Five-Point Peace Plan for Tibet,* which ever since has remained his official platform for change. These points involve turning the country into a state of peace and nonviolence, an end to repopulation policies, respect for human rights and liberties, and restoration of the natural environment to a healthy state. This last point includes protecting "what little is left" of wildlife and nature, banning nuclear weapons production and toxic dumping, and the start of restoration efforts.

In a speech describing the present environmental situation in Tibet, the Dalai Lama reflected wistfully on the environmental conditions that once prevailed in an independent Tibet:

Now, environmental problems are something new to me. When we were in Tibet, we always considered the environment pure. For Tibetans, whenever we see a stream of water, there was no question as to whether it is safe for drinking or not. . . . When we look back at our own country, Tibet, it is a big country with vast land area, with high altitude and a cold and dry climate. Perhaps these things provided some kind of natural protection to Tibet's environment, keeping it clean and fresh. In the Northern pastures, the rocky areas, the forested areas, and the river valleys, there used to be lots of wild animals, fish, and birds. As a Buddhist country, there were certain traditional laws in Tibet concerned with a complete ban on fishing and hunting.

With time, the Dalai Lama's frame of reference on environmental issues went beyond the borders of his beleaguered Tibet to include global challenges. As he traveled around the world speaking on behalf of his nation, he posited that Buddhist environmental ethics had something relevant to say about the planet's problems. And the throngs that came to hear him, as well as government leaders, listened.

Although indigenous Tibetan environmental ethics are a reflection of a Buddhist theological perspective, they constitute a uniquely Tibetan expression. As the Dalai Lama points out, the Tibetan culture and the Tibetan landscape shaped local environmental values, making them fundamentally different from the Buddhist precepts found in countries such as Japan or Thailand: "We don't live on a small heavily populated island. Historically, we have had little anxiety with our vast, low population and distant neighbors. We haven't felt as oppressed as people in many other communities."

An underlying theme in this Tibetan perspective is the centrality of compassion as the basis for human relations. Humans are basically gentle by nature, and even narrow self-interest, if framed correctly, can ultimately lead people to consider the suffering of others and offer help. The Dalai Lama calls the futility and self-destructive results of selfishness a "law of nature," and this perspective is an underlying assumption in his joyful and nonaggressive approach to social relations. This basic commitment to nonviolence and compassion must, in this view, be applied to all sentient beings.

Yet the environmental perspective that the Dalai Lama espouses is not a naïve one based on ascetics or an idealistic theology. Rather, he considers the Buddhist environmental ethic essentially pragmatic, assuming that people have the appropriate vision of self-interest. Concern for the environment per se is not necessarily holy, nor does it have to be based on sacrifice. In his book *My Tibet*, he explains: "We Buddhists express compassion for all sentient beings, but this compassion is not necessarily extended to every rock or tree or house. Most of us are somewhat concerned about our own house, but not really compassionate about it. We keep it in order so that we can live and be happy. We know that to have happy feelings in our house we must take care of it. So our feelings may be of concern rather than compassion. Similarly, our planet is our house, and we must keep it in order and take care of it if we are genuinely concerned about happiness for ourselves, our children, our friends, and other sentient beings who share this great earth with us."

Similarly his Tibetan view is far from Luddite, or even "deep-ecological," in its attitude toward technology. The Dalai Lama openly acknowledges that the world needs scientific and material development to increase the "general benefit and prosperity" of humanity; at the same time, he notes, mental peace is equally important to material well-being. His environmental ethic would attempt to restore the lost balance between the two: "These days, we human beings are very much involved in the external world, while we neglect the internal world."

The philosophical perspective of this ethic therefore is not abstract, but rooted in a physical involvement in the natural world. Ever since childhood, the Dalai Lama has found time, despite his highly regimented routine, to do his own gardening and to feed birds. (His followers report a particular affinity for tulips, and an encyclopedic knowledge of the local avian populations.) Another example of his practical perspective can be found in the Dalai Lama's opinions about overpopulation, where pragmatism again leads to surprising conclusions: "From a Buddhist perspective, it is quite simple. Each human life is very precious. From this perspective it is better to avoid or control birth, . . . but the question is of the survival of humanity at large. So therefore the conclusion we arrive at is that we must take family planning very seriously, if we are to save the prosperity of entire humanity, preferably through nonviolent means, not through abortion or killing, but by some other means. (I often half jokingly say . . . more monks and nuns.) That is the most nonviolent and effective method. So if you can't become a monk or a nun then practice other nonviolent methods of birth control."

When the Dalai Lama makes speeches, they are typically off-the-cuff and frequently full of surprises. Anecdotes pop up that often seem non sequiturs until the story comes together. Thus, he tells of Chinese soldiers, who were avid hunters, reaching Tibet; as the ducks began to recognize the uniforms and fear them, the soldiers had to don traditional Tibetan dress to lull the birds back. Or he will speak with empathy of Indian villagers forced to despoil their environment through quarrying to make a living. Anyone who comes to hear the Dalai Lama speak will most remember his beaming smile and ability to radiate joy, hope, and serenity even amid the enormous crowds who have come to listen.

When the Earth Summit was convened in Rio de Janeiro in 1992, it was billed as the largest gathering of world leaders for any meeting in history. The presence of the Dalai Lama, a global symbol of peace, patience, and environmental commitment, was a rare unifying presence for the diverse audience—with the possible exception of the unhappy Chinese government representatives. No international spiritual figure was more associated with ecological repair and protection. The Dalai Lama chose not to use the forum divisively by offering a devastating account of modern Tibetan history. Rather, he spoke of the new kind of global responsibility required for a planet that desperately needs to consider its values if it is to solve its environmental woes.

"Our Mother Earth Is Teaching Us a Lesson in Universal Responsibility"

GLOBAL FORUM, EARTH SUMMIT, RIO DE JANEIRO, BRAZIL, JUNE 7, 1992

*A*s the twentieth century draws to a close, we find that the world has grown smaller. The world's people have become almost one community. Political and military alliances have created large multinational groups; industry and international trade have produced a global economy. Worldwide communications are eliminating ancient barriers of distance, language, and race. We are also being drawn together by the grave problems we face: overpopulation, dwindling natural resources, and an environmental crisis that threatens our air, water, and trees, along with the vast number of beautiful life forms that are the very foundation of existence on this small planet we share.

I believe that, to meet the challenge of our times, human beings will have to develop a greater sense of universal responsibility. Each of us must learn to work not just for his or her own sake, family, or nation, but for the benefit of all mankind. Universal responsibility is the real key to human survival. It is the best foundation for world peace, the equitable use of natural resources, and, through concern for future generations, the proper care of the environment.

I have come to this international gathering of environmental leaders in a spirit of optimism and hope. The meetings here represent a threshold for humanity, the chance for our emerging global community to cooper-

Speech reprinted by permission of the official Agency of His Holiness the Dalai Lama in North America.

ate in an unprecedented manner. Even though it appears that the Earth Summit may, in some respects, fall short of what is needed, the very fact that it has taken place represents a tremendous achievement. That is why it is so heartening to see so many nongovernmental organizations here. Your role in forging a better future is absolutely essential, and while this role is still, within the United Nations, limited, it is expanding. . . . All of the organizations represented here have particular wants and needs, just, in fact, as individuals do. Without our collective efforts, however, the gains made here will be significantly less.

Whether we like it or not, we have all been born on this earth as part of one great family. Rich or poor, educated or uneducated, belonging to one nation, religion, ideology, or another, ultimately each of us is just a human being just like everyone else. We all desire happiness and do not want suffering. Furthermore, each of us has the same right to pursue happiness and avoid suffering. When you recognize that all beings are equal in this respect, you automatically feel empathy and closeness for them. Out of this, in turn, comes a genuine sense of universal responsibility: the wish to actively help others overcome their problems.

Of course this sort of compassion is, by nature, peaceful and gentle, but it is also very powerful. It is the true sign of inner strength. We do not need to become religious, nor do we need to believe in an ideology. All that is necessary is for each of us to develop our good human qualities.

The need for a sense of universal responsibility affects every aspect of human life. Nowadays, significant events in one part of the world eventually affect the entire planet. Therefore, we have to treat each major local problem as a global concern, from the moment it begins. We can no longer invoke the national, racial, or ideological barriers that separate us, without destructive repercussions. In the context of our new independence, considering the interests of others is clearly the best form of self-interest.

Interdependence, of course, is a fundamental law of nature. Not only myriad forms of life, but the most subtle levels of material phenomena, as well, are governed by interdependence. All phenomena, from the planet we inhabit to the oceans, clouds, forests, and flowers that surround us, arise in dependence upon subtle patterns of energy. Without their proper interaction, they dissolve and decay.

We need to appreciate this fact of nature far more than we have in the past. Our ignorance of it is directly responsible for many of the problems we face. For instance, tapping the limited resources of our world, particularly those of the developing nations, simply to fuel consumerism is disastrous. If it continues unchecked, eventually we will all suffer. We must respect the delicate matrix of life and allow it to replenish itself. The United Nations Environment Program warns, I'm told, that we are facing the most massive wave of extinctions in sixty-five million years. This fact is profoundly frightening. It must open our minds to the immense proportions of the crisis we face.

Ignorance of interdependence has not only harmed the natural environment, but human society as well.

Instead of caring for one another, we place most of our efforts for happiness in pursuing individual material consumption. We have become so engrossed in this pursuit that, without knowing it, we have neglected to foster the most basic human needs of love, kindness, and cooperation. This is very sad. We have to consider what we human beings really are. We are not machine-made objects. If we were merely mechanical entities, then machines themselves could alleviate all of our sufferings and fulfill our needs. However, since we are not solely material creatures, it is a mistake to seek fulfillment in external development alone.

Basically, we all cherish tranquility. For example, when spring comes, the days grow longer, there is more sunshine, the grass and trees come alive, and everything is fresh. People feel happy. In autumn, one leaf falls, then another, then all the beautiful flowers die, until we are surrounded by bare, naked plants. We do not feel so joyful. Why is this? Because, deep down, we desire constructive, fruitful growth and dislike things collapsing, dying, or being destroyed. Every destructive action goes against our basic nature; building, being constructive, is the human way.

To pursue growth properly, we need to renew our commitment to human values in many fields. Political life, of course, requires an ethical foundation, but science and religion, as well, should be pursued from a moral basis. Without it, scientists cannot distinguish between beneficial technologies and those which are merely expedient. The environmental damage surrounding us is the most obvious result of this confusion. In the case of religion, it is particularly necessary.

The purpose of religion is not to build beautiful churches or temples but to cultivate positive human qualities such as tolerance, generosity, and love. Every world religion, no matter what its philosophical view, is founded first and foremost on the precept that we must reduce our selfishness and serve others. Unfortunately, sometimes, in the name of religion, people cause more quarrels than they solve.

Practitioners of different faiths should realize that each religious tradition has intense intrinsic value as a means for providing mental and spiritual health.

There is a wonderful verse in the Bible about turning swords into ploughshares. It's a lovely image, a weapon transformed into a tool to serve basic human needs, symbolic of an attitude of inner and outer disarmament. In the spirit of this ancient message, I think it is important that we stress today the urgency of a policy that is long overdue: the demilitarization of the entire planet.

Demilitarization will free great human resources for protection of the environment, relief of poverty, and sustainable human development. It is my hope that the United Nations can soon help make this a reality. I have always envisioned the future of my own country, Tibet, to be founded on this basis. That would be a neutral, demilitarized sanctuary where weapons are forbidden and people live in harmony with nature. I have called this a Zone of Ahimsa or nonviolence. This is not merely a dream; it is precisely the way Tibetans tried to live for over a thousand years before our country was tragically invaded.

In Tibet, wildlife was protected in accordance with Buddhist principles. In the seventeenth century, we began enacting decrees to protect that environment, and so we may have been one of the first nations to have difficulty enforcing environmental regulations! However, mainly our environment was protected by our beliefs, which were instilled in us as children. Also, for at least the last three hundred years we had virtually no army. Tibet gave up the waging of war as an instrument of national policy in the sixth and seventh centuries.

I would like to conclude by stating that, in general, I feel optimistic about the future. The rapid changes in our attitude toward the earth are also a source of hope. As recently as a decade ago, we thoughtlessly devoured the resources of the world, as if there were no end to them. We failed to realize that unchecked consumerism was disastrous for both the environment and social welfare. Now, individuals and governments are seeking a new ecological and economic order.

I often joke that the moon and the stars look beautiful, but if any of us tried to live on them we would be miserable. This blue planet of ours is a delightful habitat. Its life is our life, its future our future. Indeed, the earth acts like a mother to all. Like children, we are dependent on [it]. In the face of such global problems as the greenhouse effect and depletion of the ozone layer, individual organizations and single nations are helpless. Unless we all work together, no solution can be found. Our mother earth is teaching us a lesson in universal responsibility.

I think we can say that, because of the lessons we have begun to learn, the next century will be friendlier, more harmonious, and less harmful. Compassion, the seeds of peace, will be able to flourish. I am very hopeful. At the same time, I believe that every individual has a responsibility to help guide our global family in the right direction. Good wishes alone are not enough; we have to assume responsibility. Large human movements spring from individual human initiatives.

The sponsor of these events, the United Nations, was founded out of the need to prevent military conflict. I am very moved that its mission has now grown to take on a new challenge—that of safeguarding the long-term health of ourselves and our planet. I hope and pray that, in the days ahead, each of us does all we can to see that the goal of creating a happier, more harmonious and healthier world is achieved.

REFERENCES

Grunfeld, Tom. *The Making of Modern Tibet.* New York: M. E. Sharp, 1996.

Gyatso, Tenzin, The Fourteenth Dalai Lama of Tibet. *Freedom in Exile: the Autobiography of the Dalai Lama.* New York: HarperCollins, 1999.

———. "Hope for Tibet's Environment." Speech by the Dalai Lama at the Endangered Tibet Conference, Sydney, Australia, September 28, 1996.

———. *The Path to Enlightenment.* Ithaca, NY: Snow Lion Publications, 1995.

———. "The Sheltering Tree of Independence— A Buddhist Monk's Reflections on Ecological Responsibility." Central Tibetan Administration web site. http://www.tibet.net/. 2003.

Gyatso, Tenzin, Dalai Lama, and Galen Rowell. *My Tibet.* London: Thames and Hudson, 1990.

Hilton, Isabel. *The Search for the Panchen Lama.* London: Viking, 1999.

Interview with the Venerable Thupten Rinpoche, Dhargyey Buddhist Centre, Dunedin, New Zealand, November 29, 2003.

Norbu, Thubten Figme, and Coliin Turnbull. *Tibet.* London: Chatto and Windus, 1969.

Shakya, Tsering. *The Dragon in the Land of Snows: A History of Modern Tibet since 1947.* New York: Columbia University Press, 1999.

Smith, Warren W. *Tibetan Nation: A History of Tibetan Nationalism and Sino-Tibetan Relations.* New York: Westview Press, 1996.

Tenzin, Sonam. "The Situation in Tibet." *http://hhdl.dharmakara.net/hhd-tibet.html.* 2004.

13. David Brower

UNITED STATES OF AMERICA

No matter where David Brower took the floor to speak about the need to change the way we treat the earth, generations of American environmentalists listened. Never was an environmental speech brought to more campaigns, campuses, conferences, and committee hearings. Never has a message been more potent in affecting the hearts, minds, and landscape of a nation.

For well over fifty years, until he succumbed to cancer in the autumn of 2000, at age eighty-eight, David Brower preached what he called "The Sermon." Constantly updated with examples and anecdotes to meet the current circumstances, the speech's fundamental appeal remained the same. Brower's was a categorical call to respect the limits and fragility of the earth, and an expression of faith that humans could yet conserve resources, preserve wilderness, and restore their planet. The message was so powerful precisely because Brower was not simply a speech maker but also an activist. He was no ordinary activist, however. There is a surprising consensus that David Brower was probably *the* most effective American conservationist who ever lived. If Ralph Nader and U.S. cabinet secretaries agree on this accolade, it must be more than mere hyperbole.

The quality that made Brower's perspective most compelling was an internal ethical compass that directed him to positions that were often considered "radical" but almost invariably were ecologically "right." Brower's uncompromising voice for preserving the dwindling corners of the planet that were still "wild" set a standard and an agenda for an American conservation movement that he was responsible for popularizing. His list of achievements spans a sixty-year career, far too long for a cursory biographical sketch.

Born in 1912, Brower grew up in Berkeley, California. His mother lost her sight when he was eight, and Brower would often take her for walks on the surrounding scenic hillsides. He would later speculate that "seeing for somebody else" may have sharpened his appreciation for beauty in natural things. But it seemed that adventure more than beauty initially brought him to nature. An accomplished mountain climber as a youth, he is credited as having made the first human ascent of some seventy peaks around the world, thirty-three in the Sierra Nevada alone. Brower was so good at climbing that the U.S. Army drafted him to teach soldiers how to climb, and eventually he won a medal of honor during World War II.

Brower joined the Sierra Club (at that time a San Francisco-based mountaineering and conservation society) in 1933, became a board member in 1941, and became editor of the organization's magazine after he returned from the war. Finally, in 1952, Brower was appointed the Sierra Club's first executive director. The organization would never be the same. His ambitious vision moved it from a relatively unknown, elitist, local, primarily hiking club with two thousand members to the largest environmental group in America. Most of all, Brower adopted a nation's conservation agenda as his own. (Today, with six hundred thousand members, the Sierra Club claims to be America's largest grassroots environmental group.)

Not every one in the club liked his style or increasingly uncompromising positions. In 1969, the Sierra Club's somewhat conservative board relieved Brower of his duties as director, ostensibly because of his penchant for politicizing environmental issues and disregard for budgets in the heat of key campaigns. Saddened but undaunted, Brower started another organization, Friends of the Earth, that soon went international and in fact exceeded the influence of the Sierra Club. With branches in seventy countries, it is the largest environmental network on the planet. Brower also founded the League of Conservation Voters, which has been extraordinarily effective at targeting and "taking out" anti-environmental members of

Congress. The Earth Island Institute is yet another Brower invention, with an international agenda of human rights and ecology. Countless other initiatives and coalitions bear his stamp.

Brower pioneered new tactics for a fledgling environmental movement. He published full-page ads in major newspapers. He produced advocacy films. He encouraged boycotts. As editing was his first formal profession, he started "exhibit format" books: oversized tomes that could only fit on coffee tables, but which paid testimony to the breathtaking loveliness of sites for which he was fighting. And he got his hands dirty in the federal politics of Washington and legislative lobbies.

Although organizations may rise and fall and tactics change, the many natural treasures that Brower almost single-handedly saved endure and are testimonies to his genius. The first campaigns that thrust him onto the national stage were intended to save the integrity of rivers in the West. The Bureau of Reclamation proposed a dam near the confluence of the Green and Yampa Rivers, creating a reservoir that would flood large parts of Dinosaur National Monument.

For the first time in modern history, Brower cobbled together a broad alliance of ecologists, sports enthusiasts, hikers, and general citizens to stop an environmentally destructive, government-sponsored initiative. The campaign challenged the technical and geological assumptions of the project as much as its existential and aesthetic impacts. With the Bureau's competency and its raison d'etre of delivering water to an arid American West under attack, the agency responded furiously. It decried Brower's "disinformation campaign," produced movies in its own defense, and galvanized its allies in Congress—to no avail. With advertisements, books, and films, Brower and his Sierra Club–led coalition managed to circumvent this bureaucracy and reach the corridors of power in Washington. The dam was cancelled and the National Park was not flooded.

The scenario was repeated again and again in what are now considered legendary battles to preserve the integrity of the Grand Canyon. Hydroelectric dams were proposed for Marble Gorge near the Utah-Arizona border, and then in the Lower Granite Gorge. Brower published full-page advertisements in the *New York Times* and the *San Francisco Chronicle* with headlines asking "Should We Also Flood the Sistine Chapel So Tourists Can Get Nearer to the Ceiling?" The public's answer resonated all the way to Capital Hill—and, sure enough, the dams were cancelled once again. Brower's victories against seemingly impossible odds catapulted him into an unrequested role as the country's leading conservationist, "the heir to John Muir." Brower's success also lost the Sierra Club its status as a tax-exempt organization, as the federal government did the Bureau of Reclamation's bidding and sought new ways to fight back.

Subsequent efforts would save key stretches in the Cascades and Great Smoky Mountains, rivers in Kentucky, wilderness areas from Maine to Alaska, as well as habitats for any number of animals.

Not all campaigns were successful, and Brower was ever critical of his own slip-ups. While a junior member of the Sierra Club board in 1949, he joined his colleagues in supporting the Bridget Canyon Dam. For almost forty years, he bemoaned his insufficient efforts to stop the Glen Canyon Dam, which flooded hundreds of kilometers of exquisite canyons around the Colorado River in Arizona and Utah. Presumably, he traded complicity on the Glen Canyon project for cancellation of the Echo Park and Split Mountain Dams, a cancellation that saved Dinosaur Park. Soon after, he would acknowledge that among the most important lessons he ever learned was not to trade away a place you don't know to save a place you care about.

Brower held an almost Romantic belief in the instincts of uncorrupted youth. Part of his inclination to start new organizations and initiatives may have been motivated by his desire to open the doorway for new leadership in the environmental movement. Rather than seek out experts, he befriended people with "fire in their bellies."

When Adam Werbach, a young Sierra Club activist at Brown University, first wrote him a letter in 1989, Brower, ever the editor, mostly responded by correcting the student's grammar. But when Werbach approached him again, right after graduating, about running for Sierra Club president, Brower immediately embraced the idea, helped craft a campaign message, and threw his prestige behind the effort. The press made much of Brower's candidate taking back the Sierra Club presidency. Werbach recalls Brower's most basic advice: "Say what you think. Don't be ashamed if you don't know everything. Don't compromise."

Although Brower was universally admired, no one claims that he was an easy person to work with. Once set on an opinion, he did not bend. His "politically incorrect" stands on issues of population and immigration occasionally left a younger generation of environmentalists uncomfortable. He seemed to take pleasure in resigning from positions over issues of principle, even on matters that seemed trivial to others. This was not a mean-spirited pedantry; he could not contain his convictions and passions, even with regards to trivial matters.

Brower brought his engaging oratorical style to what quickly became a classic environmental oration, "The Sermon." John McPhee's 1971 characterization of Brower in *Encounters with the Archdruid* remains definitive and may be the most compelling environmental biography ever written. When the book was published, Brower was almost sixty years old and ostensibly nearing the end of a brilliant career. In retrospect, however, the biography was but a mid-career report.

McPhee described Brower's presentation like this: "David Brower, who talks to groups all over the country about conservation, refers to what he says as 'The Sermon.' He travels light; he never seems far from home— one tie, one suit. He calls it his preacher suit. He has given the sermon at universities, in clubs, in meeting halls, and once in a cathedral (he has otherwise not been in a church for thirty years), and while he talks he leans up to the lectern with his feet together and his knees slightly bent, like a skier. . . . His tone of voice, soft and mournful, somehow concentrates the intensity of his words. He speaks calmly, almost ironically. . . . To put it mildly, there is something evangelical about Brower."

Brower almost invariably opened with his metaphor of Creation and the ephemeral and destructive role of human history relative to that of the earth. And he would always finish with a call to arms that centered on the personal involvement of the listeners: "Are you willing to pay more for steak, if cattle graze on level ground and not on erodable hills?" "Are you willing to pay more for electricity, if the power plant doesn't pollute air or water?" "You are villains not to share your apples with worms. Bite the worms. They won't hurt nearly as much as the insecticide does." Or, if he was in a less feisty mood, he would settle for a quote from Goethe about individual potential and responsibility. In between these fixtures, he would tackle most of the seminal challenges facing the planet, even those considered sticky or dangerous by mainstream environmental interests. What stayed the same were the clarity of the arguments, undiluted by civility or political fashions and charged with a pervasive sense of urgency.

As environmental philosopher David Orr eulogized: "These were some of the greatest contributions David made to environmental strategy and thought in recent years: avoid compromises that involved irretrievable sacrifices; stand firm, and have the courage to subordinate pragmatism to principle."

The following is a 1992 version of Brower's "Sermon." The central themes could just as easily have been lifted from one of his 1950s speeches, and they remain more relevant than ever today.

"The Sermon"

TWELFTH ANNUAL E. F. SCHUMACHER LECTURE,
STOCKBRIDGE, MASSACHUSETTS, OCTOBER 1992

I thought it would be useful to do an exercise in perspective relating to time. Squeeze the age of the earth, four-and-a-half-billion years, into the Six Days of Creation for an instant replay. Creation begins Sunday midnight. No life until about Tuesday noon. Life comes aboard, with more and more species, more variety, more genetic variability. Millions upon millions of species come aboard, and millions leave. By Saturday morning at seven, there's enough chlorophyll so that fossil fuels begin to form. At four o'clock in the afternoon, the great reptiles are onstage; at nine o'clock that night they're hauled off. But they had a five hour run.

Nothing like us appears until three or four minutes before midnight, depending on whose facts you like better. No Homo sapiens until a half-minute before midnight. We got along as hunter-gatherers pretty well, but the population couldn't have been very big; for those of you concerned about how many hunter-gatherers the Earth can sustain, the range I've heard is between five [million] and twenty-five million people. Then we got onto this big kick: we wanted *more* of us, we wanted to push forests out of the way so we could feed more people. We wanted to shift from hunting and gathering to starch, and thereby start the first big energy crisis (because the greatest energy shortage on earth is of fuel wood). So we got into agriculture one-and-a-half seconds before midnight. That recently. By the next half-second, we had been so successful that the forests ringing the Mediterranean Sea, for example, were reduced to the pitiful fragments that are the Cedars of Lebanon. That was in one half-second. At about the end of that half-second—we're now one *second* before midnight—after all this time of life being on earth, we began to invent religions.

If I could go back to a point in history to try to get things to come out differently, I would go back and tell Moses to go up the mountain again and get the other tablet. Because the Ten Commandments just tell us what we're supposed to do with one another, not a word about our relationship with the earth (at least not according to any of the translations I've seen so far). Genesis starts with these commands: multiply, replenish the

Speech reprinted with permission of Kenneth, Robert, Barbara, and John Brower.

Earth, and subdue it. We have multiplied very well, we have replenished our population very well, we have subdued all too well, and we don't have any other instruction. The Catholic Church just put "stewardship" in its vocabulary within the last seven or eight years!

So here we are now. A third of a second before midnight: Buddha. A quarter of a second: Christ. A fortieth of a second: the industrial revolution. We began to change ecosystems a great deal with agriculture, but now we can do it with spades—coal-powered, fossil-fuel-powered spades. We begin taking the earth apart, getting ideas about what we can do, on and on, faster and faster. At one-eightieth of a second before midnight, we discover oil, and we build a civilization that depends on it. Then, at two-hundredths of a second, we discover how to split the atom, and we begin the GNP race. (I've been told it was the Soviets who started it, and the United States didn't want anybody to have a grosser national product than ours.) But that's not the race we need; we must change how we think about GNP.

That reminds me of a paradigm shift I've had in mind recently. Through the years I've been quoting Adlai Stevenson in the last speech he gave as our ambassador to the United Nations. It was July 1965 when he said: "We travel together, passengers on a little space ship, dependent upon its vulnerable reserves of air and soil, all committed for our safety to its security and peace, preserved from annihilation only by the care, the work, and I will say the love we give our fragile craft. We cannot maintain it half fortunate and half miserable, half confident, half despairing, half slave to the ancient enemies of mankind and half free in a liberation of resources undreamed of until this day. No craft, no crew can travel safely with such vast contradictions. On their resolution depends the survival of us all."

I wish every person who ever occupied the Oval Office had heard this passage and committed it to memory and done something about it; it would be a totally different world right now if that had happened. But I think Adlai Stevenson, if he were here now, might accept an editorial suggestion or two. One, we have not liberated resources; we are extirpating resources. Two, let's rethink: our global conditions are not so clearly defined as to be half one way and half another way; it's more like 5 percent and 95 percent in the inequity quotient of this earth.

What is happening? I think we're getting better and better at having despair and needing to have it. But I'll tell you about the people of Ladakh, the place in India where Helena Norberg-Hodge has been working for half of every year for the past seventeen years. She is trying to bring information from Ladakh to us while also trying to prevent too much of our information from getting to *them* (unfortunately, she's losing that struggle a little bit). The Sierra Club has just come out with a book entitled *Ancient Futures*, with pictures of the people in Ladakh. When you look at these pictures, there's no great evidence of wealth there, but there is evidence of something else. You see some of the most beautiful faces; you see some of the nicest smiles; you see some inner happiness that you don't see in our supermarkets or on Park Avenue. Where is the despair?

Another thing that is happening is that we are not getting the truth. This is "the Era of Disinformation." Let me tell you a true story about a Cree Indian who came down to a city for the first time, to a courtroom, and sat in the witness chair and was asked, "Do you promise to tell the truth, the whole truth, and nothing but the truth?" And his answer, according to the interpreter, was: "I can't tell the truth; I can only say what I know." That is so beautiful. It has something in it that we, including environmentalists, lack an awful lot of: it has humility. It's true for all of us, because we don't know the truth.

To take that further, it seems to me that the more we know, the less we know. I have a beautiful example of that, relating to genetic diversity. When Bernie Frank was the head of the Division of Forest Influences, United States Forest Service—and this must have been during the late 1950s—he said, "We know next to nothing about forest soils." If there was anything known about forest soils, that's where it would have been known. Four years ago, at a conference in Berkeley on restoring the planet earth, we had some experts on mycorhizal fungi, fungi that live in symbiotic relationships with the roots of most tree and plant species. These experts have been studying them for quite awhile; they're learning more and more about how many different species of mycorhizal fungi there are and how complicated the relationships are between the fungi and the roots, but they still can't define these relationships exactly. As for the general knowledge of forest soils in the forest industry, forestry schools, and Forest Service today, it is even less than it was thirty-five years ago.

E. O. Wilson tells us in *The Diversity of Life* that there are something like four thousand different species of bacteria per pinch of soil. We are familiar with the concept of genetic diversity—according to Wilson we have identified 1.4 million species of plants and animals—but we have no idea how many more exist. The estimates I've heard range from 5 to 80 million! So, as we discover more, we discover that we know less and less about more and more. This is something that should instill some humility into us. It should give us the idea that our agricultural binge—our whole Industrial Age binge—cannot go on. We need to rethink, and our institutions are not ready for it.

To return to the "instant replay": let's back up to a hundredth of a second before midnight. That's when I was born. I mention this for one reason: a huge amount of environmental destruction has taken place since the early 1900s. The population of the earth has tripled. The population of California has gone up by a factor of twelve. The earth as a whole has used four times as many resources in those brief eighty years as in all previous history. In our great state of California we had, when I was born, six thousand miles of salmon streams; now we're down to two hundred. We had roughly 80 percent of the original stand of redwoods, which grow nowhere else but California (except for a few migrants that slipped into Oregon, not knowing what they were doing); that 80 percent is down to 4.5 percent. I go into these numbers because all of this has happened in eighty years.

In the past twenty years, we have created enough new, man-made deserts—I say "man-made" because women had very little to do with it— to equal the area of cropland in China. We've lost soil through erosion, paving, development, condominiums, suburbia, and inundation by such things as the nonrenewable hydroelectric development in Quebec (the first stage of which, in the James Bay project, inundated four thousand square miles of forest). Now, if you've just learned that there may be four thousand species of bacteria per pinch of soil and you think of the things we're throwing at that soil to get more and faster productivity, you realize that we're on the wrong track. We're wiping out species before we have the foggiest idea that they're there. As Noel Brown of the United Nations Environment Program put it, we may already have destroyed the cure for AIDS. Jay Hair of the National Wildlife Federation tells that, when his daughter was three, her doctor said, "She has four days to live," and, when he told that story a few years ago, she was then in college, doing all right. The medicine that cured her disease was derived from the rosy periwinkle, which grew only in Madagascar and is now extinct. We're wiping out species everywhere we can possibly reach.

Now it's midnight, and there's a new day coming. What are you going to do with it? *You're* going to have an important role in what happens in this new day or the next six days or whatever it may be.

But I don't think we're quite ready for it. To begin with, we feel that we have to blame somebody. It's none of us—none of us is guilty for all this, of course—so let's blame the economists. I quote Hazel Henderson: "Economics is a form of brain damage." I heard Fritz Schumacher, when he was lecturing out in Marin County, California, tell this story: There were three people arguing about whose profession was the oldest. The doctor said, "Mine is the oldest, because it took a procedure to get Eve out of Adam." The architect said, "But it took an architect to build a universe out of Chaos." And the economist said, "And who do you think created Chaos?" That is a beautiful story, and it should be carved in stone where the E. F. Schumacher Society has its headquarters. Hazel is an economist, and Fritz was an economist, and even they blame the economists!

Economists are in trouble because they leave out of their calculations two terribly important factors, which they name and do nothing about: the cost to the earth and the cost to the future. In fact, as David Orr pointed out in his lecture, they discount these factors. That implies they're essentially of no value. Leave out the cost to the earth; leave out the cost to the future, and whatever your final number is, it's worthless. We're getting worthless advice from those economists who are giving most of the advice about how to run our government, including advice about the General Agreement on Tariffs and Trade. One of my definitions of GATT is that it's the end run around the environmental gains of the last century. It is just pure gravy for the transnationals.

We've got to do something about one of our worst addictions: the addiction to growth. All of the candidates running for office are saying, "We must have a growing economy." If they want to keep it growing the way it has been growing, we absolutely must not have a growing economy. We must have a *sound* economy, a *sustainable* economy. They haven't come up with one single notion of how to move it in that direction. What are we going to do besides grow, grow, grow? In your own body, where the wildness within you puts in a control factor, you have a thymus. Civilization needs a thymus. It needs the word for "enough." But "enough" doesn't sound strong enough; Italian has the right word, "*basta.*" We must say basta to the kind of growth we've been practicing.

Another thing we need, as Adlai Stevenson pointed out, is love for the fragile craft Earth and all its inhabitants. We haven't been good about that. One small way we could show love would be not just to criticize somebody who's done something we don't like but to thank somebody who's done something we do like. We don't thank the people who deserve it. Think back to Richard Nixon when he first came into office: he made the best speech on population control any president has ever made, before or since. He hedged it a little bit, but nobody has touched what he did. Certainly not Ronald Reagan or George Bush. John Ehrlichman told me in 1969, "That speech was a dud. It bombed at the box office. No support."

So I have asked many of my audiences, "How many people think we have a population problem?" Hands up all over the place. "How many people thanked Richard Nixon for what he did?" On the average, only one hand in a thousand.

Jimmy Carter got into the same kind of box on the subject of nuclear power and whether or not to build breeder reactors. Legislation favoring these reactors had passed Congress. He wanted to veto it but felt that he had no alternative except to sign it. I was one of thirteen people who met with Carter to discuss the bind he was in, and eventually it was a letter I signed, which was written by Jeff Knight, Friends of the Earth's energy specialist, that convinced Carter he could veto it. He did. I have also asked audiences, "How many thought that legislation needed to be vetoed?" Almost everybody. "How many thanked Jimmy Carter?" One in a thousand. Yet this is one way we can show a bit of love, by thanking somebody doing something right. We don't all have to do everything right, but if a person does one thing right, then maybe, with thanks, that person will do something else right. Just think for a moment what might have happened to Richard Nixon if that speech had had the support it deserved—he might have been a completely different Richard Nixon.

I have my own axiom: not to love thy neighbor as much as thyself but to love thy neighbor more than thyself. This might be quite useful to practice, because out of that behavior something else happens. For example, it could help us be more aware of "the Law of the Minimum": that it doesn't matter how many plants there are if you don't have land; it doesn't matter how much land you have if you don't have soil on it; it doesn't matter how much soil you have if you don't have water for it; it doesn't matter how much water you have if you don't have air; it doesn't matter how much air if you don't have oxygen; or how much oxygen if you don't have judgment; or how much judgment if you don't have love. It would certainly help our transnationals and the "Misfortune 500" if they considered the Law of the Minimum.

This interrelation is terribly important, and there are parts of it that we're not thinking about. I'll just touch for a moment on oxygen. The amount of oxygen on earth is decreasing because we're getting rid of the world's forests as fast as we possibly can. While a tree is alive, chlorophyll locks up carbon and frees oxygen. But when a great tree falls, it may take two thousand years—or, depending on its chemistry and climate, maybe only two hundred or five hundred or nine hundred years—for it to turn into soil again. During that time it's going to require back all the oxygen it freed so that it can feed Robert Frost's "slow, smokeless burning of decay." This decay is absolutely essential to complete the continuing revolution of the cycles of life, particularly the carbon cycle, but it does require oxygen. Simultaneously, we are releasing the carbon that was buried and became fossil fuels over the course of five hundred million years.

We have quite a bit of locked-up carbon that could *stay* locked up, and what do we do with it? We dig it up as fast as we can and put it out as many tailpipes as we can, and we say, "This is jobs." If you're worried about the ozone barrier, then you've got to realize that the damage is going to continue for a long time. CFCs are migrating up; they are destroying ozone now and will continue to destroy it for a hundred years even if their use is stopped today. (I got this number out of the special fall 1992 issue of *Time*, "Beyond the Year 2000: Preparing for the Next Millennium.")

So for you twenty-year-olds I've got a lot of sympathy. People my age can "check out" reasonably soon, but what is going to happen as this atmospheric imbalance continues to worsen? What is going to heal it? I don't know enough high-school chemistry to know anything but this: if you want O_3 back, you've got to have some O_2 to play with. But we're getting rid of it. So what do we do? People are talking about a carbon tax and other measures, but what we need to do is pay the people who have forests and pay the countries that are storing fossil fuels to keep them where they are. We need to slow down their use as fast as we possibly can, to use every bit of science and technology and humanity we can to slow it down. To say basta to what we've been up to. It's terribly important, if you like to breathe. And what are we going to do about the soil if they keep doing to the soil what they've done? There's a big constituency out there of people who like to eat, who like to breathe, and we've got to organize this group. . . .

We're going on the idea, the myth, that hydroelectric energy is renewable, but it's *not* renewable, because it depends on reservoirs. It's a one-shot thing. It's mining the dam site: you use the dam site up, and that's it. And it's messing around with rivers, taking the meanders out. Rivers know what they're doing; meanders slow the river down, rechanneling it and recharging aquifers. When aquifers can't recharge, what happens? The Kissimmee River in Florida: the Corps of Engineers straightened it out. Now that they've realized their mistake, they're spending fifty million dollars to put the bends back in. Well, that's jobs.

We've got to find alternative forms of energy, certainly alternatives to wasting energy. We've got to cut off these hydroprojects right now. Only God can make a dam site, and we've occupied a lot of them already. We don't need to go on in China, in India, in Japan. I want Hetch Hetchy dam in Yosemite down so that we get another Yosemite Valley in our park. That can be done. Because of the numbers I was throwing at you just now—the resources used up, the population increased—we need a completely new look, a new insight, a new vision of what we're going to do. We've got to worry about numbers. We've got to worry about our appetite, and the best place to start is right at home with our overconsumption.

We can stop overconsuming immediately. Just keep your wallet in your pocket, and we'll cut consumption down fast. Yet, as E. O. Wilson says about these numbers, we aren't willing to do anything really drastic. In the case of population control, an acceptable limit is no more than two children per family. I would prefer just one per family, but that means in a short time there will be no cousins anymore. So leave it at two per family, in the families that want them and can take care of them. I firmly believe in life after birth; population control enhances life.

The big pressure is *our* pressure, our overconsumption. And we have our own Third World, as you know; the homeless aren't using much, people in the ghettoes aren't using much. But those of us who aren't poor are the problem. Buy, buy, buy; consume, consume, consume; toss it away, toss it away.

This brings me to a key area for action: we have to free the media, break the sound barrier. We've got to get the word out, and the media *can't* get the word out because most of them are indentured. The alternative press, of course, is not indentured, and there are two specific, contrasting examples of fairly "free" magazines. *Ms.* magazine carries no ads. Its editors made that decision because they wanted to be free to speak. They didn't want advertisers looking over their shoulders, and they had firm ideas about what they wanted to tell their audience. They needed to have a circulation of 150,000 to make it work without ads, and, as I understand it, they have 250,000, and it's working. That's one way to freedom.

But the other way, strangely enough, is in a magazine that is absolutely loaded with ads—and I don't approve of all of them, by any means—*The New Yorker.* Remember what *The New Yorker* did under William Shawn? It gave an entire issue to John Hershey's *Hiroshima.* One issue, maybe it was two, on Rachel Carson's *Silent Spring.* Three issues to *Encounters with the Archdruid,* John McPhee's interview with me. Again and again, *The New Yorker* carries pieces that are hard-hitting. I haven't seen it for the past three weeks—I travel too much—but I understand that even with the new editor it's still hard-hitting. In "The Talk of the Town" this week there's apparently an article providing grounds for the impeachment of George Bush. They are bold. They don't give a damn what their advertisers want, but they get them anyway. Their boldness makes them a required medium for advertisers to advertise in. I wish the rest of the media would try that out.

Incidentally, taking a stand on environmental issues is one thing they don't try out. I have been interviewed seven times by *Time* magazine. They have not put in a word of what I said. The first time was when the Alaska pipeline was the cover story. I had a long interview on that. Phil Herrera (he was then the environment editor) put a lot of that material in and submitted it. But took out everything I'd said (although they left in a picture of me). Phil said it was taken out by the advertising department.

So we *do* have to free the media. They should all be willing and able to say what they think without having to look over their shoulder and wonder, "What will the advertiser think if I do this?" That goes for PBS and NPR as well as anybody else. We *must* free the media, and that will happen only when corporations learn how to operate with conscience. When the corporations do that and the media are free, we'll get our democracy back because the people running for office won't have to go to the Fortune 500 or the transnationals to fund their campaigns. We'll do more of what Jerry Brown was doing with his 800 number: no more than a hundred dollars from anybody. With that 800 number, by that process, he raised *twelve million* dollars.

What else can we do? Let me tell you about Sam LaBudde. Although you may not know the name, I think you know what he did: he took his courage and his camcorder, which had been given to him by Earth Island Institute and Earth Trust, and he got a job aboard a fishing ship, working as a cook. He said the camcorder was a toy given to him by his father and he wanted to see how it worked. In the July 1989 issue of *The Atlantic* there was a good cover story on him, written by the writing member of our family, Kenneth Brower. Sam did something that anybody could do, at least anybody who is thirty-two and a biologist. He got aboard that ship and took camcorder footage of what was going on in the industry. One of the best shots shows a set of nets surrounding a school of tuna located under dolphins, and the nets bring in three tuna and kill more than a hundred dolphins. Hundreds of thousands of dolphins have been killed by the tuna fishing industry. Sam's tape has been made into specials and news broadcasts around the world.

That tape took a Fortune 500 company, H. J. Heinz, and turned it around. After a little bit of struggle and some full-page ads, Earth Island finally got Bumble Bee to admit they weren't telling the truth about their fishing methods. So the American tuna industry is now giving you "dolphin-safe" tuna. Mexico's tuna industry continues to kill dolphins, and they accuse us of eco-imperialism for saying we will not accept their tuna because it kills dolphins. They're being supported by the GATT philosophy. GATT says Mexico is right and we are wrong to protect dolphins and to be proud of it. What we can do now is to help fund—I think Heinz could help fund—research and development by Mexico that will enable them to catch tuna, as Heinz is doing, without killing dolphins.

They might just as well learn how to do that, because if they kill all the dolphins, where will they look for their tuna? It's like the old-growth forests: if we kill all the old-growth forests for the sake of jobs, what will the lumber industry do when the forests are gone?

Next, Sam LaBudde went aboard a driftnet ship. These ships set out thirty-five thousand miles of driftnet every night. Then they haul it in. It catches fish that shouldn't be caught, that need to grow some more and go back to the streams where they came from. Whales, seals, dolphins, marine birds, and turtles are killed in the driftnets. Their lives are wasted. Sam sums it up as strip-mining the high seas. His footage on that has brought changes at the United Nations level. Japan has recently said it will stop using driftnets. Thirty-two years old, bold, with camcorder: then Sam went up to Alaska, where young Alaskans were machine-gunning walruses to trade their ivory tusks for drugs.

By this time Sam was getting a little depressed, so he came up with the idea of an Earth Corps. I've been working on that: an Earth Corps to take up where the Peace Corps leaves off. The Earth Corps would be global, whereas the Peace Corps is just a national thing; it hasn't been very interested in the environment. It's more interested now, but it still isn't willing to displease the transnational corporations. *We* want to be able to displease them, if necessary. A corps like this will help to start the paradigm shift that must come about. We cannot afford to continue feeding our economy, our greed, and what my wife calls our "greedlock."

We're running out of some of the things in the Law of the Minimum; we're going over the edge in a so-called Giant Step for Mankind that nobody needs. We've got to avoid it, to do a one-eighty, to make a tire-screeching U-turn and not go over that edge.

I can see no better way to do this than by making a major effort to go back to where we've been, leaving the wildness that remains wild, fulfilling the maxim of Henry David Thoreau, "In wildness is the preservation of the world." We must honor wildness, for as Nancy Newhall writes in *This is the American Earth,* "The wilderness holds answers to questions we have not yet learned how to ask." It's exciting to discover—it's *fun* to discover—how nature works: to find out, for example, that *we* have to make cement at 1800° Fahrenheit, while a *hen* can make better cement per unit at 103°, and a *clam* can do it at seawater temperature. What's the trick? We don't know, but I wouldn't mind finding out. Other examples: the bombardier beetle makes actual steam in an internal chamber and fires it at its enemies; another beetle does something to the surface tension of water that makes water skaters sink and become its prey. The giant water bug injects, say, a frog, with a chemical that dissolves everything inside the frog's skin—turns it into liquid—and then the bug sucks it out.

So there's all this exciting stuff to discover. We haven't spoiled it all, and we can save all that's left of it. We can go back to where we've been and do better. To science and technology, we can add humanity and compassion and go back. Who will do this? Well, we want some teams. We want to build restoration teams on which all the creeds are represented, all the colors, all the ages (I still want something to do), all the classes, and all the sexes. We want to build teams that are willing to put aside their favorite prejudices and get into a symbiotic, instead of an aggressive, relationship with others. We don't agree on a great many things, but we *can* agree that we've got to restore the damage we've done to Earth.

We're trying to get a restoration movement going at Earth Island. We want *every* institution to get involved in it. It's the alternative to war. One of the problems with peace is that it's been rather dull—it's not much fun; if you put restoration into it, it can be great fun, and it can be profit-making. If you don't think so, try taking your car to the shop or your body to your doctor, and find out who's making money. You're glad to pay it: the car works better or your body works better (you hope), so it's a good investment.

There is no better investment, whatever it costs, than getting Earth's life-support systems back in life-supporting, working order. People are worried about the taxing and spending that might be required to pay these costs, but we've been borrowing and spending as well as deferring maintenance and replacement, for the past twelve years. We need to pay for restoration because we need to save the wild. If we were to ask the twenty-year-olds and under in the audience, "Would you be willing to pay the bill for restoring the earth so we can live on it?" I think I know what the answer would be. We have the opportunity now to invest in prosperity, to invest in ecological sanity, and to invest in an understanding of how the earth works and what we have to do to help it work. We can help nature heal. But we can't be so arrogant as to think we've got all the answers, because we haven't; if we're not careful, we'll make mistakes like bringing more rabbits to Australia or something worse.

We're getting rid of wildness before we have the faintest idea of what we're eliminating. We have got to stop. We can stop by going back to where we've been and doing better there, not by going on further with the idea that we need more and more and more. I think we're getting tired of trashing wildness. It's not making us happy and it's not making us healthy; it's making us miserable and despairing.

So here's a task; it's a challenging one. I've now talked to more than 270,000 people. At the end of my pitch for restoration I have asked each audience—and now I'm asking you—"How many people in this audience would be willing to commit at least a year of their lives, out of the next ten, to volunteering for this restoration effort, either getting paid or not?" [Show of hands in audience.] That's pretty good.

The point is that this is the public wish, as I have seen it represented in these audiences. They haven't just been members and friends of the Schumacher Society; they've been media people; they've been the Physicians for Social Responsibility; they've been directors, writers, and producers in Hollywood; they've been the audiences I talked to in Japan and in the ex-U.S.S.R. Wherever I have gone, at least two-thirds of the people put their hands up. So the wish is there. The ability to *lead* needs to be worked on; we need leaders, we need organizers, and of course it would help to have a little money. If *you* follow through and help organize this and enlist others to help organize it, then it will happen. If it doesn't, we've had it. Civilization as we know it will have had it. We can't continue going that way, we've got to turn around.

We can do it; the talent is here. My old mountaineer friend, William H. Murray, in his book *The Scottish Himalayan Expedition* expresses his deep admiration for a couplet from Goethe, "Whatever you can do, or dream you can, begin it; boldness has genius, power, and magic in it."

Do you have magic in you? You bet. Because the minimum of genetic material—the amount necessary to give all the messages about where our hundred million rods and cones go, and about the whole works, conscious mind and unconscious—would fit in a sphere a sixth of an inch in diameter. That sums up the minimum genetic material needed to produce the hundred billion people who have ever lived. That magic, that miracle of life, has been passed on for three-and-a-half-billion years. In that time, millions of species went by the wayside, but we didn't. From when it began three-and-a-half-billion years ago, to everyone here: no mistakes, no failure. So a little tiny part of each of us is three-and-a-half-billion years old, and everything that's alive is related. How did this miracle happen? What shaped it? What informed it? It wasn't civilization, because there wasn't any. It was something else. It was *wilderness.* That's all there was. Trial and error, success and failure, symbiosis; wilderness made it work. Wilderness is the ultimate encyclopedia, holding, just as Nancy Newhall put it, answers to more questions than we have yet learned how to ask.

That's the magic in *you.* You've got it; let it out.

REFERENCES

Brazil, Eric. "David Brower Dies at 88, Militant Visionary Inspired a Generation to Save the Earth." *San Francisco Examiner,* November 6, 2000.

"David Ross Brower, 1912–2000." *www.earthisland.org.* 2005.

Evans, Brock. Personal communication, September 14, 2002.

Kupfer, David. "David Brower on Wilderness, Dams, and the Future." Interview. *Earth First Journal,* 2000.

McPhee, John. *Encounters with the Archdruid: Narratives about a Conservationist and Three of His Natural Enemies.* New York: Farrar, Straus and Giroux, 1971.

Orr, David. "Brower Returns to Earth." *Earth First Journal,* 2000.

"Sierra Club Mourns David Brower's Death." Press release. November 6, 2000.

Werbach, Adam. Personal communication, September 21, 2003.

14. Ken Saro-Wiwa

NIGERIA

The environmental movement has its share of martyrs. Yet, when Ken Saro-Wiwa, the Nigerian academic, politician, author, and conservation advocate, was hanged on November 10, 1994, along with eight other activists, the sense of loss and subsequent reverberations were especially profound. Ken Saro-Wiwa's struggle on behalf of his Ogoni people and their lands is one of the many instances where human and environmental rights overlap. The execution may have left a mark of infamy on an oppressive military regime in Nigeria, and exposed Shell Oil's unscrupulous despoliation of a developing country's lands for petroleum profits. But it could not erase Saro-Wiwa's call for justice, and the achievements brought by his campaign to stop the despoliation of the Ogoni people's land.

Most people do not realize that of Africa's four hundred million residents, a full quarter live in Nigeria. The Ogoni tribe constitutes but a tiny minority of five hundred thousand. They share a small 404-square-mile patch in the Niger Delta with some five million members of other tribes. And their tragedy became symbolic of the impotence of the many indigenous peoples who suffer the unhappy coincidence of living on lands that hold valuable natural resources.

For most of his life, there was little about Saro-Wiwa's diverse and flourishing vocations that would suggest he would ultimately be best known internationally as an environmental activist. Indeed, for most of his career he was a successful academic, as well as a television producer and an author of some renown. Yet it was only natural that Saro-Wiwa, as the eldest son of a leader of the Ogoni tribe, would embrace a role of community leader. Born in 1941, he was nineteen when Nigeria was granted independence by the English colonial government in 1960. In retrospect, it was the discovery of oil in the Ogoni region by Shell Oil drillers in 1958 that changed his life forever. Rather than bringing prosperity to the tribe, Shell's activities produced a litany of environmental disasters.

Between 1958 and 1993 (when Saro-Wiwa's campaign led to suspension of drilling), Shell extracted a billion barrels of oil from over a hundred wells in Ogoniland, generating revenues of sixty billion dollars. Unlike much of the world's oil, which is either drilled off-shore or in isolated desert settings, the Nigerian fossil fuel existed in the heart of a densely populated, agrarian area. The environmental consequences came swiftly.

What was once a scenic landscape of farms and wetlands in the verdant Niger Delta became a wasteland: Shell acknowledges three thousand polluted sites caused by its oil production on Ogoni soil. Between 1976 and 1980, there were 784 recorded oil spills, with dozens more occurring even after Shell stopped drilling in Ogoni in 1993. With oil flaring twenty-four hours a day non-stop from 1958 on, a hazardous combination of hydrocarbons and other gasses contaminated the air, generating acid rain that in turn fouled local streams. The forests and marshlands were transformed into an oil production zone, with high-pressure pipes criss-crossing local farms and villages. The pipes themselves, frequently substandard in quality, often burst in the middle of populated areas. (Although Shell operated in one hundred countries, 40 percent of its spills during this period were in Nigeria.) The rich African fauna and aquatic life around Ogoniland was quickly overwhelmed and obliterated by a sloppy and insensitive oil industry.

Saro-Wiwa had ostensibly escaped this desolation when he took a scholarship and proved to be an exceptional student at Nigeria's leading

University of Ibadan. Yet he brought with him enough solidarity with his people to find time to write letters protesting the abuse in his home region. Upon graduation, he took a teaching post, and initially seemed content to channel his considerable talents toward academic pursuits. But in 1967, Saro-Wiwa's attention was distracted by the Biafran Civil War, in which he joined the government against the Ibo people's fight for independence, presumably because Ibos claimed a considerable chunk of Ogoniland. (Whereas most of the world was sympathetic to the vanquished Ibo tribe, Saro-Wiwa was never apologetic and always wrote Biafra using a small "b.")

This show of allegiance would win Saro-Wiwa an appointment as administrator at the oil port of Bonny and, soon thereafter in 1968, a promotion to become the first minister of education and information in the Rivers State. But he could not abide the military governor and was not inclined to stifle his opinions. So Saro-Wiwa eventually resigned his post and returned home to work in business, where he could carve out the leisure to indulge his literary impulse. During this period, he was shockingly prolific and remarkably prosperous. By the 1980s he had produced an impressive collection of assorted writing (twenty titles all told, mostly satirical) that gained him considerable recognition.

His son Ken "Junior" Wiwa's adoring but forthright characterization of him in *In a Shadow of a Saint* describes a brilliant but driven man whose frenetic commitment to public activities frequently left little time for his family. Saro-Wiwa read compulsively and was a fanatic about the virtues of an education. He was short, favored his pipe, and happily joked about his "tall parts." But he was most of all a blunt critic of his country, convinced that Nigeria could in fact be a better place. He was a regular and consistently trenchant political columnist for Lagos newspapers and even launched the period's most popular television soap opera in Nigeria, "Basi and Company."

However, it was ultimately his tribe's condition that most troubled him, and in 1989 he founded the Movement for the Survival of the Ogoni People. The organization would be the spearhead for a mass nonviolent movement raising the banner of environmental justice. By 1991, the cause began to absorb most of his attention. The movement gained in numbers and influence. The culmination of his campaign for environmental and social justice took place on January 4, 1993, when Saro-Wiwa led three hundred thousand Ogoni people in a peaceful protest against the continued drilling for oil in Ogoni. As chief spokesperson for this movement, his speech, reprinted subsequently, was the main event at what was probably the largest environmental rally in African history.

In his autobiographical work: *A Month and a Day: a Detention Diary,*
published posthumously, he wrote:

Shortly before Dori, at Teghe, we began to see signs of the readiness of
the people to march. . . . As I drove up, a huge crowd, the largest I had
seen in my life up to that moment, emerged from the different roads
which led to the primary school at Mogho, whose football field was to
be the venue for the rally. They had apparently been at work since seven
o'clock and had gone to K. Dere, the site of the Bomu oilfield, to sym-
bolically take over the oil field with its flaming gas flare. All the Shell
workers had abandoned the area the previous day.

They bore down, these poor, denigrated Ogoni people, green twigs,
banner, or placards in their hands, songs on their lips, and anger in
their legs and faces, moving in an endless stream to the Mogho playground. But there was also pride in their faces and I felt incredibly
proud with them. . . .

The dust in the arena was incredible, as dancers, masqueraders, and
revelers continued their celebration through other speeches. I wanted
and demanded silence, and got it. When the arena was absolutely still,
I sized up the crowd and their mood and decided not to speak in English as the previous speakers had all done, but in Khana. I spoke to the
prepared script, however, and went even further on the spur of the
moment, starting with our solidarity song, *Aakan Aaken pya Ogoni
aken*—"Arise, arise Ogoni people arise."

Yet, sadly, this triumphant moment was hardly the fairy-tale ending of
another Saro-Wiwa story. The demonstration finalized Shell's capitula-
tion to local protests and the stopping of its oil production around Ogoni.
But the corporation did not give up its appetite for Nigerian oil and it began to monitor Saro-Wiwa's movements. The military regime, headed by
General Sani Abacha, chose a less subtle response.

That year, government soldiers burned eight villages, displacing twenty
thousand Ogonis. One thousand Ogonis died as a result of the government's suppressive actions, and by 1996 the related death toll would rise
to two thousand. Countless more Ogonis were beaten or raped. Saro-
Wiwa was taken into custody on several occasions in response to his nonviolent resistance activities, which included photographing scenes of the
environmental damage. Frustrated at the lack of progress, he took the
Ogoni case to global forums. After Saro-Wiwa called for tough international sanctions against the Abacha regime, the state authorities arrested

him for the last time. Saro-Wiwa and eight others were indicted, allegedly for causing the deaths (through incitement) of four pro-government Ogoni leaders who were killed by an angry mob.

For ten months, Saro-Wiwa was held in custody, literally in chains, denied visits by friends and family, medical attention, or international observers. His trial was held in front of a closed military tribunal, and many reports subsequently emerged suggesting that witnesses had been bribed to fabricate a case against him and his eight colleagues.

According to testimony before the U.S. Congress, when Saro-Wiwa's brother, physician Owen Wiwa, approached the chairman and managing director of Shell Nigeria to intervene to stop the travesty of justice, he was told that this would be "difficult but not impossible." Shell, however, only agreed to try to stop the trial if Saro-Wiwa's organization issued a press release that exonerated the corporation and stated that there was no environmental devastation as a result of Shell activities. When the demand was communicated to Saro-Wiwa, he refused to allow such a lie, even though it would save his life.

Saro-Wiwa did succeed in smuggling out of prison his plea to the tribunal. This short, eloquent statement may not have swayed a court whose verdict was clear before it heard any evidence. Yet it soon found its way to the press, and is still available at innumerable sites on the internet. The speech not only called the government to task, but focused equally on Shell's role as a polluting corporation that bankrolled the oppression required to protect its earnings. As this plea was Saro-Wiwa's last formal address, it warrants a brief excerpt:

> I repeat that we all stand before history. I and my colleagues are not the only ones on trial. Shell is here on trial, and it is as well that it is represented by counsel said to be holding a watching brief. The company has indeed ducked this particular trial, but its day will surely come and the lessons learnt here may prove useful to it, for there is no doubt in my mind that the ecological war that the company has waged in the Niger delta will be called to question sooner than later and the crimes of that war duly punished. The crime of the company's dirty wars against the Ogoni people will also be punished.
>
> On trial also is the Nigerian nation, its present rulers and those who assist them. Any nation which can do to the weak and disadvantaged what the Nigerian nation has done to the Ogoni people, loses a claim to independence and to freedom from outside influence. I am not one of those who shy away from protesting injustice and oppression, arguing

that they are expected in a military regime. The military do not act alone. They are supported by a gaggle of politicians, lawyers, judges, academics, and businessmen, all of them hiding under the claim that they are only doing their duty, men and women too afraid to wash their pants of urine. We all stand on trial, my lord, for by our actions we have denigrated our country and jeopardized the future of our children.

Following the court's verdict, the government wasted little time in carrying out the sentence. Ken Saro-Wiwa was hanged on November 10, 1995. Resigned to a martyr's death, his final words before the execution were, "Lord take my soul, but the struggle continues." He was only fifty-four years old. Nigerian news reported that hundreds of Ogonis lined the route to the prison that day and wept uncontrollably.

Sadly, the public outcry did not produce immediate results. Three days after the executions, Shell recommitted itself to General Abacha for a four-billion-dollar gas project outside Ogoniland for which the World Bank had canceled funding. Today, Ogonis continue to suffer from enormous poverty, with little of the oil revenues trickling down to local communities. The legacy of ecological abuse remains, and access to clean drinking water is still a serious environmental concern. And who knows how long the emotional trauma of the Abacha regime will cast a cloud over those who survived this dark period.

Yet Saro-Wiwa's heroism was not in vain. Initially, the commonwealth countries meeting in Auckland suspended Nigeria's membership until the human rights situation improved. When General Abacha died in 1998, apparently of natural causes, the military rule came to an end, and there was some respite from the rule of violence after a more democratic government eventually emerged. Conditions for the Ogoni are still bleak, but the first signs of restoration have begun. Shell has started to run electrical lines to the area and pave some roads (although one report suggests that the poor villagers, lacking motor vehicles and even shoes, often prefer the dirt paths).

Most importantly, Saro-Wiwa's protest, conveyed in the message he delivered before half his people, put an end to thirty-five years of ecological devastation. Oil production in Ogoni was not renewed, and today is focused off-shore, away from the Nigerian population centers. Ultimately, Ken Saro-Wiwa's unyielding call for environmental justice would ensure that the despoliation of the Ogoni tribe's land was among the rare ecological crimes in Africa that reached the world's attention and stayed there.

"A Deadly Ecological War in Which No Blood Is Spilled but People Die All the Time"

SPEECH AT BORI, NIGERIA, BEFORE A DEMONSTRATION
OF THREE HUNDRED THOUSAND OGONI PEOPLE,
JANUARY 4, 1993

*Y*our Royal Highnesses, Respected Chiefs and Elders, President of the Movement for the Survival of the Ogoni People, Ladies and Gentlemen:

I wish to thank you all for giving me the opportunity to speak on this occasion. I speak in a dual capacity as president of the Ethnic Minority Rights Organization of Africa, which promotes the human and environmental rights of indigenous and tribal peoples and ethnic minorities in Africa (EMIROAF), and as spokesman of the Ogoni people.

The year 1993 has been formally declared the International Year of the World's Indigenous People, as directed by the General Assembly of the United Nations under resolution 36/128. The opening ceremonies took place in New York on 10 December 1992, International Human Rights Day.

The declaration of the [International] Year signifies the interest which the fate of indigenous people is receiving in the international community. Although the case of indigenous people in America, Australia, and New Zealand is well known, indigenous people in Africa have received scant attention. EMIROAF hopes to fill that vacuum and it is to this end that we have given full support to the efforts of the Ogoni people to draw attention to their plight. We intend to organize further activities during this year.

Contrary to the belief that there are no indigenous people in black Africa, our research has shown that the fate of such groups as the Zangon Kataf and Ogoni in Nigeria are, in essence, no different from those of the Aborigines of Australia, the Maori of New Zealand, and the Indians of North and South America. Their common history is of the usurpation of their land and resources, the destruction of their culture, and the eventual decimation of their people.

Indigenous people often do not realize what is happening to them until it is too late. More often than not, they are the victims of the actions of greedy outsiders. EMIROAF will continue to mobilize and represent the

Speech reprinted with permission of Olivia Wiwa.

interest of all indigenous people on the African continent. It is in this regard that we have undertaken to publicize the fate of the Ogoni people in Nigeria. The Ogoni are embattled and imperiled. Since oil was discovered in the area in 1958, they have been the victims of a deadly ecological war in which no blood is spilled, no bones are broken, and no one is maimed. But people die all the time. Men, women, and children are at risk; plants, wildlife, and fish are destroyed; the air and water are poisoned; and finally the land dies. Today, Ogoni has been reduced to a wasteland.

Unfortunately, the international community has not yet awakened to the grim nature of this sophisticated, if unconventional, battle. For a multinational oil company, Shell, to take over thirty billion dollars from the small, defenseless Ogoni people and put nothing back but degradation and death is a betrayal of all humanity.

For the Nigerian government to usurp the resources of the Ogoni and legalize such theft by military decree is armed robbery.

To deny the Ogoni the right of self-determination and impose on them the status of slaves in their country is morally indefensible. The stunning silence and insincerity, the primitive harassment and intimidation, which the looter of Lagos and the bandits of Abuja have visited on the Ogoni people since they began to demand their rights peacefully, indicate that the Nigerian government lacks the ability or will to solve the problem, and that only the international community can help the Ogoni people.

I therefore call upon the community once again to come to the aid of the Ogoni, before they are driven to extinction by the combined activity of the multinational oil companies and the oppressive, greedy rulers of Nigeria.

Oil has been mined in Ogoni since 1958. It is a wasting asset. When the oil finally runs out in ten years or so, what will the Ogoni people do? Who will come to their aid? Something must be done *now* to save Ogoni.

I congratulate the Ogoni people on their taking upon themselves the historic responsibility for saving themselves, their land, and their environment, late in the day as this may have been.

I call upon you, my brothers and sisters, to fight relentlessly for your rights. As our cause is just, and God being our helper, we shall emerge victorious over the forces of greed, wickedness, and obduracy.

God bless you all.

REFERENCES

Barry, John Byrn, et al., ed. *Environmentalists Under Fire: Ten Urgent Cases of Human Rights Abuses.* Report for Amnesty International and Sierra Club, 2000.

Iloegbunam, Chuks. "The Death of a Writer." Obituary by a Nigerian journalist. Compiled by the Coalition against Dictatorship. 1995. Reprint at http://www.hartforshire.com.

"Man in the News: Ken Saro-Wiwa, Writer and Rights Crusader." *Reuters,* 1995.

Mills, Stephen (Sierra Club, Washington, DC). Personal communication, August 6, 2003.

Montague, Peter. "Crimes of Shell." *Rachel's Environment and Health Weekly* 546, May 15, 1997.

Okonta, Ike, and Oronto Douglas., *Where Vultures Feast: Shell, Human Rights, and Oil in the Niger Delta.* New York: Random House, 2002.

Phido, Gbnewa. "The Ogoni Story." Paper delivered to University of Leeds Student Union, March 2001.

Saro-Wiwa, Ken. *A Month and a Day: A Detention Diary.* London: Penguin, 1995.

Streiker, Gary. "Execution of Nigerian Activist Remains an Emotional Issue." CNN World News, December 25, 1995.

Wiwa, Ken. *In the Shadow of a Saint: A Son's Journey to Understand His Father's Legacy.* London: Black Swan, 2001.

Wiwa, Dr. Owen. Testimony before the Joint Briefing of the Congressional Human Rights Caucus and the Congressional Black Caucus, January 30, 1996.

15. Charles, Prince of Wales

UNITED KINGDOM

Photograph courtesy of the British Embassy, Washington, D.C.

Prince Charles is increasingly recognized as a thoughtful and unyielding spokesperson for environmental interests. Probably no international public figure has made as many speeches on as broad a range of environmental issues. The general public in Great Britain may have only become aware of the depth of his concern for the planet's health and the breadth of the issues with which he was involved when he launched the film "Earth in the Balance" for the BBC in 1990. But the record shows that the Prince was passionate about ecological issues even before the modern environmental movement emerged in Europe; some biographers attribute this interest to the encouragement of his father, Prince Philip, an active wildlife enthusiast.

In 1970, "European Conservation Year" was declared. Although only twenty-one years old at the time, Prince Charles was appointed chair of the Countryside Committee for Wales. It was in this capacity that he wrote and delivered his first speech on the subject; he spoke ingenuously about the "horrifying effects of pollution," citing numerous examples. Commenting about the inherent costs to industry caused by pollution control requirements, and the ultimate manifestation of such costs in increased prices for consumers, he raised the fundamental question faced by all societies when considering environmental challenges: "Are we prepared to accept these price increases to see our environment improved? Are we also prepared to discipline ourselves to restrictions and regulation that we feel we ought to impose for our own good? We must be prepared to do so."

Conservation Year would come and go, but Prince Charles would continue to address environmental issues. He questioned the wisdom of developing a Concorde jet, given its noise and its pernicious environmental impacts. Soon thereafter, following a disturbing visit to Melbourne, Australia, he openly criticized its polluted beaches. As one of the rare celebrities who read seriously and voraciously, Prince Charles stayed abreast of key developments and studies in ecology during the 1970s. At the same time, as heir to the throne of England, he availed himself of opportunities for unusual encounters with nature, from scuba diving under Arctic ice to taking safaris throughout Africa. These undoubtedly heightened his wonder at the natural world and his growing tendency to frame environmental issues in spiritual terms.

Such candor proved courageous, as it made him an easy target for a sarcastic English press that loved to ridicule the unconventional views of the "loony Prince." When Charles voiced support for the technological optimism in E. F. Schumacher's noted book, *Small Is Beautiful,* even the progressive *Guardian* caricaturized him as an "eco-king" who would bring windmills to power Buckingham Palace. It would take years for green issues to become sufficiently trendy in England that the Prince's environmental beliefs strengthened his popularity.

Although Prince Charles may have enjoyed the considerable warmth he received from the environmental community, the dismissive scorn that his views engendered in many circles, especially the media, was often abusive. In general, he did not seek the role of ecological gadfly. The Prince once wrote a friend about the angst he suffered around a controversial speech, saying that while it would be easier to stay out of the fray, "I would not be true to myself if I did stay quiet instead of taking the risk and accepting the challenge. . . . Anyhow, I hope what I said helps to stir up the debate and raise some people's awareness." This he did, addressing topics where vested interests would take umbrage, as in his well-known advocacy of preservation and architectural integrity. Never did he "stir up debate" more, however, then when he chose to weigh in on the controversy surrounding the genetic modification of crops.

Prince Charles enjoys the counsel of numerous environmental experts, but his views on agriculture are based on his own experience. After completing his naval service in 1977, the Prince was faced with deciding what he would be "when he grew up." Beneficiary of the *Duchy of Cornwall* estate, he had considerable land holdings, and his portfolio reportedly made him the fourteenth wealthiest individual in Britain. The estate at that time contained 240 farms, and the twenty-four hundred tenancies provided employment for approximately seven hundred people. Thus, "royal duties" could have consumed his full energies and, as heir to the throne, there certainly was no need for him to initiate new economic enterprises.

Yet, over a period of about a decade, Prince Charles evolved into a farmer. The turning point in this process was his acquisition of the Highgrove Estate in Gloucester, some 150 kilometers west of London. Restoring the grounds there would elevate gardening from a hobby to a professional passion. Although the estate's walled gardens captivated him initially, he soon got serious about farming. The 140 hectares on the estate were not enough for a commercial venture, so in 1984 he doubled the property by purchasing the adjacent lands.

His great love for his garden was recorded as part of a televised documentary on the Prince of Wales's life, where he was filmed on-site in the manicured Highgrove grounds. It was then that he made the by-now famous admission that he loved to come to his garden and talk to the plants: ". . . really—very important to talk to them"—a line that a snide press and countless comedians would seize on and distort. But he was undaunted and continued to espouse the humanistic aspects of farming, while pursuing agriculture as a fully commercial enterprise.

From the outset, Prince Charles was fascinated by the details of agricultural production. In a modern variation on a fairytale theme, he on occasion would disappear for days to work as a laborer on the Duchy-owned farms. By doing menial tasks from milking to tractoring, he could presumably become better acquainted with what was actually happening among the farmers who rented land from his holdings. Even if the Prince has not greatly influenced the neighboring estates' agricultural orientation, he did gradually transform Highgrove into the very model of an environmentally sustainable farm.

Relying on advice from John Pugsley, an active farmer and member of his council, Prince Charles established a system where his cow herd produced milk while eating almost exclusively pasture feed. By 1988 he was harvesting an organically grown field of spring beans, with increasing portions of his land gradually moving to chemical-free farming. A reedbed sewage system followed, along with a line of organic biscuit products.

While typically modest, Prince Charles cannot help but let pride slip out when speaking about the organic orientation that he brought to an operation that is still profitable and about the ecological innovations initiated on his farm. His critics paint this agricultural inclination as self-indulgence, but in fact Prince Charles champions the issue of organic farming in broader arenas. For example, he helped lobby the Ministry of Agriculture to launch a program that compensates farmers during transition from conventional to organic operations.

It was no surprise, therefore, that Prince Charles went public with his reservations surrounding genetically modified agriculture. Since the emergence of the "precautionary principle" as an axiom in international environmental law, he frequently cites this as a sound basis for formulating public policy. Thus his views on the development and introduction of genetically modified produce were a reflection of both his romantic approach toward sustainable farming and his commitment to prudence where long-term, irreversible ecological impacts could be involved. He tackled the issue of genetic modification in two speeches during the mid-1990s. Two subsequent pieces, published in the *Daily Telegraph* and the *Daily Mail* at the end of the decade, condensed these ideas into cogent and compelling essays.

But it was in the speeches that he initially expressed his apprehension, articulating several coherent reservations. Prior to his talks, criticism of "GM" was considered by the general and scientific community as radical or antiscientific—as the views solely of "deep ecology" extremists. To be sure, despite their decidedly moderate tone, the Prince's comments were not universally esteemed, and would be among the most controversial positions he ever took. The Social Issues Research Center, an Oxford-based think tank, for example, still posts on its web site a piece on the topic, *The Madness of Prince Charles,* in which his "mystical and whimsical views" and "explicit hostility towards scientific rationalism" are assailed.

Yet Charles's position resonated not only in Great Britain, but also throughout Europe, where many of his concerns would soon find expression in public opinion and tougher regulatory procedures. David Baldock, director of the Institute for European Environmental Policy in London, explains that the speech not only constituted the first thoughtful intervention by a figure of royal standing on the issue of genetically modified organisms (GMOs), transforming genetic modification into a legitimate mainstream topic for public debate. He also took the discourse beyond concern for environmental and health impacts, embracing a broader resistance toward unaccountable corporate agendas in driving future technologies.

Prince Charles first spoke about genetic modification at the International Biodiversity Seminar, Lancaster House, London, December 12, 1995. There, he framed the issue within the general context of depleted biodiversity. He aired many questions that were troubling him and that promoters of the new technology had yet to address:

> There are, of course, plenty of people (not all employed or supported by the agrochemical industry) who see genetic engineering as the most promising way forward for agriculture. And it is certainly one way of maximizing the use of our total genetic resources. But am I really alone in feeling profoundly apprehensive about many of the early signals from this brave new world, and the confidence—bordering on arrogance— with which it is promoted? When I read that most of the genetically engineered species released so far in the U.S.A. have been billed as 'new crops for old herbicides,' having been developed by the major agrochemical companies seeking farmer loyalty to their own particular weed-control chemicals, my heart sinks at the prospect.
>
> And how much biodiversity would the scientists here tonight expect to discover in a field of genetically engineered sugar beets, after the regular applications of the "Roundup" to which it alone is resistant? And if these applications of genetic engineering are not enough to send a cold chill down the spine, then I suggest that you take a look at the situation in China, where such releases are already routine, with minimal controls on a vast scale.

Ultimately, Prince Charles did not endorse a blanket rejection of genetic modification, saying: "I am not, for a moment, decrying all uses of such technologies, nor do I believe that the controls which exist in this country are anything other than adequate to the perceived risks. But as a strong supporter of the precautionary principle, I think it is timely to recall the almost entirely damaging effects of introductions of alien species to new environments. It is too late to ask those responsible whether they really thought it was a good idea to introduce the rabbit and the cane toad to Australia, or the grey squirrel to this country."

Several months later, in a speech to commemorate the fiftieth anniversary of England's Soil Association, Prince Charles raised the issue in a broader ideological context. The speech integrated concerns about genetic modification as part of a vision of where agriculture is and where it should go. This speech, by a royal practitioner of sustainable agriculture, is reprinted here.

"We Venture into Realms That Belong to God, and to God Alone"

THE 1996 LADY EVE BALFOUR MEMORIAL LECTURE, FIFTIETH ANNIVERSARY OF THE SOIL ASSOCIATION, THE BANQUETING HALL, LONDON, SEPTEMBER 19, 1996

I was delighted to be asked to give this year's lecture in memory of Lady Eve Balfour, in the fiftieth anniversary year of the Soil Association which she helped to found. Lady Eve was a working farmer in Suffolk, and her intention was clear. She sought to investigate something that was simple but far-reaching: the existence of a vital relationship between the condition of the soil and health—of the crops which are grown in it, of the animals that are raised on it, and of the people who eventually consume them as food. Based on her research, Lady Eve penned the immortal line: "the health of soil, plant, animal, and man is one and indivisible."

Fifty years later, that statement seems glaringly obvious to many of us, convinced as we are of the need to think ecologically. But in 1946, when the Soil Association was formed, the mood of the nation was quite different from what it is today.

Our country had just emerged from a war during which our isolation had forced us to produce as much food as we possibly could, from our own resources. Starvation had been a real risk. Science and technology had helped us to win that war, and it was perhaps not surprising that people gained the idea that science could do almost anything for humanity. And

Speech reprinted with permission of H.R.H. the Prince of Wales's Press Office, London.

where better to apply those new-found skills than food production? One new development followed another with bewildering speed, and it must soon have seemed as if our mastery of modern science could increase output, banish weeds, pests, and diseases, and keep us one step ahead of whatever temporary setbacks might arise, indefinitely.

The period from that day to this spans fifty years, which encompasses many of our lifetimes and the entire history of the Soil Association. During those years farmers have done an admirable job—and I mean an admirable job—in meeting those clearly stated requirements for reliable supplies of inexpensive food, and they should be congratulated for this.

Working with a strong scientific supporting cast, they have achieved dramatic increases in yields; utilizing breakthroughs in plant breeding and agrochemicals, combined with improvements in a wide range of agricultural technologies. Together, these have been so successful that there is now overproduction across Europe. But the prevailing mood during that period has been that man can dominate nature and win—not only that human beings are at the top of the food chain, but that manipulation and domination of the natural world is somehow our destiny, even our duty. That, I think, is where things have gone wrong.

The Kentucky farmer and philosopher Wendell Berry summed up what I believe to be the true situation when he wrote: "Farming cannot take place except in nature; therefore if nature does not thrive, farming cannot thrive. But we know too that nature includes us. It is not a place into which we reach from some safe standpoint outside it. We are in it and are a part of it while we use it. If it does not thrive, we cannot thrive. The appropriate measure of farming then is the world's health and our health, and this is inescapably one measure."

Only now, after fifty years, is the evidence of that measure beginning to emerge from the process (some might say the experiment) in which we have all, somewhat unwittingly, taken part: in other words, the progressive industrialization of agriculture. And the results look profoundly disturbing. Today we are surrounded by evidence of what has happened to our farmland when husbandry-based agriculture is replaced by industrialized systems and where traditional management gives way to specialization and intensification. We see the consequences of treating animals like machines; seeking ever greater "efficiency" and even experimenting (catastrophically, as we now know) with totally inappropriate alternative "fuels," in the form of recycled animal proteins, with which to "power" them.

The loss has been gradual, insidious, just slow enough for us to convince ourselves that the lost rural idyll some of us may remember from our childhood was probably just a rose-tinted and romanticized dream. Perhaps in some respects it was, but, unfortunately, the losses are all too real. Degraded environmental capital is not something one can easily reinstate. We have burdened ourselves and our children with the task of rebuilding what we have destroyed. I fear it may take them most of their lifetimes to do so. And the cost, both for us and for them, will be immense.

In 1992, the Office of Water Services estimated that one billion pounds of capital investment would be required by the water companies to remove pesticides from drinking water, but in addition the monitoring and removal of pesticides from contaminated water supplies is already costing us 121 million pounds every year. Nobody knows what the future costs will be of so much officially sanctioned use of organophosphates and organo chlorines, or of the routine dosing of livestock with antibiotics. In addition, there is the huge but unquantifiable loss of landscape quality, wildlife, and cultural diversity which reduces our genetic resources, depresses the human spirit, and makes our lives less interesting and less fulfilling.

These hidden costs have never been linked to the price of conventionally grown food. The illusion has been maintained that intensive farming practices have at least given us cheap food. But the real sums are never done. If you add in the production subsidies, the degradation and loss of our environmental capital, and all the costs of cleaning up, then what started out looking like cheap food is actually nothing of the sort. At this point I can't resist commending the work of the Office of National Statistics in attempting to do at least some of these sums. In what they admit is a first step, the authors of a recent report calculated that agriculture contributes about 2 percent to our economy, but produces 10 percent of the acid rain and 4 percent of greenhouse gas emissions.

Fair competition, in the shape of a "level playing field" and proper application of the "polluter pays" principle, difficult though that might be, would make things look very different. At the moment, I believe we tend to look at only one side of the balance sheet, thereby making it difficult for ourselves to reach a balanced judgment on the costs and benefits of current agricultural systems. Is it not time to remove these distortions and give those farmers who have opted to farm in a less intensive fashion, and who by and large don't inflict those hidden costs on the rest of us, a fair chance to compete in the marketplace on equal terms?

There are those who believe that the consequences of GATT, which will assist the globalization of trade in agricultural products, will be wholly beneficial, with the fittest surviving in a glorious utopian era of perpetual growth. And then there are those who revel in the prospect of harnessing the awesome power of biotechnology to assist the relentless progress of high-tech agriculture. I suspect that few of you will be surprised to hear that none of these feature in my vision of sustainable agriculture—or of sustainable anything else, for that matter!

Of course, biotechnology, genetic engineering, release of GMOs, call them what you will, are aspects of a particularly emotive subject, and I do not intend to stoke those emotions tonight. I shall content myself with quoting from the January 1996 report on the Government's Panel on Sustainable Development. They acknowledge, as I do, that genetic manipulation could lead to major advances in medicine, agriculture, and the good health of the environment. Then they go on to say, crisply and clearly, that—and I quote— "The introduction of GMOs must proceed with caution to ensure that any benefits now are not made at the expense of the safety and well-being of future generations and their environment. Once released, . . . a GMO cannot be recalled: the action is irreversible. More than in other areas there is uncertainty about the long-term outcome of human actions and of human ability to deal with the consequences. Introduced genes may over time spread to other organisms with consequences that cannot necessarily be foreseen."

And they end with a stark warning when they say—and again I am quoting their words—"Unfortunately there are many recent examples of failure to anticipate problems arising from the use of new technologies (such as CFCs, asbestos, pesticides, and thalidomide). Potential consequences are more uncertain where self-replicating organisms are introduced into the environment."

I am not sure I have much to add to that; except to say that I believe that we have now reached a moral and ethical watershed beyond which we venture into realms that belong to God, and to God alone. Apart from certain medical applications, what actual right do we have to experiment, Frankenstein-like, with the very stuff of life? We live in an age of rights; it seems to me that it is about time our Creator had some rights, too. . . .

I am sure that the government's response to this report, in the shape of a consultative process and a national conference, will be a great help. And it is, of course, reassuring to know that in this country we already have one of the most open and thorough regulatory systems in the world for assessing possible consequences of releasing GMOs into the environment. But that system has not been designed to weigh up the benefits of this dramatic new technology against the risks, nor can it compare the biotechnological approach with more conventional ways of achieving the same ends. At the moment, as is so often the case with technology, we seem to spend most of our time establishing what is technically possible, and then a little time trying to establish whether or not it is likely to be safe, without ever stopping to ask whether it is something we should be doing in the first place. I believe that this particular technology is so powerful and so far-reaching that we should seek ways of engaging a wide range of people and interests in a thorough ethical debate about how and where it should be applied. . . .

I think that we must recognize that, for the last fifty years, we have given our farmers a remarkably narrow set of goals and accompanying incentives to help them get there: economic performance without environmental accountability; maximum production without consideration of food quality and health; intensification without regard for animal welfare; specialization without consideration of the maintenance of biological and cultural diversity. The signals we sent said what we wanted: cheap food, and plenty of it. We can hardly blame our farmers now for their outstanding success in achieving those goals. But if we want to modify and add to those goals in the light of experience and changing public expectations, we are only going to be able to do so with the support of a further reformed Common Agricultural Policy (CAP). . . .

Well, there are some people (notably the free marketers, who are wholly in favor of GATT and the further globalization of trade in agricultural products) who would prefer to see the CAP abolished altogether. For this group, farming has no special claim to be treated any differently from the steel and mining industries. But they are still, thank goodness, outnumbered by those who recognize that agriculture is unique, with responsibility not only for feeding us, but for the custody of a precious natural resource, as well as cultural and social dimensions that cannot be ignored. Farmers play a crucial role, not only in safeguarding the health of the nation and the environment, but also in maintaining the vitality and viability of our rural communities. Few would dispute the need to encourage farmers to become more responsive to their markets, but, if we want farmers to adopt more environmentally sustainable methods, it is clear that we could use the mechanisms of the CAP to encourage moves in this direction, together with training and encouragement, just as we used them in the past to encourage maximum production.

There are always going to be aspects of farming, such as maintaining the fabric of our landscape, where the costs cannot easily be passed on to the consumer. It is difficult to ignore evidence such as the recent Gallup poll which showed that "the countryside" came second only to "free speech" as the attribute most valued in Britain today. Yet it is impossible, and counterproductive, to attempt to attach a monetary value to such intangible aspects of our existence. So we need to find new ways in which all farmers can be supported for providing these services to society as a whole. There seems to be a growing consensus that the best way would be to make specific payments to farmers who commit the whole of their farms to environmentally sound methods, and to ensuring food safety, nutritional quality, and animal welfare. This might form the heart of a future Common Agricultural Policy.

With only around eight hundred organic farms in this country, and a growing and unsatisfied market for organic foods, there would appear to be a tremendous opportunity for many more farms to convert. . . . Ladies and gentlemen, I am now, you will no doubt be relieved to hear, more than two-thirds of the way through this lecture—and I have just mentioned organic farming for the first time. This is not an accident, nor an omission on my part. I am, of course, inextricably identified with the organic movement (which probably won't do its reputation any good at all), but when I first started farming organically my real aim was to explore the best ways of developing a sustainable system of food production. Organic farming was, and still is, the most effective system of applying what I thought to be the principles of sustainable agriculture. It is only much more recently that organizations as diverse as the Ministry of Agriculture, Fisheries and Food, and our main environmental organizations have confirmed the benefits to conservation of organic farming (partly, I have to say, based on research at Highgrove).

Now I have certainly never suggested that organic farming could "feed the world," which is, in any case, a problem of economics and politics as much it is of agriculture and technology. But, on the other hand, I am a firm believer that "seeing is believing," and skeptics are regularly invited to come and look at the crops and livestock at Highgrove and suggest what sort of farming system could be more sustainably productive. You may—you will—find ways of producing more in the short term, but what about the long term? And isn't the long term the only thing we should be thinking about?

And that is all I have to say about organic farming at present, except to suggest that, even if they have no wish to face the challenge of conversion, conventional farmers could still learn a lot from their organic colleagues about how to apply at least some of the principles of sustainable farming. Sadly, the word "sustainability" itself is in danger of taking on rather technical connotations. It is an important word in more than a technical sense. There is an element of circularity to it. We must sustain the world if it is going to sustain us. We must act generously towards the soil which has been generous to us. Our lives are not sustainable if the world in which we live is not itself sustained—by us. If we come to understand that again, a certain dignity will I think return to our lives. We will no longer regard our planet as a treasure chest to be raided at will, but as a world that will nurture us if we will nurture it.

"The poetry of earth is never dead," John Keats wrote in his sonnet on the humble grasshopper. I hope that remains true and that we have not left things too late. The line itself—the poetry of earth is never dead—is full of optimism, even though it refers to a dimension of our relationship with the natural world which has been utterly abandoned in the purely technological agriculture which now surrounds us. It is a dimension, which needs to be remembered, and rediscovered.

REFERENCES

Baldock, David. Personal communication, August 12, 2003.

Dimbleby, Jonathan. *The Prince of Wales: A Biography.* London: Little Brown and Company, 1994.

Hamilton, Alan. *The Real Charles.* London: Collins, 1988.

Holden, Anthony. *King Charles III: A Biography.* New York: Weidenfeld and Nicolson, 1988.

Lean, Geoffrey. Personal communication, Johannesburg, August 27, 2002.

"The Madness of Prince Charles." Social Issues Research Center (Oxford) web site. *http://www.sirc.org/articles/madness_of_prince_charles.html.*

Official internet site of H.R.H. the Prince of Wales. *http://www.princeofwales.gov .uk/speeches/agriculture.*

16. Ecumenical Patriarch Bartholomew

TURKEY

Photograph used with permission of his All-Holiness, Ecumenical Patriarch Bartholomew. Photograph by Nicholas Manginas.

In 1966, University of California at Los Angeles professor of history Lynn White published a controversial essay in *Science* magazine, "The Historical Roots of Our Ecological Crisis." White considered the unaccommodating posture and even destructive influence of religion on the troubling environmental dynamics of the time. Since then, many environmentalists have characterized organized Western religion as a fundamentally anti-environmental force.

Of course religious tradition in general, and the Bible in particular, contain mixed ecological messages. Even though the Pentateuch does authorize humans to "subdue" other creatures, it also prescribes stewardship through crop rotation, open spaces around cities, and sustainable forestry, even in times of war. Ultimately it is the interpretation that religious leaders choose, and what they actually preach, that determines whether a particular religious creed or denomination is a force for healing or damaging the planet.

In fact, enlisting organized religion as a full partner in environmental efforts constitutes a key step toward disseminating a universal environmental ethic, one that not only targets government or industrial accountability, but also highlights the personal responsibility of the individual. Orthodox Christianity would not have been an obvious choice for a church that might take a leadership role on this issue. But, largely because of its present spiritual leader, it has.

In recent years, Ecumenical Patriarch Bartholomew (analogous to the pope, in the Orthodox faith) has begun to redefine his church's approach to the natural world, and to silence critics who perceive Christianity as environmentally obtuse. The remarkable ecological conviction that Bartholomew brings to his tenure as spiritual leader for three hundred million Orthodox Christians places this segment of Christianity in an almost radically ecological light. Bartholomew has consistently acted to earn his nickname of "the Green Patriarch."

Bartholomew was born Dimitrios Arhonodis on February 29, 1940, on the Aegean island of Imvros. His father was a barber and coffee-shop owner. Turkey had only recently resumed control of its part of the island that was predominantly inhabited by Greek Christians. After completing his conventional studies in Imvros and Constantinople, he was accepted to the prestigious Theological School in Halki, where he graduated with honors at age twenty-one and given the name Bartholomew. Subsequently he spent two years completing compulsory service as an officer in the Turkish Army Reserves.

From 1963 to 1968, Bartholomew studied in numerous theological centers, eventually completing a doctorate in canonical regulations at the Gregorian University of Rome and emerging as an expert in ecclesiastical law. When a new ecumenical patriarch was elected in 1972, he pulled the young Bartholomew from the role of an assistant dean at Halki and thrust him into a leadership position. Soon thereafter, Bartholomew was appointed bishop for all of Asia Minor. In subsequent years, he became the patriarch's personal secretary and chief advisor. In this capacity, he worked to start the "greening" of the Orthodox church, declaring September 1 an annual day of prayer for protection of the environment among Orthodox Christians. Following the patriarch's death in 1991, Bartholomew was the natural successor.

Upon assuming the position of patriarch in Constantinople (Istanbul), Bartholomew launched his drive to make environmental protection a central theme in Orthodox theology. He initiated innumerable environmental conferences and ecological seminars for church leaders and priests. Frequently these classes were held on the open sea, as he would bring his message, via cruise ships, to environmentally troubled areas.

Eventually these marine missions attracted a broader cadre of activists. This happened during Bartholomew's 2003 trip to the Baltic, where, in the presence of two hundred scientists, political leaders, and journalists, he declared protection of the ocean to be "God's work." Indeed, in 1997 he brought European Union and World Bank officials to the Black Sea, in a successful attempt to renew the funding for its protection.

Bartholomew's environmental commitment is so remarkable because it was so unanticipated. Orthodox Christianity is composed of several "autonomous" churches: Greek, Russian, Bulgarian, Serbian, and Romanian. These countries have not been in the forefront of environmental innovation and involvement internationally. Moreover, traditionally the Orthodox church has preferred to maintain a nonpolitical, somewhat detached profile. This is a far cry from Bartholomew's insistence on environmental relevance. The patriarch has utilized his new environmental dogma (and his own fluency in seven languages) to unify the disparate factions and Orthodox churches, albeit not without resistance from the conservative rank-and-file clergy. This initiative went beyond the Orthodox world when he signed the Venice Declaration of Environmental Ethics with Pope John Paul II, a rare moment of ecumenical accord between these rival denominations.

Perhaps Bartholomew's most dramatic theological move took place in 1997. At a symposium hosted by the Greek Orthodox church in Santa Barbara, California, Bartholomew went a step further than before, calling crimes against the natural world "a sin." This marked the first time that the head of a major Western religious movement would be so unequivocal in admonishing ecological offenders. The speech is printed here almost in its entirety.

The gathering itself was part of a religious initiative to raise the issue of environmental justice. But the thousand participants included leaders from industry, science, government, and education who had come to talk about broadening the community of environmental interests. Bartholomew was billed as the event's main attraction and he did not disappoint. Not content to leave "environmental sin" an amorphous precept, Bartholomew went on to list specific ecological transgressions. They include the causing of: species extinction; climate change deforestation; wetland destruction; disease; and contamination of water, land, and air with poisonous substances.

First-World environmentalists are often criticized by their Third-World colleagues for conveniently focusing on issues such as pollution control and population explosion while ignoring the issue of profligate consumption and its environmentally destructive impact. Patriarch Bartholomew places this issue at the very heart of his speech, explaining that overconsumption reflects an estrangement from self, land, life, and God. Rather, he calls for people to "work in humble harmony with creation and not in arrogant supremacy against it." In this context, he casts asceticism in a new light, as a fundamentally sustainable and environmentally responsible way of life and thinking.

"To Commit a Crime against the Natural World Is a Sin"

ADDRESS OF HIS ALL-HOLINESS ECUMENICAL PATRIARCH, BARTHOLOMEW, AT THE ENVIRONMENTAL SYMPOSIUM, SAINT BARBARA GREEK ORTHODOX CHURCH, SANTA BARBARA, CALIFORNIA, NOVEMBER 8, 1997

*O*ur Beloved Brother in Christ, Archbishop Spyridon of America; Our Beloved Brother in Christ, Bishop Anthony of San Francisco; the Honorable Secretary of the Interior, Mr. Bruce Babbitt; Distinguished Scholars; Learned Guests; Beloved Friends and Children in the Lord:

It is with deep joy that we greet all of you, the honorable delegates and attendees of this blessed Symposium on the Sacredness of the Environment. Here in this historical city of Santa Barbara, we see before us a brilliant example of the wonder of God's creation. Recently, that God-given beauty was threatened by an oil spill. We are proud that the effort to restore the damaged beauty of Santa Barbara's seas was led by Orthodox Christians, Dan and Candy Randopoulos.

The Ecumenical Throne of Orthodoxy, as a preserver and herald of the ancient Patristic tradition and of the rich liturgical experience of the Orthodox Church, today renews its longstanding commitment to healing the environment. We have followed with great interest and sincere concern the efforts to curb the destructive effects that human beings have wrought upon the natural world. We view with alarm the dangerous consequences of humanity's disregard for the survival of God's creation.

It is for this reason that our predecessor, the late Patriarch Dimitrios, of blessed memory, invited the whole world to offer, together with the

Speech reprinted by permission of his All-Holiness, Ecumenical Patriarch Bartholomew.

great church of Christ, prayers of thanksgiving and supplications for the protection of the gift of creation. Since 1989, every September 1, the beginning of the ecclesiastical calendar, has been designated as a day of prayer for the protection of the environment throughout the Orthodox world.

In these and other programs, we have sought to discover the measures that may be implemented by Orthodox Christians worldwide, as leaders desiring to contribute to the solution of this global problem. We believe that, through our particular and unique liturgical and ascetic ethos, Orthodox spirituality may provide significant moral and ethical direction toward a new generation of awareness about the planet.

We believe that Orthodox liturgy and life hold tangible answers to the ultimate questions concerning salvation from corruptibility and death. The Eucharist is at the very center of our worship. And our sin toward the world, or the spiritual root of all our pollution, lies in our refusal to view life and the world as a sacrament of thanksgiving, and as a gift of constant communion with God on a global scale.

We envision a new awareness that is not mere philosophical posturing, but a tangible experience of a mystical nature. We believe that our first task is to raise the consciousness of adults who most use the resources and gifts of the planet. Ultimately, it is for our children that we must perceive our every action in the world as having a direct effect upon the future of the environment. At the heart of the relationship between man and environment is the relationship between human beings. As individuals, we live not only in vertical relationships to God, and horizontal relationships to one another, but also in a complex web of relationships that extend throughout our lives, our cultures, and the material world. Human beings and the environment form a seamless garment of existence, a complex fabric that we believe is fashioned by God.

People of all faith traditions praise the Divine, for they seek to understand their relationship to the cosmos. The entire universe participates in a celebration of life, which St. Maximos the Confessor described as a "cosmic liturgy." We see this cosmic liturgy in the symbiosis of life's rich biological complexities. These complex relationships draw attention to themselves in humanity's self-conscious awareness of the cosmos. As human beings, created "in the image and likeness of God" (Genesis 1:26), we are called to recognize this interdependence between our environment and ourselves. In the bread and the wine of the Eucharist, as priests standing before the altar of the world, we offer the creation back to the Creator in relationship to Him and to each other.

Indeed, in our liturgical life, we realize by anticipation the final state of the cosmos in the Kingdom of Heaven. We celebrate the beauty of creation, and consecrate the life of the world, returning it to God with thanks. We share the world in joy as a living mystical communion with the Divine. Thus it is that we offer the fullness of creation at the Eucharist, and receive it back as a blessing, as the living presence of God.

Moreover, there is also an ascetic element in our responsibility toward God's creation. This asceticism requires from us a voluntary restraint in order for us to live in harmony with our environment. Asceticism offers practical examples of conservation.

By reducing our consumption—in Orthodox Theology, *encratia,* or self-control—we come to ensure that resources are also left for others in the world. As we shift our will, we demonstrate a concern for the Third World and developing nations. Our abundance of resources will be extended to include an abundance of equitable concern for others.

We must challenge ourselves to see our personal, spiritual attitudes in continuity with public policy. Encratia frees us of our self-centered neediness, that we may do good works for others. We do this out of a personal love for the natural world around us. We are called to work in humble harmony with creation and not in arrogant supremacy against it. Asceticism provides an example whereby we may live simply.

Asceticism is not a flight from society and the world, but a communal attitude of mind and way of life that leads to the respectful use, and not the abuse, of material goods. Excessive consumption may be understood to issue from a worldview of estrangement from self, from land, from life, and from God. Consuming the fruits of the earth unrestrained, we become consumed ourselves, by avarice and greed. Excessive consumption leaves us emptied, out of touch with our deepest self. Asceticism is a corrective practice, a vision of repentance. Such a vision will lead us from repentance to return, the return to a world in which we give as well as take from creation.

We invite Orthodox Christians to engage in genuine repentance for the way in which we have behaved toward God, each other, and the world. We gently remind Orthodox Christians that the judgment of the world is in the hands of God. We are called to be stewards, and reflections of God's love by example. Therefore, we proclaim the sanctity of all life, the entire creation being God's and reflecting His continuing will that life abound. We must love life so that others may see and know that it belongs to God. We must leave the judgment of our success to our Creator.

We lovingly suggest, to all the people of the earth, that they seek to help one another to understand the myriad ways in which we are related to the earth and to one another. In this way, we may begin to repair the dislocation many people experience in relation to creation.

We are of the deeply held belief that many human beings have come to behave as materialistic tyrants. Those that tyrannize the earth are themselves, sadly, tyrannized. We have been called by God to "be fruitful, increase, and have dominion in the earth" (Gen 1:28). Dominion is a type of the kingdom of Heaven. Thus it is that St. Basil describes the creation of man in paradise on the sixth day as being the arrival of a king in his palace. Dominion is not domination. It is an eschatological sign of the perfect kingdom of God, where corruption and death are no more.

If human beings treated one another's personal property the way they treat their environment, we would view that behavior as antisocial. We would impose the judicial measures necessary to restore wrongly appropriated personal possessions. It is therefore appropriate for us to seek ethical, legal recourse where possible, in matters of ecological crimes.

It follows that to commit a crime against the natural world is a sin. For humans to cause species to become extinct and to destroy the biological diversity of God's creation, for humans to degrade the integrity of earth by causing changes in its climate, by stripping the earth of its natural forests or destroying its wetlands, for humans to injure other humans with disease, for humans to contaminate the earth's waters, its land, its air, and its life with poisonous substances—these are sins.

In prayer, we ask for the forgiveness of sins committed both willingly and unwillingly. And it is certainly God's forgiveness which we must ask, for causing harm to His own creation.

Thus we begin the process of healing our worldly environment, which was blessed with beauty and created by God. Then we may also begin to participate responsibly, as persons making informed choices, both in the integrated whole of creation and within our own souls.

In just a few weeks the world's leaders will gather in Kyoto, Japan, to determine what, if anything, the nations of the world will commit to do to halt climate change. There has been much debate back and forth about who should and should not have to change the way they use the resources of the earth. Many nations are reluctant to act unilaterally. This self-centered behavior is a symptom of our alienation from one another and from the context of our common existence.

We are urging a different and, we believe, a more satisfactory ecological ethic. This ethic is shared with many of the religious traditions represented here. All of us hold the earth to be the creation of God, where He placed the newly created human "in the Garden of Eden to cultivate it and to guard it" (Genesis 2:15). He imposed on humanity a stewardship role in relationship to the earth. How we treat the earth and all of creation defines the relationship that each of us has with God. It is also a barometer of how we view one another. For if we truly value a person, we are careful as to our behavior toward that person. The dominion that God has given humankind over the earth does not extend to human relationships.

As the Lord said, "You know that the rulers of the Nations lord it over them, and their great ones are tyrants over them. It will not be so among you; but whoever wishes to be great among you must be your servant, and whoever wishes to be first among you must be your slave; just as the Son of Man came not to be served but to serve, and to give his life as a ransom for many." (Matthew 20:25–28)

It is with that understanding that we call on the world's leaders to take action to halt the destructive changes to the global climate that are being caused by human activity. And we call on all of you here today to join us in this cause. This can be our important contribution to the great debate about climate change. We must be spokespeople for an ecological ethic that reminds the world that it is not ours to use for our own convenience. It is God's gift of love to us, and we must return his love by protecting it and all that is in it.

The Lord suffuses all of creation with His divine presence in one continuous legato from the substance of atoms to the Mind of God. Let us renew the harmony between heaven and earth and transfigure every detail, every particle of life. Let us love one another, and lovingly learn from one another, for the edification of God's people, for the sanctification of God's creation, and for the glorification of God's most holy Name.

Amen.

REFERENCES

Chryssavgis, John. "Bartholomew, Ecumenical Patriarch." *Encyclopedia of Religion and Nature.* Ed. Bron Taylor. London: Continuum International, 2005.

Ecumenical Patriarchate of Constantinople web site. *http://www.patriarchate.org.*

McCann, John. "Ecumenical Patriarch Bartholomew Named 2002 Winner of the Sophie Prize for Leadership on the Environment." *World Wide Earth News,* April 22, 2002.

National Council of Churches of Christ, USA. "NCCCUSA Leaders Participate in Orthodox Environmental Conference." Press release, October 10, 1997.

White, Lynne. "The Historical Roots of Our Ecological Crises." *Science* 155(1967): 1203 1207.

Woodard, Colin. "Orthodox Leader Blesses Green Agenda." *Christian Science Monitor,* July 24, 2003.

17. Ian Kiernan

AUSTRALIA

As disposable products have come to dominate world markets, litter has grown from an urban nuisance to a global scourge. The main engine behind the phenomenon is the sheer volume of rubbish generated by today's consumer-driven society. Notwithstanding progress in recycling technologies and awareness, there is simply more garbage produced than ever before. In 1960, for example, U.S. citizens produced a little more than a kilogram per person per day of garbage. Within forty years, that amount had doubled to two kilograms. In Europe, where recycling is more widely embraced than on any other continent, 2.5 billion tons of garbage are still produced each year.

Many are the reasons why people toss their trash to the public domain. Keep America Beautiful, perhaps the world's most experienced organization in the field of litter, cites several factors: lack of "ownership" and an alienation from public property; a presumption that someone else (a park maintenance or highway worker) will pick up after them; or the perception that litter has already accumulated, so another piece won't matter. Some add to this a healthy element of human laziness and juvenile delinquency. Yet studies suggest that the litterbugs do not fit not the stereotype of a post-adolescent male in a pick-up truck, but come in all shapes, sizes, and demographics.

There is probably not a country on earth without a law that prohibits littering. As literally hundreds of millions of people break these laws, trashing public spaces, the environmental challenge appears to be less regulatory and more educational in dimension. Anyone who visits the immaculate alternatives of Switzerland or Japan understands intuitively that there is a cultural component to how societies value cleanliness.

Inasmuch as the litter problem has been on the environmental agenda for decades, it is also fair to assume that convincing the general public to change its behavior towards refuse and its attitude toward its public spaces is no simple matter. Although major environmental groups often shun litter as a "light-weight" problem that cannot compete with toxic contamination or irreversible ecological disasters, there are a few people who have taken on the issue and made a difference. Notable, for example, was Lady Bird Johnson, the wife of American President Lyndon Johnson, who adopted the issue as part of her 1960s "beautification" campaign, bringing the problem to the doorsteps of a nation. But no single individual has made his country—and eventually his planet—care about the issue of litter more than Ian Kiernan.

Among the world's many accidental environmental heroes, Ian Kiernan can certainly compete for the least likely. A World War II baby, he grew up in Australia, the vast and largely empty continent where the seemingly unlimited resources left him (in his own words) "an environmental vandal at seventeen." Kiernan skipped university to make his fortune restoring slum housing in the booming Sydney economy, tossing corrugated iron roofs into the harbor with the hope that the salt water would corrode them away.

Kiernan's construction business was initially a huge success, and he led a very good life for most of the 1960s. When his over-leveraged twenty-million-dollar real estate empire began to crash during the economic slump of the early 1970s, he left his family behind and found solace among the waves, sailing from Tahiti to Hawaii.

What began as a hobby became an obsession, and his skills as a sailboat captain reached world-class levels. Kiernan kept his business sufficiently afloat to support his passion, and eventually was good enough to be picked to sail the *Spirit of Sydney* in the BOC (British Oxygen Company) challenge. The ultimate yachting race, the challenge pits the world's best sailors against each other as they single-handedly sail around the world. Although Kiernan did not win the race, his strong showing (sixth in a field of twenty-five), along with his colorful, authentically Australian persona catapulted him into his country's public eye.

While Kiernan thrived throughout the demands of the reclusive adventure, he had one very unhappy surprise during his time at sea. In the most remote regions of the planet, he sailed through trash. In his autobiography "Coming Clean," he writes of his entrance into the Sargasso Sea on the last leg of his round-the-world journey: "I can't overstate my disgust when I sailed into this pristine place of smoky blue water dotted by semi-submerged golden weed so vital to the marine food chain, this sea of magic and myth . . . and found it littered with rubbish. First a rubber thong, then a toothpaste tube, a comb, a plastic bag. As *Spirit* cut through the almost glass-like sea, propelled by the lightest of breezes, the rubbish popped upon both sides of the bow . . . it took me back to the Sydney Harbour I knew as a boy, and the one I knew forty years later, with broken glass at the tide line and plastic bags covered with green slime on the surface."

After the race, Kiernan resumed life as a real-estate developer. But, by now a public figure, with a keen sense of the growing dissonance between humans and the planet's environment, he found his heart going beyond business. A vague idea of cleaning up his beloved Sydney harbor began to take hold. His vision was to engage citizens in a massive cleanup, instilling in them a sense of ownership and empowerment. The government officials that Kiernan initially approached were less than enthusiastic. But the seaside suburb of Mosman was willing to humor the ebullient skipper, as Kiernan had flown their rowing club's flag on his famous craft.

The notion of cleaning Mosman's seventeen beaches was ultimately too modest for Kiernan's hefty appetite. A friend connected him with the head of the local McDonald's, who was won over by Kiernan's sincerity and charm. Armed with a $25,000 sponsorship, he told the press that on January 8, 1989, he was going to lead a cleanup that would take on all of Sydney Harbor. Kiernan was later shocked to discover that there were no less than 270 kilometers of foreshore associated with that harbor, most in need of a very serious cleanup.

Like so many successful environmental advertising campaigns, Kiernan's targeted children, approving a moronic jingle, "Yuckie Yuckie Poo," that caught the fancy of the town. Kiernan and his volunteers estimated that one hundred to two hundred tons of rubbish would be pulled out of the sea and the beaches. The army of forty thousand who turned up around the city found a good deal more trash than that. An early count set the quantity of garbage collected in one day at five thousand tons—including three thousand syringes. That quantity was far beyond Kiernan's collection capacity and there was concern that many of the trash bags left on the beach would be washed away with the morning tide. Miraculously, "a bloke named Harry" called up out of the blue and offered his eight-wheel "bogey tipper," and Kiernan and the organizers played garbage crew all night to finish the job.

By the time the 1990 cleanup came around, the initial success at Sydney had led to hundreds of thousands of dollars in additional sponsorship from corporate giants, from Westpac bank to Telecom. Within a year, Kiernan's idiosyncratic impulse had burgeoned into a national operation that was then called "Clean Up Australia." In the second year, Kiernan attracted 320,000 volunteers in 450 cities, bringing in over twenty thousand tons of rubbish, including two thousand car bodies. Word got out that something special was happening down under, and Mostafa Tolba, the director general of UNEP, invited Kiernan to his offices in Nairobi to explore how to make the project a global initiative.

September was picked for holding "Clean Up the World," as this was the optimal time globally for people to be outdoors. UNEP provided seed money, but it was Kiernan who went banging on corporate doors around the world to make it happen by meeting an anticipated budget of three million dollars. The momentum continued, with cleanup operations taking place in eighty countries, with thirty million volunteers picking up trash from the Congo to South Korea. Today, 114 countries actively participate in the annual event.

Kiernan was suddenly the head of Australia's largest citizens group, with 750,000 citizens joining his annual cleanup campaigns. Polls showed "Clean Up Australia" enjoyed more public trust than any other organization in the country. Kiernan was expected to be an environmental expert, and he plunged into the issue.

His group began to publish an annual "Rubbish Report" whose statistical analysis tried to identify trends and a more intelligent strategy for addressing the country's litter syndrome. Quickly, Kiernan realized that his successful cleanups were in fact only dealing with symptoms, and that he could no longer ignore the causes of an international syndrome. "How garbage is generated," consumerism, and a "disposal culture" became issues he pondered and brought to his expert Environmental Advisory Committee. Soon the organization was taking on issues of sewage, industrial effluents, and water conservation, and was involved in a war against plastic bags. But notwithstanding Kiernan's expanded agenda, the many campaigns shared the same fundamental aspects of engaging the public.

By 1994, Kiernan was awarded the prestigious Australian of the Year award by the prime minister. His image didn't suffer when he spontaneously leaped off the award stage to apprehend a would-be assassin who was running toward him with a gun pointed at the visiting Prince Charles. Four years later, he won the Susakawa Environmental Prize, an award administered by UNEP. His brief acceptance speech brought together the basic principles behind his Clean Up initiatives, which had already become an international network: "A simple formula of local empowerment and harnessing human nature that prefers living in clean surroundings."

In interviews Kiernan plays down his ecological credentials: "I don't see myself as a nuts and berries greenie. Just an ordinary bloke who's made an environmental commitment to improve my environmental behavior." Australia is a vast, largely unpopulated continent; whether it is filled with garbage or not depends entirely on its citizens and the ongoing effectiveness of this unlikely but highly successful leader.

"It's All about Taming Greed"

SPEECH TO THE UNITED NATIONS UPON RECEIVING THE SASAKAWA ENVIRONMENT PRIZE, NEW YORK, N.Y., NOVEMBER 16, 1998

*T*his is a very exciting night for those of us who conceived of Clean Up the World. I've always believed in pursuing a dream, and while I acknowledge that sometimes that can get you into trouble, what I have found is tenacity will, more often than not, deliver more than you ever expected. Clean Up the World, our latest dream, is not a modest project. Fortunately, it's one that doesn't rest solely on my shoulders.

My awakening to the pressure being put on our fragile world came through sailing. I got to see parts of this world few of us have the privilege to see—and everywhere I saw evidence of humanity's lack of respect for this miracle which is our world. Since then, I've been reading about how the global environmental crisis is deepening. The challenge for business, government, and communities is creating action from dialogue, giving the community ownership of their local environmental issues together with the resources and support to get involved in solving these issues. What's the point about boasting about higher short-term growth if you can't breathe the air, drink the water, or safely swim at your local river or

Speech reprinted with permission of Ian Kiernan.

beach? Clean Up the World is certainly not the answer to these problems, but it's a start . . . and it starts right at the grass roots. You see, I firmly believe that the state of our environment is at the base of our survival, and that every person on this planet has a responsibility to care for our environment.

When we took the concept of Clean Up to the people of Australia, they welcomed us with open arms. It then struck me that we had an idea that is exportable, because it has universal appeal. The common denominator is galvanizing people with a renewed desire for action—delivering financial, social and heath benefits.

While developing our campaign, I've become a strange tourist, attracted to the type of places you seldom see on the tourist maps. Whether it be in major cities like New York, where civic efforts are focusing on restoration and rebuilding, to developing communities like the slums of Tondo in metropolitan Manila, where more than twenty thousand people used to live on the rubbish heap of Smokey Mountain in disease ridden squalor, there are new settlements and new hope.

This is all due to the mobilization of armies of people out there—some in corporations or government, others attached to the United Nations or other environmental NGOs, or in suburban homes or villages. That's what Clean Up the World is about. It's about educating people, raising community awareness, and giving ordinary citizens the opportunity to play a significant role.

While the Sasakawa prize is a check made out to me, it's not going into my bank account. It's going straight back into Clean Up, into a special fund we intend to grow to repair industrial and agricultural land using the best science and technology in partnership with communities and government.

Why? Because I firmly believe that people's efforts, coupled with good policy and partnership with business, can deliver the solution. Our world is a constantly changing place, and we have to meet those changes with our own actions. Old attitudes no longer apply. Just look at sewage and solid waste, major problems facing us today. The old attitude was to find minimal ways of treatment followed by a convenient dumping ground.

Today, the water companies say: how much dirty water can I buy from you? And the progressive solid waste companies say it's not a rubbish tip . . . it's a recovery facility. The key is converting a waste stream into a resource stream. That way, business is driving an environmental agenda and making profit at the same time.

I guess you could say it's all about taming greed. Greed, ignorance, and fear are the base causes of so many of our environmental problems. You just need to look at the opponents of action and policy to control global warming, to understand that. If an economic incentive and disincentive can be applied, . . . you'll satisfy the greed.

Ignorance can be overcome through education, whether it's in schools or in the boardroom or at a village meeting. Fear is our biggest enemy, fear of personal poverty or short-term national economic setbacks. How we overcome this fear is our biggest challenge.

I see the environment as the absolute primary issue if we want to look at a sustainable world for our children and our children's' children. If it hadn't been for the United Nations Environment Program's early support, we wouldn't have been able to export the Clean Up program from Australia. My own team at Clean Up has seen the project through, despite small budgets and many obstacles. And the support I've had from my long-suffering family has been paramount, allowing me the time to dedicate to Clean Up.

This award is for the forty-million-plus people who participate in Clean Up around the globe each year, and we're going to continue our efforts with renewed vigor. Our goal is to build on the investment we've made over the past ten years and to take Clean Up the World to as many nations as we can in the new millennium.

I thank you for your support and for this great honor. Our commitment is unwavering in our resolve.

REFERENCES

Clean Up the World web site. *http://www.cleanup.com.au.*

"Ian Kiernan, a Short Biography." *Top Achievers. http://www.achievers-odds .com.au /topachiever/ikiernanfull.htm.*

Keep America Beautiful. "Litter Prevention." *http://www.kab.org/.* 2004.

Kiernan, Ian. Personal communication, September 3, 2003.

Kiernan, Ian, and Phil Jarratt. *Coming Clean.* Sydney: MacMillan, 1995.

United Nations. Commission on Sustainable Development. Report of the Secretary–General. "Sustainable Human Settlements Development and Environmentally Sound Management of Solid Wastes." New York, 2001.

United Nations Environmental Program (UNEP). "United Nations Premier Environmental Prize Awarded to Ian Kiernan of Australia, Founder of 'Clean Up the World' Campaign." Press release, 1998.

U.S. Environmental Protection Agency. *Municipal Solid Waste in the United States: 2001 Facts and Figures.* Washington, 2003.

18. Vandana Shiva

INDIA

*T*he obstacles faced by environmentalists in developing countries are often as much geographical as they are economic. Frequently, the source of their ecological problems lie far across the ocean in corporate boardrooms worlds away from their realm of influence. It was no surprise when globalization evolved into a major theme among green activists around the world. Environmental groups were among the more passionate participants in the extraordinary November 1999 protests at the Seattle meeting of the World Trade Organization. At issue was the emerging supremacy of free trade over environmental and other values. In the poorer nations of the planet, people are increasingly concerned about losing ground to "economic imperialism." They feel helpless when faced with the power of multinational corporations to control their industrial sectors, their consumer products, the way they farm even the very plants on which they have traditionally relied.

The debate surrounding ratification of the Convention on Biological Diversity in the early 1990s was a harbinger of the coming storm. The disagreement boiled down to divergent perceptions of intellectual property rights. Developing countries challenged provisions demanded by Western countries. They claimed that the new rules would protect the profits of commercial, corporate plant breeders, while not remunerating farmers who had been improving and developing plant genotypes from time immemorial. When corporations began to receive patent rights for genetically modified seeds and to sell them aggressively in developing countries, many people saw this activity in the broader historical context of colonialism and exploitation.

No individual has been as important in raising questions about agriculture, the environment, and the social impacts of free trade and multinational corporate abuse as Vandana Shiva. The fact that she is a scientist and frames her arguments in terms of biodiversity and agricultural productivity provide legitimacy to a cause typically caricatured by opponents as extremist and irrational.

Dr. Shiva's curriculum vitae is an impressive document. Like many figures in the environmental and organic movements, she may be considered a second-generation activist. She was born in the scenic region of Dehradun near the Himalayas in 1952; her father was the Conservator of Forests in her region and her mother was a farmer. Sent to Christian schools, she gravitated towards the sciences.

Shiva's subsequent training was far from the applied, interdisciplinary orientation that would make her famous. Rather, she completed a Ph.D. in physics at the University of Western Ontario and submitted a dissertation on the relatively arcane topic of "Hidden Variables and Non-locality in Quantum Theory." Returning to the Indian Institute of Science and Indian Institute of Management in Bangalore, however, her research took her in completely new areas, and she began to consider biological systems and agriculture.

By age thirty, Shiva felt constrained by conventional academic frameworks, so she founded her own Research Foundation for Science, Technology, and Ecology in New Delhi. The foundation serves as a center that addresses the ecological and social issues that she saw as interrelated. This open framework unleashed her startling productivity. Shiva has since published over three hundred articles and several books on a range of topics, from the failure of the Green Revolution and seed diversity to ecofeminism and genetic engineering.

Her candor and lack of hesitation to go beyond scientific analysis quickly made her a highly sought-after speaker all over the planet. Indeed, no individual received more nominations for inclusion in this book from more countries than she did, with any number of her "critical speeches" cited. Shiva continues to bring together and galvanize a new coalition of environmental, organic, and antiglobalization factions that share her dissatisfaction with industrialized agriculture and corporate behavior.

Multinational corporations have born the brunt of her attack. The speech in this book was given by her in New Delhi, part of a series of five talks about sustainable development by speakers scattered around the globe. The BBC covered her lecture live. In this presentation, Shiva takes aim at a series of multinational corporations involved in developing agricultural commodities, including Dupont and Cargill. But she saves her most devastating critiques for Monsanto, perhaps her ultimate corporate antagonist.

In truth, Shiva's attack could have been aimed at any number of powerful transboundary consortiums. For instance, in one televised interview she took on the fast food industry, characterizing the McDonald's experience as "the experience of eating junk while thinking you are in heaven because of the golden arches, which is supposed to suggest you enter heaven." Her critique not only included the environmental ramifications of the corporation's food production, but the child labor policies as well.

Shiva does more than merely pontificate. At the International Conference for Women in Beijing in 1995, her lecture instigated an impromptu demonstration to kick the McDonald's outlet off the convention grounds. Shiva was at the front of the picket line.

Shiva is hailed not just as a leader of the environmental camp, but also as a feminist leader. From her perspective, the two causes are inextricably linked. For example, she frequently cites the fact that it is *women,* who do most of the work on small farms in the developing world, who have rejected monocultures. When asked whether preserving germ plasm should be left to the specialists, she agreed—but explained that these happen to be the women of developing nations, who are the true preservers of crop biodiversity.

It was this sort of willingness to go where her analysis would lead that brought Shiva in 1998 to the St. Louis headquarters of Monsanto so that she could launch the first American gathering of activists concerned about genetic modification. In taking on Monsanto, as she does without blinking in her speech reprinted here, two year's later, Shiva remained focused on the biggest biotech industry giant, a company that posts sales around the planet of billions of dollars annually.

Monsanto made a strategic decision to embrace the biological engineering technologies that could modify crops genetically, as a way to move beyond its original orientation as a chemical company. Starting in 1996, the corporation systematically spent over eight billion dollars purchasing biotechnology and seed companies globally, then merged with other corporations to form the largest life science company in the world. Genetically modified seeds were at the heart of the new corporate mission.

In many countries, farmers were responsive to the new products. In the United States, Latin America, and China, for example, some sixty million hectares of genetically modified crops are being grown today. Cotton production leads the way, with GM rubber, palm oil, and rape seeds commercially marketed as well.

Europe, however, continues to be more circumspect. With Shiva and other activists raising a long list of concerns, large segments of the European public refused to embrace the new seed technologies and their produce. Most countries in Europe have placed serious restrictions on the use of genetically modified crops. Indeed, in 2001, the Italian police raided a Monsanto stockpile of genetically modified maize, which had been banned there.

Monsanto for its part expressed befuddlement at the viciousness of Shiva's attack, justifying their "GM" innovation on environmental grounds: genetic modification would reduce reliance on pesticides, and ultimately improve yields and save open spaces. As Monsanto's former CEO, Robert Shapiro, mused: "The application of biological knowledge to issues like food and nutrition and human health has to occur, for the same reasons that things have occurred for the past ten millennia. People want to live better, and they will use the tools they have to do it. Biology is the best tool we have."

Other Shiva critics were nastier: "If developing-world farmers took her one-tenth as seriously as do Western activists, her proclamations would lead inexorably to massive famine," scoffed Michael Fumento, a senior fellow at the Hudson Institute. "She was born into wealth and her soft palms have never worked a plow. Hunger to her is something she reads about in the newspapers."

But Shiva remained undaunted, and her fears increasingly became part of consumer culture in Europe. In England, for example, following a spate of food-related scares, the public was suspicious of industry and government alike. In her study of the factors leading to current opposition to food biotechnology, Georgetown University's Kim Brooks explained: "What the private sector did not anticipate was the role the activist and green parties would play in 'outing government,' providing consumers with a watchdog. The unavailability of scientific studies to bolster corporate claims that genetic engineering was safe placed government and industry in precarious positions."

In India itself, Shiva's positions began to enjoy grassroots support. In 2002, farmers and activists in South India burned copies of the government's new agricultural policy law. The protests focused on the introduction of genetically modified seeds that they saw as leaving them economically and agronomically more vulnerable. The protests came in the wake of mass suicides by cotton farmers, who killed themselves by consuming pesticides. The campaign adopted the slogans "Cremate Monsanto" and "No Patents on Life."

The debate over genetically modified crops and the role of transnationals in "transforming" agriculture in the developing world has yet to be resolved. Certainly, there are many compelling environmental reasons why innovations in developing drought- and pesticide-resistant strains should be explored. But Vandana Shiva's vigilance has helped change the terms of the debate and has forced industry to honor a long list of consumer and environmental concerns as it promotes its new products. Her tireless crusade for economic justice and sustainable agriculture for the farmers of the developing world helped redefine genetically modified food, from a technical biological innovation to a complex social issue that is very much a part of the world's environmental and agricultural agenda.

"Sharing and Exchange, the Basis of Our Humanity and Our Ecological Survival Has Been Redefined as a Crime"

THE REITH LECTURE, THE NEHRU MUSEUM, DELHI, INDIA, APRIL 27, 2000

*R*ecently, I was visiting Bhatinda in Punjab, which used to have fertile soils and prosperous farmers. Today every farmer is in debt and despair. There has been an epidemic of suicides. Vast stretches of land have become waterlogged wasteland. And, as an old farmer pointed out, even the trees have stopped bearing fruit, because heavy use of pesticides has killed the pollinators—the bees and butterflies.

Speech reprinted with permission of Dr. Vandana Shiva.

Last year I was in Warangal, Andhra Pradesh, where farmers have also been committing suicide. Farmers who traditionally grew pulses and millet and paddy have been lured by seed companies to buy hybrid cotton-seeds referred to as "white gold." Their native seeds have been displaced with new seeds, which cannot be saved, and need to be purchased every year at a high cost. Hybrids are also very vulnerable to pest attacks. Expenditures on pesticides in Warangal have increased 2,000 percent, from $2.5 million in the 1980s to $50 million in 1997.

The corporations are now trying to introduce genetically engineered seeds that will further increase costs and ecological risks. That is why farmers like Malla Reddy had uprooted and burned Monsanto's genetically engineered Bollgard cotton trials.

It is experiences such as these tell me that we are so wrong to be smug about the new global economy. I will argue in this lecture that it is time to stop and think about the impact of globalization on the lives of ordinary people. This is vital if we want to achieve sustainable development.

Last year in Seattle, many strands of my life came together and crystallized into one of those moments when you see things clearly. Seattle and the World Trade Organization protests have forced everyone to look again at the process of globalization. Throughout this lecture series, people have referred to different aspects of sustainable development, taking globalization for granted. For me it is now time radically to reevaluate what we are doing. For what we are doing in the name of globalization to the poor is brutal, so come down to earth with me here in India.

Who feeds the world? My answer is very different to that given by most people.

It is women and small farmers working with biodiversity who are the primary food providers in the Third World.

The rich diversity and sustainable systems of food production have been destroyed in the name of increasing food production. However, with the destruction of diversity, rich sources of nutrition disappear. When measured in terms of nutrition per acre, from a different perspective, that of biodiversity, the so-called "high yields" of industrial agriculture do not imply more production of food and nutrition.

Yields usually refer to production per unit area of a single crop. Output refers to the total production of diverse crops and products. Planting only one crop in the entire field as a monoculture will of course increase its yield. Planting multiple crops in a mixture will have low yields of individual crops, but will have high total output of food. Yields have been defined in such a way as to make the food production on small farms by small farmers disappear. It hides the production by millions of women farmers in the Third World—farmers like those in the Himalayas who fought against logging in the Chipko movement, who in their terraced fields grow Jhangora (barnyard millet), Marsha (amaranth), Tur (pigeon pea), Urad (black gram), Gahat (horse gram), soybean (glycine max), Bhat (glycine soya), Rayans (rice bean), Swanta (cow pea), Koda (finger millet). From the biodiversity perspective, biodiversity-based productivity is higher than monoculture productivity.

The Mayan peasants in the Chiapas are characterized as unproductive because they produce only two tons of corn per acre. However, the overall food output is twenty tons per acre when the diversity of their beans and squashes, their vegetables and fruit trees, are taken into account.

Research done by the United Nations Food and Agriculture Organization (FAO) has shown that small, biodiverse farms can produce thousands of times more food than large, industrial monocultures. In Java, small farmers cultivate 607 species in their home gardens, with an overall species diversity comparable to a deciduous tropical forest. In sub-Saharan Africa, women cultivate as many as 120 different plants in the spaces left alongside the cash crops. A single home garden in Thailand has more than 230 species, and African home gardens have more than 60 species of trees. Rural families in the Congo eat leaves from more than 50 different species of trees.

A study in eastern Nigeria found that home gardens occupying only 2 percent of a household's farmland accounted for half of the farm's total output. Similarly, home gardens in Indonesia are estimated to provide more than 20 percent of household income and 40 percent of domestic food supplies.

Because biodiversity produces more than monocultures, for ten years I have been working with farmers to conserve biodiversity and diverse farming systems.

The blindness to diversity, the blindness to nature's production, production by women, production by Third World farmers, allows destruction and appropriation to be projected as creation.

Take the case of the much flouted "golden rice" or genetically engineered vit. rice as a cure for blindness. It is assumed that without genetic engineering we cannot remove vitamin A deficiency. However, nature gives us abundant and diverse sources of vitamin A. If rice were not polished, rice itself would provide vitamin A. If herbicides were not sprayed on our wheat fields, we would have bathua, amaranth, mustard leaves as delicious and nutritious greens.

Women in Bengal use more than 150 plants as greens. Hinche sak (*Enhydra fluctuans*), Palang sak (*Spinacea oleracea*), Tak palang (*Rumex vesicarious*), Lal Sak (*Amaranthus gangeticus*), Champa note (*Amaranthus tristis*), Gobra note (*Amaranthus lividus*), Ghenti note (*Amaranthus tennifolius*), Banspata note (*Amaranthus lanceolatus*), Ban note (*Amaranthus viridis*), Sada note (*Amaranthus blitum*), Kanta note (*Amaranthus spinosus*), Bethua sale (*Chenopodium album*), Brahmi Sak (*Bacopa monrieri*), Sushin Sak (*Marulea quadrifolio*), to name but a few.

But the myth of creation presents biotechnologists as the creators of vitamin A, negating nature's diverse gifts and women's knowledge of how to use this diversity to feed their children and families.

The most efficient means of rendering the destruction of nature, local economies, and small autonomous producers is by rendering their production invisible. Millions who work and produce in partnership with nature are declared unproductive. In contrast, a minority of people who gamble on the global casino are declared "wealth creators." Globalization has created a system in which work and wealth have been totally separated from each other.

Women who produce for their families, children, and nature are treated as non-productive and economically inactive. The devaluation of women's work, and of work done in subsistence economies, is the natural outcome of a system constructed by capitalist patriarchy. This is how globalization destroys local economies, and the destruction itself is counted as growth.

And women themselves are devalued. Because, for many women in the rural and indigenous communities, their work cooperates with nature's processes, and is often contradictory to the dominant market driven "development" and trade policies. And because work that satisfies needs and ensures sustenance is devalued in general, there is less nurturing of life and life-support systems.

That is why I ask, who feeds the world?

The devaluation and invisibility of sustainable, regenerative production is most glaring in the area of food. While patriarchal division of labor has assigned women the role of feeding their families and communities, patriarchal economies and patriarchal views of science and technology magically make women's work in providing food disappear. "Feeding the World" becomes disassociated from the women who actually do it, and is projected as dependent on global agribusiness and biotechnology corporations. Without global free trade and genetic engineering, we are told, the world will starve.

However, industrialization of food, globalization of trade, and genetic engineering in agriculture are recipes for creating hunger, not for feeding the poor.

Everywhere, agriculture is becoming a negative economy, with farmers spending more on production than the price they receive for their produce. The consequence is rising debts and epidemics of suicides in both rich and poor countries.

The globalization of nonsustainable industrial agriculture is literally evaporating the incomes of Third World farmers through a combination of devaluation of currencies, increase in costs of production, and a collapse in commodity prices.

Farmers everywhere are being paid a fraction of what they received for the same commodity a decade ago. In the U.S., wheat prices at the farm dropped from $5.75 a bushed to $2.43, soybean prices dropped from $ 8.40 to $ 4.29, and corn prices dropped from $4.43 to $1.72. In India, from 1999 to 2000, prices for coffee dropped from Rs. 60 to Rs. 18 per kg.

The Canadian National Farmers Union put it like this in a report to the senate this year: "While the farmers growing cereal grains—wheat, oats, corn—earn negative returns and are pushed close to bankruptcy, the companies that make breakfast cereals reap huge profits. In 1998, cereal companies Kellogg's, Quaker Oats, and General Mills enjoyed return on equity rates of 56 percent, 165 percent and 222 percent, respectively. While a bushel of corn sold for less than $4, a bushel of corn flakes sold for $133. In 1998, the cereal companies were 186 to 740 times more profitable than the farms. Maybe farmers are making too little because others are taking too much."

At the same time, the costs of production are shooting up.

Economic globalization is leading to a concentration of the seed industry, the entry of global corporations into agriculture, the increased use of pesticides, and, finally, increased debt, despair, and sometimes suicide among small farmers. Capital-intensive, corporate-controlled agriculture is being spread into regions where peasants are poor but, until now, have been self-sufficient in food. In the regions where industrial agriculture has been introduced through globalization, higher costs are making it virtually impossible for small farmers to survive.

Simultaneously, the prices for consumers are not coming down. In India, food prices have doubled between 1999 and 2000, and consumption of food grains has dropped by 12 percent in rural areas, increasing the food deprivation of those already malnourished, and pushing up mortality rates. Rural poverty has increased by 10 percent since the beginning of economic reforms. Half India is now below the poverty line. When growth increases poverty, when real production becomes a negative economy, and speculators are defined as "wealth creators," something has gone wrong with the concepts and categories of wealth and wealth creation.

The real economies of nature and food production are being undermined for the growth of the bubble economy of fictitious finance. This is creating a totally nonsustainable situation both because the rising inequalities create nonsustainability and because the bubble itself can burst anytime. Pushing the real production by nature and people into a negative economy implies that production of real goods and services is declining, creating deeper poverty for the millions who are not part of the dot.com route to instantaneous wealth creation.

Women, as I have said, are the primary food producers and food processors in the world. However, their work in production and processing has now become invisible.

According to the McKinsey corporation, "American food giants recognize that Indian agrobusiness has lots of room to grow, especially in food processing. India processes a minuscule 1 percent of the food it grows compared with 70 percent for the U.S., Brazil, and Philippines." McKinsey only sees 1 percent of agroprocessing carried out by large corporations through industrial processes.

The 99 percent food processing done by women at household level, or by a small cottage industry is not counted because it is not controlled by global agribusiness. Since 99 percent of the food economy, dominated by women and small producers, does not just disappear by discounting it, it must be wiped out by force and coercion, manipulation and violence. Pseudohygiene laws that shut down the 99 percent economy based on local small-scale processing under community control are part of the arsenal of global agribusiness for establishing market monopolies.

In August 1998, small-scale local processing of edible oil was banned in India through a "packaging order" which made sale of open oil illegal and required all oil to be packed in plastic or aluminium. This shut down tiny "ghanis" or cold-pressed mills. It destroyed the market for our diverse oilseeds—mustard, linseed, sesame, groundnut, and coconut.

On World Food Day, women of the Delhi slums organized protests against the criminalization of their food system and the dumping of genetically engineered soybean.

The takeover of the edible oil industry has affected ten million livelihoods. The take over of "atta," or flour, by packaged, branded flour will cost one hundred million livelihoods. These millions are being pushed into new poverty.

The forced use of packaging will increase the environmental burden of millions of tons of plastic and aluminium.

The globalization of the food system is destroying the diversity of local food cultures and local food economies. A global monoculture is being forced on people by defining everything that is fresh, local, and hand-made as health hazards. Human hands are being defined as the worst contaminants, and work for human hands is being outlawed, to be replaced by machines and chemicals bought from global corporations. These are not recipes for feeding the world, but stealing livelihoods from the poor to create markets for the powerful.

People are being perceived as parasites, to be exterminated for the "health" of the global economy.

In the process, new health and ecological hazards are being forced on people through genetic engineering.

Recently, because of a WTO ruling, India was forced to remove restrictions on all imports.

Among the unrestricted imports are carcasses and animal waste parts that create a threat to our culture and our public health.

The U.S. Centers for Disease and Prevention (CDS) in Atlanta has calculated that nearly eighty-one million cases of food borne illnesses occur in the U.S. every year. Deaths from food poisoning have more than quadrupled due to deregulation, rising from two thousand in 1984 to nine thousand in 1994. Most of these infections are caused by factory-farmed meat. The U.S. slaughters ninety-three million pigs, thirty-seven million cattle, two million calves, six million horses, goats, and sheep, and eight billion chickens and turkeys.

Now the giant meat industry of the U.S. wants to dump contaminated meat produced through violent and cruel methods on India.

The waste of the rich is being dumped on the poor. The wealth of the poor is being violently appropriated through new and clever means like patents on biodiversity and indigenous knowledge.

Patents and intellectual property rights are supposed to be granted for novel inventions. But patents are being claimed for rice varieties, such as the basmati, for which my Doon Valley, where I was born, is famous, or pesticides derived from the neem, which our mothers and grandmothers have been using.

Rice Tec, a U.S.-based company, has been granted patent number 5,663,484 for basmati rice lines and grains.

Basmati, neem, pepper, bitter gourd, turmeric—every aspect of the innovation embodied in our indigenous food and medicinal systems is now being pirated and patented. The knowledge of the poor is being converted into the property of global corporations, creating a situation where the poor will have to pay for the seeds and medicines they have evolved and have used to meet their needs for nutrition and health care.

Humans do not create life when they manipulate it. Rice Tec's claim that it has made "an instant invention of a novel rice line," or the Roslin Institute's claim that Ian Wilmut "created" Dolly, denies the creativity of nature, the self-organizational capacity of life forms, and the prior innovation of Third World communities.

Such false claims to creation are now the global norm, with the Trade-Related Intellectual Property Rights Agreement of WTO forcing countries to introduce IPR [intellectual property rights] regimes that allow patenting of life forms and indigenous knowledge.

Instead of recognizing that commercial interests build on nature and on the contribution of other cultures, global law has enshrined the patriarchal myth of creation to create new property rights to life forms just as colonialism used the myth of discovery as the basis of the takeover of the land of others as colonies.

Patents and intellectual property rights are supposed to prevent piracy. Instead, they are becoming the instruments of pirating the common traditional knowledge from the poor of the Third World and making it the exclusive "property" of western scientists and corporations.

When patents are granted for seeds and plants, as in the case of basmati, theft is defined as creation, and saving and sharing seed is defined as theft of intellectual property. Corporations like Monsanto, which have broad patents on crops such as cotton, soybeans, and mustard, are suing farmers for seed saving, and hiring detective agencies for finding out if farmers have saved seed or shared it with neighbors.

Sharing and exchange, the basis of our humanity and our ecological survival, has been redefined as a crime.

Nature has given us abundance; women's indigenous knowledge of biodiversity, agriculture, and nutrition has built on that abundance to create more from less, to create growth through sharing. Women farmers share seeds freely; and, with sharing as a base, there can never be scarcity. The giving and sharing of food in abundance has been the basis of ensuring food security.

The giving and sharing of knowledge has been the basis of the growth and evolution of knowledge. An economy of sharing is an economy of abundance.

Criminalization of sharing makes us all poor. The poor are pushed into deeper poverty by being made to pay for what were their resources and knowledge. Even the rich are poorer because their profits are based on theft and on the use of coercion and violence. This is not wealth creation but plunder.

Sustainability requires the protection of all species and all people, and the recognition that diverse species and diverse people play an essential role in maintaining ecosystems and ecological processes. Pollinators are critical to fertilization and generation of plants. Biodiversity in fields provides vegetables, fodder, medicine, and protection to the soil from water and wind erosion.

As humans travel further down the road to nonsustainability, they become intolerant of other species and blind to their vital role in our survival. In their so-called global village being shaped by globalization, corporations view peasants saving seeds, bees pollinating crops, plants converting the sun's energy into food, fodder, and medicine as "thieves."

In 1992, when Indian farmers destroyed Cargill's seed plant in Bellary, Karnataka, the Cargill chief executive stated, "We bring Indian farmers smart technologies which prevent bees from *usurping* the pollen." When I was participating in the United Nations Biosafety Negotiations, Monsanto circulated literature which claimed the "weeds *steal* the sunshine." In its advertisements in India, Monsanto refers to weeds and biodiversity as "thieves." A worldview that defines pollination as "theft by bees" and claims that biodiversity "steals" sunshine is a worldview which itself aims at stealing nature's harvest by replacing open, pollinated varieties with hybrids and sterile seeds, and destroying biodiverse flora with herbicides such as Monsanto's Roundup.

The threat posed to the Monarch butterfly by genetically engineered bt. Crops is just one example of the ecological poverty created by the new biotechnologies. As butterflies and bees disappear, production is undermined. As biodiversity disappears, with it go sources of nutrition and food. When giant corporations view small peasants and bees as thieves, and through trade rules and new technologies seek the right to wipe them out, humanity has reached a dangerous threshold. The imperative to stamp out the smallest insect, the smallest plant, the smallest peasant comes from a deep fear—the fear of everything that is alive and free. And this deep insecurity and fear is unleashing violence against all people and all species.

This worldview is based on scarcity, which in turn creates scarcity and conflict and poverty. It cannot create abundance.

A worldview of abundance is the worldview of women in India who grow food not just for humans, but for all species. They leave food for ants on their doorstep, even as they create the most beautiful art in kolams, mandalas, and rangoli with rice flour. This view of abundance recognizes that, in giving food to other beings and species, we maintain conditions for our own food security. In feeding the earthworms, we feed ourselves. In feeding cows, we feed the soil, and in providing food for the soil, we provide food for humans.

This worldview of abundance is based on sharing and on a deep awareness of humans as members of the earth family. This awareness that, in impoverishing other beings, we impoverish ourselves, and in nourishing other beings, we nourish ourselves, is part of our present ecological knowledge and ancient wisdom.

The global free trade economy has become a threat to sustainability and the very survival of the poor and other species, not just as a side effect or as an exception but in a systemic way through a restructuring of our worldview at the most fundamental level. Sustainability, sharing, and survival are being economically outlawed in the name of market competitiveness and market efficiency.

I want to argue here tonight the need urgently to bring the planet and people back into the picture.

The sustainability challenge for the new millennium is whether global economic man can move out of the worldview based on fear and scarcity, monocultures and monopolies, appropriation and dispossession, and shift to a view based on abundance and sharing, diversity and decentralization, and respect and dignity for all beings.

Sustainability demands that we move out of the economic trap that is leaving no space for other species and most humans. Globalization has become a war against nature and the poor. We must bring this war to an end.

Since Seattle, a frequently used phrase has been the need for a rule-based system. Globalization is the rule of commerce, and it has elevated Wall Street to be the only source of value, and as a result things that should have high worth—nature, culture, the future—are being devalued and destroyed. The rules of globalization are undermining the rules of justice and sustainability, of compassion and sharing. The rules of free trade must give way to the rules of the biosphere to set the limits and boundaries of economic activity to ensure it respects ecological processes and human life and dignity. We have to move from market totalitarianism to an earth democracy.

We can survive as a species only if we live by the rules of the biosphere—and the rules of sharing and caring. The biosphere has enough for everyone's needs if the global economy is bounded by the limits set by sustainability and justice.

As Gandhi had reminded us, "The earth has enough for everyone's needs, but not for some people's greed."

REFERENCES

Bower, Christopher. "Monsanto Lifted by Rising Sale of Modified Seeds." *Financial Times,* April 24, 2002.

Brooks, Kim. "History, Change, and Policy: Factors Leading to Current Opposition to Food Biotechnology." *Georgetown Public Policy Review* 5 (2000): 153.

"Italian Police Raid Monsanto GM Stockpile." BBC News, March 28, 2001.

Natrajan, Balmurli. "Interrogating Globalization: The Impact on Human Rights; Legitimating Globalization: Culture and Its Uses." *Transnational Law and Contemporary Problems* 12 (spring 2002): 127.

Quaim, Martin, and David Zilberman. "Yield Effects of Genetically Modified Crops in Developing Countries." *Science,* February 7, 2003: 900.

Rathbone, Sharon. "Biting the Hand That Feeds You." *Euroinvest,* summer 2003: 37.

Scopacasa, Paolo. "Fighting Monocultures of the Mind." *EcoWorld: Global Environmental Community,* 2002.

Shiva, Vandana. "Monsanto's Expanding Monopolies." *http://www.vshiva.net.* July 1, 2001.

19. Karl-Henrik Robert

SWEDEN

The environmental movement has seen innumerable models of public interest activism by individuals who started nongovernment initiatives. The diversity is hardly surprising; the objectives and tactics often reflect the variety of local cultural and political realities.

Every so often a new approach emerges and produces results. During the last decade, the Natural Step has emerged as a unique Swedish contribution to the growing environmental global network. Using a synthesis of science, philosophy, and consensus building, the Natural Step has managed to transcend the adversarial dynamics with industry that many interest groups thrive on but that also can stymie environmental progress.

The organization, and its methods and ideology, are a reflection of its founder, Karl-Henrik Robert, a pediatric oncologist. Within five years of completing his medical degree, he became head of the Hematology and

Oncology Unit at the Huddinge Hospital. Not just a clinician, he emerged as one of Sweden's leading cancer researchers, and in the span of only a few years wrote ninety scientific publications about leukemia, lymphoma, and lung cancer. But Robert took little satisfaction from his findings and the improved survival rates of his patients, for any clinical progress was overshadowed by the gnawing concern associated with the unmistakable increase he noted in childhood leukemia and other malignancies. These trends and the clear proliferation in damaged human cells could only be explained by environmental factors.

Robert also noticed that the same parents who would sacrifice anything to help their dying children did not exhibit a similar selfless ethos when they were faced with environmental choices. He became increasingly concerned that he was dealing with symptoms rather than with the cause of the growing cancer morbidity.

Then a sequence of dreams began to haunt him, in which a tempting, beautiful woman beckoned to him; several nights later, the woman became transformed into a witch and attacked him. Fortunately, he did not have to go far to have the nightmare interpreted. His wife, Rigmor, a therapist, understood the dream as a manifestation of his frustration at not setting up some sort of organization that could field a comprehensive response to the present crisis.

This was in the late 1980s, a time when Geo Brundtland's U.N. commission launched "sustainable development" as a central global environmental objective. "Sustainability" quickly took its place in green jargon worldwide. Unfortunately, the very vagueness of the concept that allowed it to be embraced by so many stakeholders ensured that it meant very little. Although amorphous definitions abounded, few constructive policy approaches or operational decision guidelines emerged from it. Within this context, Robert's intellectual contribution can be more fully appreciated.

Being a scientist, Robert was not inclined to establish an NGO based on the aggressive, adversarial model. Indeed, Robert was already weary of the paralysis and petty scientific controversies that conventional advocacy had brought to environmental issues. In an oft-quoted analogy, he likened Europe's environmental debates to monkeys chattering in the withering leaves of a dying tree: "In the midst of all this chatter about the leaves, very few of us have been paying attention to the environment's trunk and branches. . . . We must learn to deal with environmental problems at the systematic level. If we heal the trunk and the branches, the benefits for the leaves will follow naturally."

So in 1989, still deeply immersed in cancer research, Robert broadened the scope of his inquiry. His ambitious objective was to create a set of systematic guidelines that could help greens and industrialists alike analyze environmental dilemmas. Relying on the universal proclivity of professors to offer critiques and comments, Robert decided to elicit responses from the top scientific minds of Swedish academia for what he called "a consensus report."

Eventually, one hundred scientists participated in the process. The document ultimately went through twenty-one iterations, but by the twenty-second, Robert had a system for environmental decision making that has subsequently been considered by a range of scientific forums in other countries and has survived the peer review.

The resulting Natural Step system relies on fundamental scientific axioms, in particular the laws of thermodynamics and common sense. The scientists agreed that there were some axioms, which Robert called "system conditions," that characterize the present environmental challenge:

1. *Substances from the earth's crust, like fossil fuels, metals, and minerals, must not be systematically introduced into nature.* If they are, eventually they will create problematic pollution problems. Extraction must drop to replacement levels.

2. *Substances produced by society must not systematically increase in nature.* Here, objections focus on the composition of modern products that are neither biodegradable nor recyclable, and their release into nature. When the release of plastics or nuclear wastes intensifies, it violates this system condition.

3. *The physical basis for productivity and diversity of nature must not be systematically deteriorated.* Human reliance on ecosystem services mandates restoration of these life support systems.

4. *Human society needs to be fair and efficient in meeting basic human needs for all of humanity.* When poverty leads to unsustainable production methods, the resulting loss of habitat and human and natural resource exploitation eventually affects the entire planet's health.

Once Robert had a document, he set his sights on dissemination. His approach again reflected a signature Natural Step style for moving environmental initiatives. Although Robert is a physician with no formal training in marketing, his promotion of the Natural Step program may constitute the best publicity campaign ever undertaken on behalf of an environmental manifesto.

He started by enlisting top Swedish entertainers to produce a nationally televised show on the subject. Once they were on board, Swedish Television could not help but agree to allocate prime time for the unveiling of the guidelines, on the last day of April 1989. With momentum growing, the King of Sweden even agreed to offer "royal" sponsorship for the initiative. Of course, as with many environmental nongovernment initiatives, the critical piece of the puzzle would ultimately be funding. But by the time Robert went to Swedish industry to support his initiative, so many ducks were in place that a great many firms decided to participate.

A videocassette and pamphlet were produced, and the funding from industry allowed Robert to deliver them to each of the 4.3 million homes and schools in Sweden. Strategic constituencies such as nurses, doctors, attorneys, musicians, teachers, architects, and policy makers were targeted for special attention. In contrast to most nongovernment groups, which gather strength gradually, the Natural Step hit Sweden in April 1989 with a very big bang.

The Natural Step soon introduced innovative ways to reach out to the public. In schools, children began to run natural-cycle greenhouses with organic products and composting toilets. Paraphernalia and gimmicks that in most countries are associated with commercial superstars like Harry Potter were launched. Natural Step songs, Natural Step plays, Natural Step interactive board games and community environmental calendars, Natural Step eco-fairs, self-teaching CD-ROMs—and support for the three thousand eco-labeled products on the shelves of Swedish stores—created a very high profile.

Unlike the directors of many NGOs, Robert steered away from exclusively preaching to the converted. Rather, his outreach prioritized industry. Advocating a pragmatic position of picking the "low hanging fruit," Robert argued that focusing on the easiest and most profitable environmental changes could start an institutional movement. He devised industry-specific action plans that stressed a four-stage process. The program started with awareness and mapping of present practices, and moved on to establish a vision and an action plan. .

More than sixty industries initially answered the call, including IKEA (the world's largest producer of furniture), Electrolux (the appliance king), Swedish Railways, supermarket chains, hotels, and even the Swedish McDonald's franchises. Some twenty professional groups, from architects to doctors and lawyers, were formed to integrate the Natural Step program into their activities. A Natural Step consensus document on farming broke

through the polarization created by the conventional versus organic farming debate and, within ten years, led to a 75 percent reduction in pesticide
use in Sweden.

Robert would eventually introduce the Natural Step beyond Sweden,
establishing branches in England, Holland, Australia, Japan, and North
America. Interface, the American carpeting giant, became the U.S. Natural Step poster child. Its CEO, Ray Anderson, like many converts, began
to spread the word among his corporate colleagues. So enthusiastic were
participating corporations that one journalist even called Natural Step
training sessions (never provided for free) "cult-like."

The substance of Robert's Natural Step breaks little new scientific
ground; its major innovation is procedural. As an example of the consensual approach, Robert offers the following dialectic: a hypothetical politician might query as to whether the reproductive organs of seals are destroyed by the chemical PCB. Should the question be answered directly,
the scientific uncertainty would lead to a chorus of conflicting and con-
fusing responses. An iterative dynamic, however, can produce much
more effective results, particularly when it links the answers back to the
"system conditions." His example is instructive:

> For instance: *Is PCB a naturally occurring substance?* No, it is artificially
> manufactured by man. All scientists agree on that. *Is it chemically stable
> or does it quickly degrade into harmless substances?* It is stable and per-
> sistent. On that they all agree as well. *Does it accumulate in organs?* Yes
> it does. *Is it possible to predict the tolerance limits of such a stable, un-
> natural substance?* No, since the complexity of ecosystems is essentially
> limitless. Nevertheless, it is known that all such substances have limits,
> often very low, which cannot be exceeded. *Can we continue to introduce
> such substances into the ecosystem?* Not if we want to survive.

Given his experience with Natural Step, Robert left medicine and is now
an adjunct professor at two universities, where he develops the intellectual underpinnings and expands the application for his work.

The speech included here is a relatively recent presentation that reflects
Robert's growing inclination to take his vision beyond Sweden. Delivered
in Sydney, Australia, as the Jack Beale Lecture at the University of New
South Wales, it was rebroadcast on the radio to a national audience. The
address goes beyond Robert's usual description of Natural Step evolution
and ideology to reveal a hopeful societal and political analysis of the requirements for entering an era of sustainability. Using sustainable energy

as his key example, he focuses on the role of the media in transforming "business as usual" into a sustainable economy.

"Problems Are Not Enough in Themselves to Create a Momentum for Change"

JACK BEALE LECTURE AT THE UNIVERSITY OF NEW SOUTH WALES, SYDNEY, AUSTRALIA, SEPTEMBER 27, 2001

I believe that we are on the verge of a paradigm shift, and what the leaders in that new paradigm do and say—the ones who are invisible on the cutting edge today—will soon be seen as mainstream. The new visibility of those leaders will be the first fall of a domino that will bring the others crashing down in their turn. The subsequent dominos to fall involve primarily the destructive imbalance between the Western traditional political parties' attitudes toward sustainability issues, and the institutions that are obsolete when it comes to the protection of oceans, atmosphere, ecosystems, and social equity on a global scale.

During a sequence of several decades, almost a century, industrialism and free enterprise have harvested great success. The subsequent deterioration of the environment represents a problem that the green movement often calls the "prisoners' dilemma." Since ancient times, man has encountered this problem whenever the economy has expanded—for instance, when the pressure on pastureland has grown beyond its carrying capacity. The individual farmer says, "Why should I reduce the number of animals in my herd, if I cannot get guarantees from my neighbors that they will do the same?" If no public institutions existed that were strong enough to establish and enforce rules, the environment was destroyed and people had to move off the land. What is unique today is that this time the "environment" is the whole biosphere, and there is nowhere to go.

In an attempt to get some initiative back, politicians on the right often claim that private ownership is the best guarantee for safeguarding the environment: "You protect what is yours." But who owns the ozone layer? As long as our life-supporting domains of the biosphere are at risk, and as long as only parties on the left have the problem as a top priority on the agenda, it seems inevitable that we will keep the "red-green" mess.

Historically, industrialism developed from a stage of profound poverty. It developed as a strong and dynamic power, and created security for the nourishment of our lives (in Swedish, "business" is called *"närings-livet,"* nourishment for life). But now it seems to have reached its senile stage, "consumerism" or "economism." In this stage we seem to have forgotten what it was all about. Whatever we call this senile stage, it is threatening the values it was once designed to protect.

Are the new challenges, in our time of affluence and threatened biosphere, so fundamentally different that we need fundamentally different visions, institutions, and traditions? We may not know the answer yet, but surely it should be possible to envision a rich world, where the whole culture is tailor-made to create the best conditions for quality of life and security, in a sufficiently large perspective, geographically and in time. Whether we can make it or not, it seems to me that there are three preconditions to find that vision and start going for it.

The first precondition is that we can successfully maintain democracy and the necessary balance between right and left. Democracy should be a verb, rather than a noun. Seeing it as a noun may lead us to think of it as something we "have," and that we can relax once we have it. The balancing act of democracy should rather be a verb—something we do and must continue to do and protect, if we are to keep it. The first sign of deterioration of democracy is something we could call "manipulative," rather than "participative," democracy, when decisions are made over the heads of people. If the public, or investigations that are conducted afterward, find that the decisions were wrong, they get the chance to correct their points of view in the next election or investigation. Most of us in Europe have experienced this sort of decision making, when large infrastructural constructions threaten natural values.

In Sweden, we have recently seen even more frightening signs. A couple of national economists have, seemingly independently of each other, and with leading newspaper coverage, suggested that we should limit the rules of democracy (at a time when we need them the most). They were to be changed by various experts and certain business corporations, who could design the society for us—because otherwise the experts and the firms may leave us, and move abroad with their assets.

The second precondition is that we succeed in finding new traditions and institutions. The balance between right and left is not enough as an idea, but must be operationalized through institutions and traditions that are relevant for the problems at hand. Most proactive people, also in business, believe that we need new rules that are more suited for the new situation we are in. Our freedom to choose is, for instance, threatened by a cynicism that is not all that uncommon in certain large transnational firms and organizations, whose values are flying in the face of the moral beliefs of most people. Sometimes institutions, constituted in a vague and obscure way, are the owners. So there is no geographical and social responsibility, and no one in particular to blame when things go wrong—things like destruction of the environment, greedy squandering of nature, and social battering. If we could just agree that we have a problem, then we can explore it together.

Many transnational companies really have so much power, and use it in such a destructive way, that they can be perceived as threats to the common good. But it would be no solution to forbid them in a democratic process. It may not even be desirable, since a number of big and strong transnational companies give us all hope. They have benefited from taking a clear social and ecological stand, and the very size of these companies has contributed to spreading that good example on the global scale. However, again my point is that firms are not people that you can say hello to and love or hate. They are constituted by people, and some of the employees at companies such as Interface, Electrolux, IKEA, and Shell are launching projects every day that are driven by attractive visions, and that use the power of their organization while doing so.

Likewise, most of us have also seen that being a large corporation does not guarantee success. Swedish businessman Lars Bern, in his book *Sustainable Leadership,* has elaborated on the vulnerability of the transnational companies. They too have an Achilles heel. During the last decades, we have entered a trademark economy, where almost all of a firm's assets are in its trademark, and relatively much smaller parts are in real estate. This makes them vulnerable, since the trademark can easily be linked to images of bad morals. When people in the market exercise the power they get from this, firms can suffer considerable financial losses.

We have seen a number of examples of such stigmatization on the market that have cost business corporations billions in bad will. And we have seen other examples of companies that change the situation to play a more constructive role. Some large oil companies' reputations have suffered, with consequent stock price losses, as a result of events such as huge oil spills, paying money to lobby against effective political actions for sustainability, violations of environmental and ethical standards in developing countries, and so on. But today these same large companies are investing billions in photovoltaics, are withdrawing from anti-climate-change groups, and are making positive statements about green taxes on fossil fuels.

Our hope is, of course, that such anecdotes will become the common cultural norm. There are many powers that try to channel the good work in various networks and institutions to make that happen faster and more powerfully. Consumers' associations of various kinds, green and social NGOs, ethical funds, international business charters and agreements, banks, and insurance companies with ethical core values—there are many examples, and they seem to grow in numbers and influence by the hour. If the right takes on the challenge to support such institutions in competition with the left, it may reestablish a meaningful balancing act between left and right, and may empower the transnational companies to be means for people, not the opposite way around.

The third precondition, and the most difficult, is to find a "story of meaning" in exchange for the feeling of emptiness that so many people harbor today. Without it, it is difficult to imagine a revitalization of democracy or the growth of effective institutions. If, on the other hand, we find such a vision, the other two preconditions are likely to evolve by themselves. The Swedish theoretical physicist Karl-Erik Eriksson used to talk about the necessity of a global "taking-care-of-the-planet culture." It would be the basis of new cultures anywhere we need them, and it would build on some common characteristics from all vital and long-lasting cultures from history. For it to be successful, it must at the same time allow room for our true modern values, and be open to local, regional, and national differences.

But finding a meaningful myth, a "story of what it is all about," that would fit a modern society, is not easy. It is probably not even possible, since cultures cannot be engineered. Cultures must grow organically— when the time is right for it to happen, and when people want it. But how can the evolution of such stories be promoted? How can a story like that be authentic enough to win the hearts of modern people in the age of information technology and big cities? This is when we need leaders. Where are they?

The Western industrial world must take the lead to develop sustainable techniques and lifestyles that can be applied anywhere, and show that they will pay off even in the short term. If not, how can we help the developing countries? Do we really want them to repeat our mistakes? Or would we rather develop a new paradigm together with them, learning from each other, and heading towards visions that are so attractive that we all would long for them? For many hundreds of years, European/American economic development has undermined, sometimes even destroyed, many cultures around the world. Today it is time to do our best to pay some of the debt back. Poor countries in the South cannot enter a path of sustainable development by themselves. Their acute problems (lack of sustainable sources of fresh water, food, and energy) rest in the lap of the rich world. If we cannot do this together, we will go under together; the biosphere sees no boundaries.

There are two acute problem areas to tackle:

- Nature's functions, which give us food, fresh air, clean drinking water, and renewable resources, are squandered more and more while we simultaneously produce more and more people on earth. Today, one billion people don't have access to safe drinking water and enough nourishment. Erosion, asphalt covering fertile land, losses of groundwater, deforestation, and over-fishing are examples of problems that increase globally, while population expands and inequity problems increase. Or, to put it more simply: global, life-sustaining production is decreasing at the same time our demand for it is increasing and the social divide between rich and poor is widening.
- Nature is becoming more and more polluted. The problem is not that we are just generally untidy, but that concentrations of various compounds that are "left over" are *increasing systematically*—molecular garbage that increases the greenhouse effect, deteriorates the ozone layer, causes acidity, poisons biological systems, and is radioactive.

In spite of all the easily grasped underlying evidence of these problems, debate about sustainability and what it means is still unclear. Bickering about details, and misleading questions—such as, for instance, whether sustainable development is preferable to economic growth—throw us off course and make us forget what sustainable development is really all about. And particularly what it will mean if we fail. The problem is partly caused by confusion. The minute we begin to draw logical conclusions about the need for a human evolution that does not depend on atomic energy or increasing amounts of concrete, a host of uninformed nay sayers suddenly appear to deny the problems.

Most government authorities and all professional institutions working with sustainability issues are at last agreed on the nature of the problem. Those who provide flawed arguments and flawed information have been marginalized in their own fields. Their negative influence can be attributed to society's extreme reluctance to change itself. Society is receptive to even the most amateurish resistance. As long as the resistance is only strong enough to slightly hamper the pace of change, it may even be constructive and help us avoid mistakes. In other words, problems are not enough in themselves to create a momentum for change. We need expertise and vision.

The continuous deterioration of civilization's conditions for survival can be laid at the door of our decision makers, who still have a poor understanding of fundamental principles and therefore lack strategic competence in four fields that encompass the great tasks of our time:

- To change energy systems
- To phase out the use of certain chemicals and metals that nature cannot assimilate
- To manage the life-supportive ecosystems in a sustainable way—fresh water flows, forests, fields, and fishing waters
- To heal the battered and broken cultures around the world.

The positive aspect here is that the fourth area, the problem of broken cultures, can be merged with the other three areas into one overall task. Experience shows that, when people who are faced with great challenges move together with shared vision, the other problems virtually solve themselves, and vice versa. If everyone is aware of great systemic problems in society, without any call for fundamental industrial or economic reforms to be put into place, social and political instability will tend to increase. The general feeling of emptiness and apathy in the face of mounting global problems may well prove to be one of the most significant concerns of our time.

So just "getting rid of our problems" cannot serve as a sufficient vision. Meaningful development, as pointed out by the American systems thinker Peter Senge, is like a rubber band stretched between present-day reality on the one hand and attractive, utopian dreams on the other. The tension cannot be maintained forever, and there are only two options: either give up the dreams and go back to the old weary plod, or stubbornly stick to our visions long enough for the other end of the rubber band to start moving. This is when the leaders must enter the scene, because it is their job to see and interpret and communicate visions, and to be stubbornly sustainable in doing so.

So, where are the leaders? It seems to me that good leaders are everywhere, and they are growing in numbers! The problem is not that they don't exist, but that their good examples are not yet allowed to become the norm. If they are seen at all, they are perceived as unrealistic dreamers, whom we may admire or not. In spite of all the rhetoric backed up by exhaustive facts, our present culture still evaluates everything according to the rules of the old order. It is true that encouraging words are heard every now and then. But when most decisions in society are made, and when we see the daily news on TV, it's still more of the same. The other stuff is not "realistic." Will it ever be?

In this early stage of transition, the true leadership is visible largely on the local level. It is in certain business corporations, or municipalities, where people are optimistic and committed. In their case, neither "getting rid of problems" nor "increased GNP" form the story. These people are envisioning something new, and their vision is the engine of change. They are longing for it—it's that simple. And the leaders, as well as the visions, are so trustworthy that the rubber band can lose its tension only by everybody moving in the direction of the vision. People are united through a common cultural identity that provides a sense of meaning.

As the invisible leadership grows stronger, the old establishment's response becomes increasingly irritable. But suddenly, a few leaders from the old paradigm's defense lines start changing sides. They realize that it is time to listen, and that it is time not only to let go, but to be helpful in the demounting of the old paradigm. There are many examples of such "heroes of retreat" that can serve as examples. Gorbachev is one. The German author Hans Magnus Enzensbergers has written a thoughtful thesis on the phenomenon. In Sweden, the prime minister, Göran Persson, began his term by talking about an attractive, ecologically sustainable society as a new vision for Sweden, and the U.S. vice president, Al Gore, has taken a clear stand for similar visions. This is bold, because there is no guarantee that the pendulum will not swing back again.

And indeed, the Swedish prime minister has been object of a fair amount of ridicule from various people defending their entrenched positions in the old order, on the left as well as on the right. I believe that the change of paradigm will not be complete until it is acknowledged by the mass media as the new norm.

In the industrial society, the distance between people is paradoxically wider than ever. We may not think so, as we sit in front of the TV and learn about President Clinton's private life. But we generally know much less about our neighbors. We hardly meet with people, at least not when it is about sharing our thoughts on values and longings, or about the shaping of a new and better world. These things are taken care of by soap operas and political leaders once we have made it home to the TV after another hard day's work. Because of this, a lot of intuitive feelings that we may all share never become generally accepted. So we won't have a new culture until it is seen by the mass media, because only then can we trust that others see it too.

In Europe, at least, we don't really trust either of these substitutes—soap operas, and politics mirrored in TV—for an active participation in the creation of our culture. The reason is simple: we may be amused, but we don't really feel that we are represented. It's as if everything we see on TV is rhetoric, while most of us feel that there are fundamental errors in the societal system that need attention but don't get addressed. The problem is that we sit there and think this, but we don't *say* it often. We don't sit with the others in the tribe around the fire anymore. We fall asleep in front of the TV.

In spite of what many people believe, the mass media are in fact part and parcel of the establishment, representing an "insider" view, usually with a condescending and sometimes even derisive stance towards new ideas. For example: the Western world has changed energy systems twice in history, from wood to coal, and from coal to the energy systems we use today—petroleum and nuclear power. It took about forty years each time, and each time the transition was met with scornful resistance from those who had the largest investments in the old energy systems. Now, we are there again. But this time, the resistance is stronger than ever, mainly because the investments are larger than ever. And as could be expected, the daily news media are viewing the early stages of change through their old glasses, and perceive the supporters and actors of the new energy systems—windmills, bioenergy, and photovoltaics—as a new breed of eccentrics.

Through those old glasses, it appears that a stark choice must be made between fossil fuels and nuclear power. However, certain other areas never seem to come under scrutiny: issues such as time scales, the future availability and potential of various alternative energy sources, and how we should be linking tomorrow's energy systems with energy systems being put into place today. In fact, the mainstream news media don't even report on the development of new energy systems on the market *right now.*

Instead, the supporters of the only energy systems that are growing strongly today, photovoltaics and windpower, are generally called enemies of progress, while the supporters of the only traditional energy system that isn't growing at all, nuclear power, are referred to as progressive. The idea that today's problems could be solved by any other thinking than what created them is regarded as naive. And yet it is clear that things are starting to change, if only at the edges. Journalists with courage, ability, and insight are appearing in the Sunday supplements, the cultural pages, some scientific journals, and the local press.

Unlike many people, I don't believe there is a conspiracy between the news media and those in power. The inertia of television and the large newspapers has another explanation.

The acclaimed French sociologist Pierre Bourdieu has posited that an increasing commercialization of the media, with ever-greater numbers of newspapers and competing TV channels, has paradoxically resulted in a "dumbing-down" of the coverage. All that frantic jostling about to bring out news before anyone else creates high insecurity. Journalists are anxiously watching to see what others publish or broadcast, and match what they see, thus creating uniformity. That's why we see the same material and the same people on the sofas commenting on it, regardless of what channel we watch or newspaper we read. News coverage is adapted to what the media believe the public will take. Wearing their journalist spectacles, media professionals are free to go for the quick and easily digested stories while remaining myopic to anything that requires more time and reflection. The discussion of the emerging new worldview obviously belongs in this latter category.

President Clinton's private life, a Swedish minister buying a piece of chocolate on her official business card, or the Mayor of Stockholm drinking wine with his lunch are examples of events that are easier to understand than the fact that photovoltaics on 10 percent of the Sahara desert would produce as much electricity as the whole world's expenditure of energy, including all energy sources. Likewise, it is easier to digest than the fact that big petroleum companies like BP, Shell, Amoco, and Enron are spending billions on photovoltaics, are buying up cheap desert land to put these photovoltaics on, and are making positive statements about green taxes on petroleum. But what is most sensational?

From whence will the new culture come? If we won't endorse the new culture until the mass media does, who will present it to the media? *Business*, that's who.

For the long term, we must find ways of getting the time needed to consider and debate more subtle issues, like our future, and what we really want to get out of our lives. Where will these more subtle conversations take place, if not in the mass media? In our jobs, of course. In the modern world, where we don't sit around the fire with our neighbors anymore, business and our jobs make up the new communities. And they can be wonderful. That's why we need to make our hidden leaders visible, to speed up the process of making the new paradigm—the taking-care-of-the-planet culture—the norm.

In conclusion, the good news is that we do not need to stop being interested in sensations or scandals. The growth of the new paradigm, and the fact that we already have some leaders who are operationalizing it, can be sensational enough. We just need to start regarding the growth of the new vision as the new normality. And when reality is mirrored through journalist glasses which regard the new vision as normal, we can trust that it is not only at our working place that the shift of paradigm has taken place. Then the old paradigm is finished.

Will the mass media resist this? I don't think so. They have their own rubber band. Their vision could be, of course, to play their role of observers and reporters on the establishment, and to play this role to its full extent. To that end, one task would be to reveal that the old emperor is nude in front of the new paradigm, with its demanding challenges. Certainly, that should be a more attractive and perhaps more sensational task than reporting on the cut of his clothes.

REFERENCES

Gips, Terry. "Take the Natural Step." *Conscious Choice.* September 1998. See *http://www.consciouschoice.com.*

Montague, Peter. "The Natural Step." *Rachel's Environment and Health Weekly,* no. 667, September 9, 1999.

Robert, Karl-Henrik. *The Natural Step Story: Seeding a Quiet Revolution.* Gabriola Island, BC: New Society Publishers, 2002.

———. "Planning from Principles for Success." Commemorative lecture for the Blue Planet Prize Award, Tokyo, 2000, sponsored by Asahi Glass Foundation.

———. "Educating a Nation." *Making it Happen* 28 (spring 1991).

20. Wangari Maathai
KENYA

Photograph by Martin Rowe.

Desertification may be the most heartless and avoidable global environmental problem. But because it does not affect most developed countries, it tends to receive precious little international attention and funding. Human imprudence lies behind the massive degradation of arable lands in arid and semiarid climates. As deserts continue their silent, relentless march forward, the economic base of some 250 million people across the planet is systematically jeopardized. A billion more are considered to be "at risk" as fertile lands give way to erosion and soil loss. Sadly, the victims of desertification are frequently among the most destitute and disempowered inhabitants on the planet. They simply do not have the capacity to combat the phenomenon.

Most people are surprised to discover that drylands cover over a third of the planet's landmass. In contrast to their harsh and tough image, these territories are quite fragile ecologically. Rainy regions tend to be robust, able to rebound after sustaining damage. Desert ecosystems are not. When deforestation, overgrazing, sprawl, and inappropriate irrigation conspire together, drylands become barren. For most residents, the impact is perceived as a one-directional, irreversible march to oblivion. And yet, combating desertification is a relatively feasible challenge. It can start with something as simple as planting a tree.

Kenya is a typical example of a country where a spiraling population and logging interests have elevated desertification to a critical issue. Eighty-eight percent of the country has sufficiently low rainfall to be designated as "drylands." In these scenic savannas, there are not only about a third of the thirty million Kenyans, but also three-quarters of the wildlife and half the livestock. Periodic droughts and the relentless subdivision of lands by large families into small, unsustainable parcels are part of the problem. But deforestation is the dominant piece of the puzzle. Since British colonial logging and farming began 150 years ago, three-quarters of the country's woodlands have been cleared. Today only about 2 percent of the Kenyan lands enjoy forest cover. And the demand for wood for burning is growing. Dung and crop residues are simply inadequate as a fuel alternative.

Wangari Maathai was an exceptional woman even before she attracted international attention as an environmentalist, political dissident, government leader, and ultimately Nobel Peace laureate. She was born in 1940 in the relatively remote village of Tetu, near Nyeri, Kenya (about two hundred kilometers north of Nairobi). Maathai was an exceptionally gifted student in the Colonial Girls' School System, talented enough to win university scholarships in the United States for undergraduate and graduate studies. From there, she began to accrue a long series of "firsts" for African women:

- first African woman to receive a Ph.D. in science
- first female professor at the University of Nairobi
- and, when she was appointed chair of Veterinary Anatomy at the University of Nairobi, first female university department head.

But the state of her country and continent were too grim to leave her satisfied with the relative tranquility of an academic career. And university politics in Kenya were not always congenial for women. As a pioneering female faculty member, Maathai had to fight for equal opportunity from the start. By the mid-1970s she emerged as a natural leader in the National Council of Women in Kenya, a group she chaired between 1981 and 1987. Like many feminists, Maathai sensed that it was women who paid a disproportionate price for the ecological damage taking place in Kenya. For example, women were the ones who were walking farther and farther to find a scanty piece of wood to cook meals and to provide heat for their families.

Trees offered a natural nexus between her professional background in the biological sciences and her growing stature in Kenya's nascent women's movement. In 1977, Maathai began to advocate tree-planting as a very practical form of ecological empowerment for women. She started small, with a simple nursery in her back yard. But trees have a way of growing, and within a decade the Green Belt Movement that she began could count some twenty million trees planted. Ten million more have been added, since. Today, Maathai's movement has also sprouted into a national network of three thousand tree nurseries, offering three thousand part-time jobs.

In characterizing the ideology behind the Green Belt initiative, Professor Maathai explains to listeners that East Africa's proximity to the Sahara desert makes its environment particularly vulnerable, as the desert could expand southward: clearing remaining patches of forests is, "in essence, creating many micro-Sahara deserts." Maathai claims that in any given group of one hundred Kenyan farmers, thirty will be able to identify streams that have dried up in their lifetimes.

But Maathai has always envisioned the Green Belt Movement as much more than a narrow "silviculture" initiative. The implicit message is also political. It is one of empowerment. Planting trees builds environmental awareness through civic participation. Because they are visible, Maathai calls the trees her movement's ambassadors.

In a 1993 speech at New York University, Professor Maathai described how the idea for her movement originated. It began with hearing a talk on regional distribution of ill health:

The speaker described causes of malnutrition, illnesses, and where the condition was prevalent. We were surprised to hear that the diseases were common in areas which had a high income from cash crops (coffee, tea, pyrethrum, etc.), therefore an affluent community. That is not where one expected to find malnutrition and associated illnesses. But because trees had been cut to make way for this high-potential and income-generating agriculture, there was no firewood. Poor women used agricultural residues to cook, and therefore families opted for fast-cooking and partly processed foods, all of which were rich in carbohydrates and poor in proteins and vitamins. This link between the availability of wood fuel and the choice of diet made me think about women and the possibility of them planting trees so that they could have adequate energy to cook the right kind of food for their families.

We could have chosen to initiate a campaign to educate women about balanced diets and different types of food which they needed to plant and eat. But something said, "Get to the root cause of the problem—i.e., lack of firewood. These women need energy, not knowledge!" Immediately we started contacting rural women, especially from the affected areas, to plant trees.

But the Green Belt Movement quickly sprouted beyond its rural roots to embrace quality of life for the crowded residents of Kenya's cities. Nairobi, the Kenyan capital, exhibits all the pathologies of rural–urban migration: poverty, sprawl, and loss of open spaces. The Uhuru Park, a rare patch of green in the city's northern district, served as almost an isolated haven to the crowded local residents amid the growing density. Families frequented the site; children played there; Nairobi residents had a small corner in which to breathe. But by 1998 the lonely green park could also offer "mega" profits for developers of a proposed mega-office development in its heart. The Kenyan government, for its part, was a firm supporter of building Africa's tallest skyscraper there. It had not, however, counted on Maathai's stubbornness nor the extent of her popular support.

Although a zoologist and veterinary expert, Maathai in her environmental ideology puts people first. "We can provide parks for rhinos and elephants. Why can't we provide open spaces for people?" she would ask. Leading a coalition that included architects, curators of the National Museum, and legions of her Green Belt infantry, she succeeded in attracting world-wide attention to her campaign. Maathai told the television reporters: "We already have a debt crisis: we owe billions to foreign banks now. And the people are starving. They need food; they need medicine; they need education. They do not need a skyscraper to house the ruling party and a twenty-four-hour TV station."

Rather than address Maathai and the Green Belt's substantive arguments, Kenyan president Daniel Arap Moi preferred personal attacks, calling her a "mad woman" and a "threat to order and security." Maathai's status as a divorced woman was derided, and her "womanhood" unabashedly called into question. Less obstreperous opponents condescendingly questioned her naïveté and lack of sophistication about development. Maathai didn't blink, but simply responded that, though she might not understand development, she knew that cities need open spaces.

When Maathai did not back down to the initial intimidation tactics, the Green Belt Movement itself became a target. Within twenty-four hours of her press conference, the government saw to its eviction from the offices it had worked from for ten years. But the retaliation was too late. In the face of the Green Belt's demonstration and mounting international pressure to stop the "Park-Monster," the foreign investors withdrew their support. President Moi's government eventually declared the park a National Heritage Site.

This was just the opening round in a string of confrontations. Beyond her proactive afforestation efforts, Maathai visited forests to stop logging, and brought protesters with her. She was routinely detained and often physically attacked by the proxies of logging companies. Once again, the line between environmental rights and human rights became blurred. It was then that Maathai began to enter the political arena, becoming active in the Kenyan opposition. When her efforts to unify the disparate parties into a single coalition failed in 1992, she ran against Moi, though unsuccessfully, for president.

During a fifteen-year ordeal, Maathai endured break-ins at her home, being clubbed into unconsciousness, innumerable arrests, and merciless public attacks. But the abuse only seemed to increase her resolve, as well as her standing within Africa and overseas. Indeed, by the late 1990s, the Green Belt Movement became a Pan-African phenomenon. Dozens of affiliates were established across sub-Saharan Africa. As time went on, Maathai's broader political interests made her spokesperson for good governance within all of Africa.

Environmentally, Maathai is associated with trees, but it is important to emphasize that her efforts always had people and quality of life as their ultimate objective. "If we can't protect our own species, what's the point of protecting tree species?" she often asks. Indeed, the twenty thousand Kenyan farmers (mostly women) who plant Green Belt trees are themselves the most immediate beneficiaries of her work. No less important are the jobs created by afforestation efforts, in a country where 60 percent of the population are below the age of twenty and unemployment is a scourge.

"The Green Belt Movement introduced a procedure which the women and the community followed to make sure that not only were the trees planted, but they were also followed to make sure that they survived," she explained in one speech:

> This enthusiasm for tree-planting in a campaign which allowed tree seedlings to be issued to farmers' free of charge, made the Green Belt Movement quite popular. . . . Although farmers get seedlings free of charge, the women who grow them get paid a token of appreciation of about forty cents per seedling that survives on farmers' land. The counting of the surviving seedlings for payment may take months after the women issued the seedlings to the farmers. This is little money compared to the work which the women do, but it is meant to be an encouragement. . . . Women appreciate the funds they get and indeed will abandon the tree nurseries if they are not given even the forty cents they get.

In seeking the secret behind Maathai's stamina, one is not surprised to find a spiritual dimension. Like many environmental leaders, she is open about a deeply religious component to her work, even if not affiliated with a formal church: "All of us have a God in us, and that God is the spirit that unites all life, everything that is on this planet. It must be this voice that is telling me to do something, and I am sure it's the same voice that is speaking to everybody on this planet—at least everybody who seems to be concerned about the fate of the world, the fate of this planet."

Although environmental degradation in Kenya remains a daunting and disturbing challenge, we can, in Maathai's case, finish a personal story with a happy ending. The decision of President Moi to step down issued in a new era in Kenyan politics. In the first open election in Kenyan history, in December 2002, Maathai's National Rainbow Coalition swept into power. In her home district, Maathai swamped all opponents (taking 27,992 votes, against 554 for the candidate from the ruling Kenyan African National Union.) She was one of eight women who broke into the parliament, traditionally a club limited to Kenyan males. After a decade of continuous harassment of her environmental policies and visions, Maathai enjoyed the ultimate triumph, and in 2003 was appointed Kenya's Assistant Minister for Environment, Natural Resources, and Wildlife. A year later, she was awarded a Nobel Peace Prize, the first individual to receive this ultimate accolade for environmental achievements.

Maathai has always perceived Africa's environmental and desertification crisis as a symptom of a larger series of problems. "Bottlenecks to Development," her analysis of the African condition, was presented as a speech in numerous forums during the 1990s. This analysis quickly departs from the specific environmental issues of deforestation, desertification, or overpopulation with which Maathai is identified. Good governance, she argues, constitutes the key prerequisite to meaningful environmental improvement.

Unlike many advocates from the developing countries, Maathai does not dwell excessively on the colonial past and the scars of the slave trade, but places an equal burden of responsibility on failed local leadership. Ultimately she seeks solutions, not incrimination: "The poor do a lot of damage, and they over-mine the environment to try to sustain their lives. And the rich and those who live a lifestyle where they over-consume the world's resources are also doing a lot of damage. So both ends of the spectrum need to come together and develop a partnership."

In the growing field generically called "environmental security," Maathai has also been among the most outspoken advocates linking environmental stress with violence and international instability. Her web site features a quote at its heading: "If we did a better job of managing our resources sustainably, conflicts over them would be reduced. So protecting the global environment is directly related to securing peace." This belief is very much at the heart of her movement's effort to reclaim degraded African lands. When one considers her personal stamina and relentless commitment to nonviolent organizational tactics, the Nobel Committee's decision to award her the coveted Peace Prize and its formal rationale has a powerful logic: "Peace on earth depends on our ability to secure our living environment. Maathai stands at the front of the fight to promote ecologically viable social, economic, and cultural development in Kenya and in Africa. She has taken a holistic approach to sustainable development that embraces democracy, human rights, and women's rights in particular. She thinks globally and acts locally."

Maathai celebrated the news by planting a tree at her home in Nyeri, across from Mount Kenya. She took the opportunity to call on those around the world who cared for the environment to each plant a tree.

Maathai's Nobel Prize acceptance speech offers an overview of the basic principles behind the Greenbelt Movement, expressing convictions and hopes that go far beyond the Kenyan borders to encompass the entire African continent. The perspective brings together ecological and economic sustainability, the status of women, issues surrounding AIDS, as well as African cultural integrity and economic equity. Of course, at the heart is a call to concrete action: to planting trees and to education.

Although a scientist, Mathaai has always framed Kenya's problems in a political context. Her willingness to stay engaged in a political process and withstand enormous psychological and physical intimidation, along with her steadfast commitment to democratic and environmental change, would prove the key to her personal victory and Nobel Prize recognition.

"The Challenge Is to Restore the Home of the Tadpoles and Give Back to Our Children a World of Beauty and Wonder"

NOBEL PRIZE LECTURE, OSLO, NORWAY,
DECEMBER 10, 2004

*Y*our Majesties, Your Royal Highnesses, Honorable Members of the Norwegian Nobel Committee, Excellencies, Ladies and Gentlemen: I stand before you and the world humbled by this recognition and uplifted by the honor of being the 2004 Nobel Peace laureate. As the first African woman to receive this prize, I accept it on behalf of the people of Kenya and Africa, and indeed the world. I am especially mindful of women and the girl child. I hope it will encourage them to raise their voices and take more space for leadership. I know the honor also gives a deep sense of pride to our men, both old and young. As a mother, I appreciate the inspiration this brings to the youth, and urge them to use it to pursue their dreams.

Although this prize comes to me, it acknowledges the work of countless individuals and groups across the globe. They work quietly and often without recognition to protect the environment, promote democracy, defend human rights, and ensure equality between women and men. By so doing, they plant seeds of peace. I know they, too, are proud today. To all who feel represented by this prize, I say use it to advance your mission and meet the high expectations the world will place on us.

This honor is also for my family, friends, partners, and supporters throughout the world. All of them helped shape the vision and sustain our work, which was often accomplished under hostile conditions. I am also grateful to the people of Kenya, who remained stubbornly hopeful that democracy could be realized and their environment managed sustainably. Because of this support, I am here today to accept this great honor.

I am immensely privileged to join my fellow African Peace laureates: Presidents Nelson Mandela and F. W. de Klerk, Archbishop Desmond Tutu, the late Chief Albert Luthuli, the late Anwar el-Sadat, and U.N. Secretary General Kofi Annan. I know that African people everywhere are encouraged by this news. My fellow Africans, as we embrace this recognition, let us use it to intensify our commitment to our people, to reduce conflicts and poverty and thereby improve their quality of life. Let us embrace democratic governance, protect human rights, and protect our environment. I am confident that we shall rise to the occasion. I have always believed that solutions to most of our problems must come from us.

In this year's prize, the Norwegian Nobel Committee has placed the critical issue of environment and its linkage to democracy and peace before the world. For their visionary action, I am profoundly grateful. Recognizing that sustainable development, democracy, and peace are indivisible is an idea whose time has come. Our work over the past thirty years has always appreciated and engaged these linkages.

My inspiration partly comes from my childhood experiences and observations of nature in rural Kenya. It has been influenced and nurtured by the formal education I was privileged to receive in Kenya, the United States, and Germany. As I was growing up, I witnessed forests being cleared and replaced by commercial plantations, which destroyed local biodiversity and the capacity of the forests to conserve water.

Excellencies, ladies and gentlemen: in 1977, when we started the Green Belt Movement, I was partly responding to needs identified by rural women, namely lack of firewood, clean drinking water, balanced diets, shelter, and income.

Throughout Africa, women are the primary caretakers, holding significant responsibility for tilling the land and feeding their families. As a result, they are often the first to become aware of environmental damage as resources become scarce and incapable of sustaining their families. The women we worked with recounted that, unlike in the past, they were unable to meet their basic needs. This was due to the degradation of their immediate environment as well as the introduction of commercial farming, which replaced the growing of household food crops. But international trade controlled the price of the exports from these small-scale farmers, and a reasonable and just income could not be guaranteed.

I came to understand that, when the environment is destroyed, plundered, or mismanaged, we undermine our quality of life and that of future generations. Tree planting became a natural choice to address some of the initial basic needs identified by women. Also, tree planting is simple, attainable, and guarantees quick, successful results within a reasonable amount of time. This sustains interest and commitment. So, together, we have planted over thirty million trees that provide fuel, food, shelter, and income to support their children's education and household needs. The activity also creates employment and improves soils and watersheds. Through their involvement, women gain some degree of power over their lives, especially their social and economic position and relevance in the family.

This work continues. Initially, the work was difficult because historically our people have been persuaded to believe that, because they are poor, they lack not only capital, but also knowledge and skills to address their challenges. Instead, they are conditioned to believe that solutions to their problems must come from "outside." Further, women did not realize that meeting their needs depended on their environment being healthy and well managed. They were also unaware that a degraded environment leads to a scramble for scarce resources and may culminate in poverty and even conflict. They were also unaware of the injustices of international economic arrangements.

In order to assist communities to understand these linkages, we developed a citizen education program, during which people identify their problems, the causes, and possible solutions. They then make connections between their own personal actions and the problems they witness in the environment and in society. They learn that our world is confronted with a litany of woes: corruption, violence against women and children, disruption and breakdown of families, and disintegration of cultures and communities. They also identify the abuse of drugs and chemical substances, especially among young people. There are also devastating diseases that are defying cures or occurring in epidemic proportions. Of particular concern are HIV/AIDS, malaria, and diseases associated with malnutrition.

On the environment front, they are exposed to many human activities that are devastating to the environment and societies. These include widespread destruction of ecosystems, especially through deforestation, climatic instability, and contamination in the soils and waters, that all contribute to excruciating poverty.

In the process, the participants discover that they must be part of the solutions. They realize their hidden potential, and are empowered to overcome inertia and take action. They come to recognize that they are the primary custodians and beneficiaries of the environment that sustains them.

Entire communities also come to understand that, while it is necessary to hold their governments accountable, it is equally important that, in their own relationships with each other, they exemplify the leadership values they wish to see in their own leaders, namely justice, integrity, and trust

Although initially the Green Belt Movement's tree planting activities did not address issues of democracy and peace, it soon became clear that responsible governance of the environment was impossible without democratic space. Therefore, the tree became a symbol for the democratic struggle in Kenya. Citizens were mobilized to challenge widespread abuses of power, corruption, and environmental mismanagement. In Nairobi's Uhuru Park, at Freedom Corner, and in many parts of the country, trees of peace were planted to demand the release of prisoners of conscience and a peaceful transition to democracy.

Through the Green Belt Movement, thousands of ordinary citizens were mobilized and empowered to take action and effect change. They learned to overcome fear and a sense of helplessness, and moved to defend democratic rights. In time, the tree also became a symbol for peace and conflict resolution, especially during ethnic conflicts in Kenya when the Green Belt Movement used peace trees to reconcile disputing communities. During the ongoing rewriting of the Kenyan constitution, similar trees of peace were planted in many parts of the country to promote a culture of peace. Using trees as a symbol of peace is in keeping with a widespread African tradition. For example, the elders of the Kikuyu carried a staff from the thigi tree that, when placed between two disputing sides, caused them to stop fighting and seek reconciliation. Many communities in Africa have these traditions.

Such practices are part of an extensive cultural heritage, which contributes both to the conservation of habitats and to cultures of peace. With the destruction of these cultures and the introduction of new values, local biodiversity is no longer valued or protected, and, as a result, it is quickly degraded and disappears. For this reason, the Green Belt Movement explores the concept of cultural biodiversity, especially with respect to indigenous seeds and medicinal plants.

As we progressively understood the causes of environmental degradation, we saw the need for good governance. Indeed, the state of any country's environment is a reflection of the kind of governance in place, and without good governance there can be no peace. Many countries which have poor governance systems are also likely to have conflicts and poor laws protecting the environment.

In 2002, the courage, resilience, patience, and commitment of members of the Green Belt Movement, other civil society organizations, and the Kenyan public culminated in the peaceful transition to a democratic government and laid the foundation for a more stable society.

Excellencies, friends, ladies and gentlemen:

It is thirty years since we started this work. Activities that devastate the environment and societies continue unabated. Today we are faced with a challenge that calls for a shift in our thinking, so that humanity stops threatening its life-support system. We are called to assist the earth to heal her wounds, and in the process heal our own—indeed, to embrace the whole creation in all its diversity, beauty, and wonder.

This will happen if we see the need to revive our sense of belonging to a larger family of life, with which we have shared our evolutionary process. In the course of history, there comes a time when humanity is called to shift to a new level of consciousness, to reach a higher moral ground. A time when we have to shed our fear and give hope to each other.

That time is now.

The Norwegian Nobel Committee has challenged the world to broaden the understanding of peace: there can be no peace without equitable development; and there can be no development without sustainable management of the environment in a democratic and peaceful space. This shift is an idea whose time has come. I call on leaders, especially from Africa, to expand democratic space and build fair and just societies that allow the creativity and energy of their citizens to flourish. Those of us who have been privileged to receive education, skills, and experiences and even power must be role models for the next generation of leadership. In this regard, I would also like to appeal for the freedom of my fellow laureate Aung San Suu Kyi, so that she can continue her work for peace and democracy for the people of Burma and the world at large.

Culture plays a central role in the political, economic, and social life of communities. Indeed, culture may be the missing link in the development of Africa. Culture is dynamic and evolves over time, consciously discarding retrogressive traditions like female genital mutilation and embracing aspects that are good and useful.

Africans, especially, should rediscover positive aspects of their culture. In accepting them, they would give themselves a sense of belonging, identity, and self-confidence.

Ladies and gentlemen:

There is also a need to galvanize civil society and grassroots movements to catalyze change. I call upon governments to recognize the role of these social movements in building a critical mass of responsible citizens who help maintain checks and balances in society. On their part, civil society should embrace not only their rights but also their responsibilities. Further, industry and global institutions must appreciate that ensuring economic justice, equity, and ecological integrity are of greater value than profits at any cost.

The extreme global inequities and prevailing consumption patterns continue at the expense of the environment and peaceful coexistence. The choice is ours.

I would like to call on young people to commit themselves to activities that contribute toward achieving their long-term dreams. They have the energy and creativity to shape a sustainable future. To the young people, I say, you are a gift to your communities and indeed the world. You are our hope and our future. The holistic approach to development, as exemplified by the Green Belt Movement, could be embraced and replicated in more parts of Africa and beyond. It is for this reason that I have established the Wangari Maathai Foundation to ensure the continuation and expansion of these activities. Although a lot has been achieved, much remains to be done.

Excellencies, ladies and gentlemen:

As I conclude, I reflect on my childhood experience when I would visit a stream next to our home to fetch water for my mother. I would drink water straight from the stream. Playing among the arrowroot leaves, I tried in vain to pick up the strands of frogs' eggs, believing they were beads. But every time I put my little fingers under them, they would break. Later, I saw thousands of tadpoles: black, energetic, and wriggling through the clear water against the background of the brown earth. This is the world I inherited from my parents.

Today, over fifty years later, the stream has dried up, women walk long distances for water—which is not always clean— and children will never know what they have lost. The challenge is to restore the home of the tadpoles and give back to our children a world of beauty and wonder.

REFERENCES

Anbarasan, Ethirajan. "Wangari Muta Maathai: Kenya's Green Militant." *UNESCO Courier*, 1999.

"Biography." *Official web site of Professor Wangari Maathai. www.wangari maathai.or.ke*. 2004.

The Green Belt Movement web site. *http://www.greenbeltmovement.org*. 2004.

"Living on Earth." Interview with Wangari Maathai. American National Public

Radio, transcript. *http://www.loe.org/archives/970627.htm#feature6.* June 27, 1997.

Morris, Jessica. "Atlantan Joins Mother in Keeping Kenya Green." *Atlanta Journal-Constitution,* July 15, 2003.

Quist-Arcton, Ofeibea. "Maathai: Change Kenya to Benefit People." *AllAfrica. com.* January 2003.

Republic of Kenya. *National Action Programme: A Framework for Combating Desertification in Kenya in the Context of the United Nations Convention to Combat Desertification.* 2002.

"Wangari Maathai." *http://www.womenshistory.about.com.*

Index

About the Author

Alon Tal founded the Israel Union for Environmental Defense, the country's leading environmental advocacy organization as well as the Arava Institute for Environmental Studies, a regional, Middle Eastern research and advanced-training center. He is author of *Pollution in a Promised Land: An Environmental History of Israel* and he recently joined the faculty at Ben Gurion University.

DATE DUE

DEC 2 3 2009			
GAYLORD			PRINTED IN U.S.A.